Maria Simma speaks with Nicky Eltz
(Authorized by Maria Simma)

"GET US OUT OF HERE!!"

*Maria Simma responds to this call
from the Poor Souls in Purgatory.*

The Medjugorje
Web http://www.medjugorje.org
2002 A.D.

First printing, May 2002:	1 -- 1,500
Second printing, August 2002:	1,501 -- 5,500
Third printing, November 2002:	5,501 -- 17,500
Fourth printing, December 2002:	17,501 -- 37,500
Fifth printing, March 2005:	37,501 -- 47,500
Sixth printing, October 2006:	47,501 -- 57,500
Seventh printing, April 2009:	57,501 -- 62,500
Eighth printing, October, 2010:	62,501 -- 67,500
Ninght printing, March 2012:	67,501 -- 72,500

Published by: The Medjugorje Web
               DeKalb, IL 60115
               USA
               http://www.medjugorje.org
               815-748-0410

ISBN: 978-0-9727445-0-8
Photography by Nicky Eltz, except:
Village of Sonntag, page 75, by Anton Näher Satan's
burn, page 76, by José-Marie Santens.
Međugorje visionaries, page 133, permission of M.P.L.
Marija Pavlović Lunetti, page 133, by Margaret Leonard.
Maria Simma and the author, page 134, unknown.

Cover photograph: Interior of steeple of St. Jerome Church in Slano, Croatia.

Printed by: Jafra Print
             Croatia
             www.jafra.hr

Dedicated with love to
ALL who have yet to feel
God's Love

"... will rise to a disciplinary curative time of punishment."

Correct translation
from Aramaic and Greek of both
Matthew 25:46 and John 5:29

* * * * *

Love extends also to those who have
died in this love, for love is the life of
the soul
as the soul is the life of the body.

St. Thomas of Aquinas

* * * * *

Our dead are among the invisible, not among the absent.

Pope John XXIII

* * * * *

What is life compared to that day which
will have no ending for the elect, or to that night
which will have no dawning for the damned?

Sister M.G. from Purgatory,
† February 1871

TABLE OF CONTENTS

PREFACE

Dear reader,

What you are now holding is a most interesting book. The world beyond is speaking. It is offering advice, asking for help and giving answers. It exists and speaks about life -- our life here on earth and of possible consequences of our behavior. It tells us that it is not the same to be humble, loving, good, merciful, loyal and honest as it is to be proud, loveless, bad, merciless, betraying and dishonest. At death this is not forgotten but rather remembered in total clarity. Not only is the punishment, or better yet the cleansing, spoken about; but also the length of this cleansing and so very much more.

Then you ask yourself, is this possible?

In the Catholic Church one speaks about a transitory state which for a very long time now has been referred to as Purgatory. Despite there being different theories, this state is always taken seriously. One needs it because one can only come before God cleansed and pure.

It is also accepted within the Catholic mystical tradition that some mystics have had similar experiences with the souls in Purgatory as does Maria Simma. So it is not entirely unknown as a phenomenon, but in these excessively rational- ized times in which there is danger of believing only that which is measurable and understandable with physical units and laws, it often becomes difficult to speak about and thus to believe. And when one adds atheism, the complete rejection of the world beyond, to this need-to-measure-everything mentality it becomes clearer yet that we are concerned here with a highly interesting book of rich content. When, in addition to all that, one discovers the author's style that is full of lively expressions and pictures, as well as an exciting imag- ination in his questioning of this visionary, one has a real joy in reading it.

Although I, as a theologian, have questions about some of the answers, all personal doubts disappeared once I too had met and spoken with Maria Simma. She is true. Her eyes and facial expression awaken in one a deep respect and a healthy trust. When her own suffering is requested by the world beyond she, by always accepting it freely, is cleansed and thus lives in deep peace.

Maria's voice showers her guest with an indescribable yearning, as does a spring rain the sprouting meadows; and within her guest the wish immediately grows to work along with her and to help those who suffer. After I had spoken with her I felt like a young person who had many questions and had found no answers. Upon Maria's advice this young man started to pray and after the prayer he said, 'I no longer have any plaguing questions despite my not having received any answers. Peace and joy are in my heart.'

Dear reader!

My wish for you is that, through reading this book, you open yourself to the world beyond. Were you then also to believe that you can help these suffering brothers and sisters, decide for it now for love, which knows no death, makes this our duty. At the end you will certainly discover, whether you are a be- liever or not, that life only then becomes truly worth living when one loves and out of this love serves.

Fr. Slavko Barbarić, OFM (†)
Parish Office, Međugorje
Bosnia and Herzegovina
July 1, 1993

INTRODUCTION

Maria Simma is a most rare and uniquely gifted woman. She has not wavered in her determination nor shaken in her understanding in spite of lifelong opposition. Her lonely furrow has resulted in a harvest that can only be understood through the veil that separates us from eternity. Her experiences have come as a gift. She did not deliberately seek this; whereas to most of us on this path, our training needs our deliberate listening, looking and knocking by which we thereby develop. These were the rules laid down by the Lord Jesus that we read in Matthew 7:7.

To most people today prayer, if any, is a hurried few words and then we rush on. But to deliberately sit still and to listen, noting down the thoughts, to look, noting down the imagery, we enter the totality of the real world and begin with the advantage of knowing what the loving boss is intending for the day. God is the maker and his instruction book is so full of love. As we explore it in trust, we see that there is a vast world of eternity going on all around us.

Maria has been made aware of the desperate need for all the wandering suffering souls, moaning their states of unfinished business, lost opportunities and of their sins while here on earth. They have not yet made it into Heaven and badger, visit, trespass, oppress and cause disease and illness amongst the living in a mostly vain attempt to get us praying and sacrificing for them. Medicine and therapies can suppress symptoms, alleviate suffering, but in a vast array of our problems this area of ancestral and other control is often at the root and at the time of onset. While this entirely different approach has been proven true, not only by the peace brought on by Maria's advice, but also by many secular as well as church counselors, it exposes most of the medical world as having used only a smoke-screen. There is neither risk of harm nor an endless pile of bills to pay in this approach; so if we follow what this book says, then we will do what Maria indicates and go to Confession, to Holy Mass, to Communion and to Adoration. There we may proxy for the wandering souls in accepting the gift of forgiveness and its resulting healing and thus accelerate their convalescent journey.

Where it concerns forgotten children the progress is quick, while among adults it is slower and may need repetitions for they are in need of far greater cleansing and atonement. And here we should also ask the angels, who await our instructions, to step in for them. As our own confessions are most healing when spoken out loud, so it is also when we write down our ancestors' sins to make the whole problem objective. In this way we who suffer from this 'Pos- session Syndrome' can dissociate from those who pressure us. As to who may conduct this search, rules to its handling or the time and place, the Lord did not advise on these points. All He said was, "Do this in remembrance of Me." The operative word is remembrance -- a renewal or re-assembly -- re-assembly of me.

With great devotion and as a labor of love, this author has worked for the benefit of all of mankind by bringing to us this dialogue with Maria Simma. It opens for us endless opportunities to bring healing and it is this for which we praise and thank Our Lord Jesus Christ.

Dr. Kenneth McAll (†)
Consultant Psychiatrist
Healing the Family Tree Min-
istry
Brook Lyndhurst
Hampshire, England
July 10, 1993

1 -- SUNDAY IN AUSTRIA

Descending westward out of the Arlberg Tunnel I am soon on another Autobahn; this one heading toward Feldkirch in the western-most Austrian Province of Vorarlberg. Was my destination beyond it, I would very soon cross the border into either Switzerland or the Principality of Liechtenstein, but finding an exit sign directing me to the Grosseswalser Valley, I turn off just beyond Bludenz and head north on smaller country roads.

Soon I am winding my way up a steep and narrow serpentine road along the northwest side of a magnificent alpine valley. Twisting and turning its way through fir trees, the road often has iron avalanche barriers just above it. At every major turn or incline, covered boxes containing 'splitt', a mix of sand and salt, also remind me of the severe winters that the farmers at these altitudes must endure. Being early spring, the snow has now melted, but still evident is the recent erosion from the masses of water that have run off these mountains in the past several weeks.

Each village I pass through has a church at its center; either with a very tall, straight-sided spire or with a plump rust-red onion shaped spire. On both sides of the valley, tan cows, a few wearing large bells, hug the slopes and nibble the young grass. Higher and higher I go, deeper still into the mountains. (City folks occasionally tell the story that the locals up here cannot travel down to the flat valley for they all have one leg considerably longer than the other.) Along the edge of the road the last few white or purple crocuses look tired, having pushed their way through the dead twigs. Way up in the distance one sees smooth, lichen-green meadows crowned by a chain of limestone and granite peaks, snow still lying in their shaded crevasses. Higher and higher I go, enjoying the well-designed roads of the Austrian engineers.

Children carrying cowhide backpacks and looking all related with their applered cheeks walk home from school in small groups. Up ahead is another village. The sign reads: Sonntag.

This is 'Sunday', Austria. Here I take a neck-breaking left turn up to the church. This last road is so steep it now requires first gear and, although no sign advises right-of-way, meeting another vehicle here would be adventurous. The road swings around the cemetery walls and up ahead, pushed into the slope, sits a small comfortable chalet-type house.

This is home for Maria Simma.

Ringing the doorbell, I soon hear the sandy but warm and friendly voice calling, "Ja, kommen Sie nur 'rauf." (Yes, just come on up.) I climb a steep staircase up onto a porch that is now at eye level with the steeple of the church.

Maria is small and stout. She wears a tight colorful kerchief, and behind glasses the crystal clarity and depth of her blue eyes tell instantly that she has seen much in her eighty-three years. At the front door hangs a large carved wooden sign in German poetry that proclaims, "Wer bei mir Kritik und Korrektur betreiben will betrete meine Wohnung nicht, denn jeder hat in seinem Leben, auf sich selber acht zu geben." (Whoever wishes to practice criticism and correction here, do not enter my house; for in his life everyone has to attend to himself.) Entering from the sunny balcony she leads me through a tight and crowded little corridor to her back room. There she offers me a rickety chair and sits down herself with a slight sigh.

Everywhere I look there are pictures or statues of the Blessed Virgin Mary, St. Michael and St. Joseph; and there is at least one crucifix in every space. As we chat about the glorious weather and the multitude of pots on the porch in which she raises flowers and spices to sell, I prepare my cassette recorder. There is a slight cozy smell of kitchen and of chickens that I heard in her basement as I stepped out of the car. When the recorder is ready, I make a point of explaining to her that I intend to record as we talk and I show her the small microphone suspended between us. I ask her if this is all right with her.

> Oh, yes, that's fine with me. And as we talk, I'll keep my fingers busy. Is that all right with you?

She bends over and pulls two open boxes up from under the table and places them in front of her. They seem to contain feathers. ——

Of course, Maria; but tell me, what are you doing there?

These are duck feathers and this is the down that I pull from them. D'you see, when I have enough I sell it to a pillow factory down in the valley. The farmers up here bring me their fowl. I butcher and clean them and for that they let me keep the innards and the feathers. I then cook and eat the innards and sell the down. This is good work to do while I speak to people for any length of time, and by what you told me this could take a while.

Well, yes; I have many questions and we can simply talk until either of us becomes tired. Is that all right with you?

Certainly.

First I'd like to thank you for your time. I am sure you have had many people come to question you over the years.

Yes, that's true; but I do it gladly because I know that many people have come closer to God through what I can tell them. So go ahead. I will answer everything to the best of my ability.

(Author's note: The following discussion is the result of the author visiting Maria Simma, today 87, more than thirty times over five years.)

2 -- MARIA'S BACKGROUND

Please, could you tell me a little about your childhood and youth?

On three different occasions I wanted to enter the convent. Already as a child I told my Mum that I would not marry. To this she said, "Just wait until you are twenty, I'll ask you then." -- "No, Mum, you will not experience that" I replied. "It is firm inside me. Either I will go into the convent or I will take work somewhere else in the world where I can help others."

It was my Mum who always cared a lot for the Poor Souls and even as a schoolgirl I too did a lot for them. Later I simply decided to do everything for them. So when I left school, I thought, "All right, I'll go into the convent. Perhaps God wants that of me."

So at seventeen I entered The Heart of Jesus Convent in Hall in the Tyrol. Already, after the first six months, they said, "We'll tell you right away, you're too weak for us." You see, at eight I'd had pleurisy and pneumonia and due to that I was still a little behind physically. So after a year I had to go, but still the Mother Superior said, "I am sure you have a call for a religious Order, but wait two or three years until you are stronger and then go enter an easier Order, perhaps an en-closed Order." From that point on I always said, "A closed Order or none at all. No, I will not wait, I want to go immediately."

The second Convent was in Thalbach near Bregenz with the Dominicans. After only eight days they said, "You're much too weak for us, you must go again." Next I heard about the Mission Sisters. "The mission, that's what I want. That's why the other two weren't right." So I registered with the Franciscan Sisters in Gossau, Switzerland. "Yes, you can come." But I also had to tell them that I had already been to two others and that both had sent me off. So they always gave me the toughest work and the other candidates would ask, "Why are you doing that all alone? We wouldn't put up with that." -- "Just watch me, the Lord will help. It's all right, I'll do anything they give me." Then one day I was told, "Today you can stay here and do something light." To this I thought, "So either I must go or they saw I could do it." But when the mistress of the candidates came down the stairs, she looked at me with such pity that I knew it immediately, "Uh oh, I must go home." She comes up to me and says, "I must tell you something." -- "Yep, I know; I must go again, right?" -- "Who already told you that?" -- "Oh, I saw it in you." -- "Yes, you are too weak for us." So I had made up my mind; if I can't stay here, I won't go into any convent. Then it's not God's will that I enter a convent. And I must say, from that moment on my soul suffered a lot. I became impatient and said to God, "Hey God, it will be Your fault if I don't do Your will." But what I didn't know was that we're not to demand miracles from Him. I was still young. I often thought that God was trying to show me what He wanted of me, but that I couldn't see it. I kept expecting to find a hand-written note somewhere hidden under a haystack.

Maria, you said your Mum cared a lot for the poor souls. Who are the poor souls and what do you mean when you say she cared a lot for them?

The Poor Souls are all the souls of the deceased who have not yet reached Heaven, the souls who are still in Purgatory. In other parts of the world they're called either Holy or Chosen and those terms are biblically more correct than Poor Souls. Then again 'poor' is also correct because they're 100% dependent upon us and the poor are truly dependent upon others.

Anyway, my mother prayed a lot for them, did many loving things for them and always had them near to her heart. She always told us children that if we ever needed any help with anything that we should give it to the Poor Souls because they're our most grateful helpers. My mother was also very close to Fr. Vianney, the Curé of Ars, and often made pilgrimages to Ars. Today I am almost certain that my mother must have experienced the souls too in some way but kept it from us children.

And so when this started in 1940, I quickly knew that this was what God wanted me to do. The first soul came to me when I was twentyfive. Until then the Lord had let me wait.

You say that a deceased soul came to you. Do you mean to tell me that it came into your room to visit with you?

Yes, and they still do today. From 1940, when it started, to 1953 only two or three came to me each year and most of those in the month of November. Back then I worked at home or with children; also as a maid on a farm in Germany and then here in a neighboring village. Then in the Marian Year of 1954 I was visited by a soul every night. And also when it comes to my health, I must admit and be grateful to God that it improved with this work. On occasion when much is happening, I do cut back a bit; but in general I've been healthy. And how often have I been grateful that He did not let me enter a convent! God always gives us what it takes to do His will.

For many years now I go and give lectures. A German woman organizes these talks and also drives me there. She calls and says: On this or that day, is it possible for you to come to this or that town? And already the first time I was invited I doubled things up and couldn't go because someone was coming here. Most of the talks are received well, but I do have to put up with a lot from the modern Priests. Older believers and, for the most part, the older Priests believe everything that I say.

So why do you think this happened to you?

I cannot really know that exactly. As I've said, I always wanted to give my life to God and therefore prayer became very important to me, and I also prayed a lot and did other things for the Poor Souls. Then I also made a vow to Our Lady to be a suffering soul especially for the Poor Souls. That could have something to do with it. Yes, that will have something to do with it.

Exactly what kind and how much schooling did you have?

I finished Public Grade School. In those years only Grade School was required of us by law, and we were poor.

So at what age did you last see the inside of a school?

Let's see. I was eleven; no, twelve. Yes, I'm sure now; I was twelve when I left school for good.

And how many children were there in your family?

I was the second of eight children, and we certainly could not afford anything higher than grade school. I remember that lunch and dinner, more often than not, consisted only of soup and bread.

I ask about your schooling because I think it is important for me to have a good idea from where your answers come. Whether they come from your visiting souls, in other words supernaturally, or whether they are opinions that you have formed in your schooling and experience and obviously the influence of others around you. Will you tell me clearly from where your answers come?

Yes, I understand. My entire life revolves around this experience but your concern is a valid one. If I say, the Poor Souls have said... then that's that. If I do not preface it that way you may presume that it is my opinion. But please, you also help me with this when you might not be entirely sure. I could at times neglect to preface it that way, because I do meet with the souls about three times a week these days; and these are, one could say, my most regular meetings with other souls. There is hardly a living person with whom I meet that often during the week, except perhaps a few neighbors here and at church, and my Priest. I live alone up here and most of my guests who come with names, questions or situations needing prayer or other help, do usually come from far away.

So may I presume that due to your relatively meager education and your humble, simple and quite secluded life up here, what you tell me is based for the greatest part on what these visiting souls have told you?

Yes, that's right. You may.

3 -- PURGATORY

Now please, what exactly is Purgatory?

Purgatory is a place and a condition that every soul experiences when it still needs to do atonement and reparation for sins that it committed during its life before it too can join Jesus in Heaven. Very little is taught about it today, and when little is taught about Purgatory it leads far more people in becoming curious on their own and without any spiritual guidance they then stumble so easily into occult practices. Usually it's said that Purgatory is only a condition. This is only partially true, for it is most definitely also a place. It is also a time for waiting where the souls yearn for God. This yearning for Him is their greatest suffering. All Poor Souls experience this no matter at what level they find themselves.

There are three main levels in Purgatory and I experience the souls that need relatively little for their deliverance into Heaven. I believe this for two reasons.

The first is something that I experienced when I was called to a house by the owner who had just lost his wife recently and where strange things were happening at night. So I agreed to go there to spend a night to see if I could help him. It didn't take long for a loud banging and thumping to start up out in the hall. I then asked as I normally do, "What can I do for you?" But the noises only became louder and louder when suddenly a huge animal appeared that I had never seen before and right behind it came a large serpent that quickly devoured the first animal. Then the whole scene disappeared. I must have been somewhat afraid because I was sweating by the time it was all over. Later on I described this to a man who knows plenty about such occurrences and it was he who identified the first animal for me. It had been a hippopotamus which is symbolic for hard-heartedness. This does not mean that the woman was in Purgatory as a hippopotamus; this was only a way for me to understand this case more clearly. Having then spoken at length with the widower, it soon became clear that his wife had kept an animosity going with another woman for some thirty years even though the latter had wanted peace between them. This refusal to forgive then earned her the deepest level of Purgatory from where I was not yet able to deliver her.

The second reason, I believe, that I usually experience the souls in the highest level of Purgatory is a diary written by a German Princess in the '20s. For several years she experienced the souls in the deeper levels and many of those descriptions are certainly monstrous and very much more painful than what I have seen (Note #1)

What might some other differences be between the higher and the lower levels of Purgatory?

In the lowest level Satan can still attack the souls whereas he can no longer do that in the higher levels. It is true that we are tested while here on earth and that testing stops with our death. However, the souls in the deepest third of Purgatory must first suffer away the sins that they committed before our prayers, Masses and good deeds can be beneficial to them. And a part of that suffering in the deeper levels is that they continue being attacked by Satan.

The many levels of Purgatory are different in the same way that all our earthly illnesses are different. One can be a mere irritation of a fingernail while another can consume the entire body like a fire. This fire exists only in the lower levels of Purgatory but not in the highest.

Can our prayers block Satan from attacking those in the lowest level of Purgatory?

Yes, they can; and especially when we directly ask St. Michael the Archangel and the lesser angels to do that.

And within these three main levels there are more levels?

Yes, a very large number, because every soul is so very different when it arrives there. There are great sufferings and there are lesser sufferings and everything in between. There are probably as many levels there as there are souls because no two people or two souls, of course, are ever identical.

When the Poor Souls suffer, do they experience joy and hope in any way?

Yes. No soul ever wishes to return here to earth because they have a realization of God that is very much clearer than ours is here. They never want to return to the darkness that we live in here.

So God puts the souls there to cleanse them of their sins not yet atoned for and repaired?

No, this is usually taught incorrectly, and false teaching such as this can so easily turn people away. God does NOT put them there! The souls judge and then assign themselves to the appropriate level. It is THEY who wish to cleanse themselves before they join God. And realizing this specific truth about God's love for us is very important.

So it is we who recognize that we're not yet pure and therefore need to be cleansed in Purgatory?

Yes, that's right.

Do souls there ever revolt against their condition? Are they patient or do some of them not want the condition that they are in?

No, they are patient and they want to suffer, knowing that through this they atone and repair everything. They become clean to arrive in front of God in a entirely brilliant condition. The more atonement and reparation that are done, the cleaner they become.

Are the sufferings of Purgatory greater than those that we suffer here on earth?

All in all, they're greater, and sometimes very much greater, especially in the bottom third. They suffer more spiritually than we do.

When I asked a soul once what he suffered there, he told me that it was a very particular suffering. For instance, a father who was too lazy to work for his family that then suffered here because of him, then had to work a great deal there. The suffering from that will be much greater than the body would suffer from appropriate work here. But our sufferings here, despite being less severe, are worth so very much more to erase our sins than those in Purgatory.

If Purgatory is also a place, do the Poor Souls spend their time at particular places here on earth?

Yes, it seems that they congregate the most often around the altar or at the spot where they died. A woman I knew in Liechtenstein saw them only around the altar and when they were no longer there she knew that they had gone on to Heaven.

The souls do not come to me or to us from Purgatory, but come to us with Purgatory. It is so many different places, not a place, and so many different conditions, not a condition.

If Purgatory is many places or a large space, then are Heaven and Hell also places?

Yes, my spiritual director had me ask about this and the answer was, "It is wrong what many theologians teach today when they say that Heaven, Purgatory and Hell are merely conditions. They are all places too."

How broad is the span of time that souls must be there before they can enter Heaven?

Oh, that's very broad. Some for a mere half-hour and others for the rest of time, to the very last day. The average, the souls say, is forty years.

So there will be a last day?

Yes.

Can a Poor Soul see and communicate with others near to it?

They are always aware of the presence of others and know that they were not alone when many have acted together to do something, but they only rarely communicate with each other.

Maria, can they read?

Yes, they can; they read spiritually. I know this because when they come to me I do not have to read the names or questions that I have for them, they simply lift them off the page.

How much do they know about their families?

I would say almost everything. They see us all the time. They hear every word that we speak about them and they know what our sufferings are. But they do not know our thoughts.

They watch their own funerals and know who is there praying for them and who is there only to be seen by the others.

Do the souls there know what is going to happenin the world?

Yes, they do know some of it; but not everything. They've told me that there is something very big just at the door, just ahead of us. For many years they said it was "in front of the door" but since May '93 they have used the term "at the door". It will be for the conversion of humanity. And in smaller ways they have told me things slightly ahead of time. In the summer of 1954 they told me about the floods that did so much damage in this area. Then they also told me once that after an avalanche there were still some people alive under the snow; and so the rescue people continued to search a while longer than they would have otherwise. And they did locate and save people for two more days after I told them to please continue searching.

It is said that time no longer exists after this life, but then you say that Purgatory is a time for yearning for God. Please explain this.

It's correct that after this life time no longer exists; but when we are told that a soul must suffer so much time there, it is being translated into time for us. They can say they must suffer more, they cannot yet be delivered or their suffering has lessened. When a time is given, or when a number of Masses is given by the souls, it symbolizes the intensity and the amount of the suffering.

Do the Poor Souls have bodies as we do here or do they have another, say, spiritual body?

They say that they do not notice that they do not have their body with them. They have a transfigured body and it can take on the form of a healed and dressed human body.

The souls regret things that they did badly while here. Do they also regret things that they did not do at all while they were here on earth?

Yes, very much so. They regret chances that they missed to do good for God and for their fellow men and they get to see what good fruits would have come from them. When we die we lose the chance to do good deeds. The Souls in Purgatory can no longer earn merits as we can here.

It's also said that the angels envy us because we can do good deeds for God; whereas they cannot do good deeds for Him either thus earning further merits. (laughter)

What happens when people who know Purgatory exists, go ahead and sin anyway thinking it won't be so bad?

That they will regret very dearly! Much more dearly than those who commit the same sin knowing nothing about its existence.

What is the deepest purpose of all for what you experience?

God has permitted this so that through my apostolate others would have a clear understanding that our life here is ONLY for us to gain entry into Heaven. Our purpose here is to be good to one another and by doing so to join God, both here and now, and then finally in eternity. With this realization, life becomes increasingly valuable to everyone and the absurdity of what a huge number of people do with it also becomes much clearer. It shows us the enormity of God's love and the glorious beauty that life can become when we work alongside of Him. So, what I have been shown should and can give people a clear and definite orientation through life if they wish to participate in God's heavenly will and in its resulting beauty.

And, in a nut-shell, what is it that you yourself have learned throughout these many years of your very rare experiences?

To love God with all my might.

4 -- SIMMA'S EXPERIENCES

Maria, what happened the first time a Poor Soul visited you?

The very first time I woke up because someone was pacing back and forth in my room. I was never scared easily and really wouldn't be unless someone actually jumped into my face. So I thought, "Who's this?" It was a complete stranger walking impatiently back and forth at the foot of my bed and I called out, "Hey! Who are you?" No answer. Then I jumped out of bed, ran at him and tried to grab him, calling, "Now see to it that you get out of here. Get lost! There's nothing here of yours!" But nothing was there! Then I thought, "I wasn't dreaming. I saw him, I heard him." And as soon as I was in bed again, there he was the same as before, pacing back and forth. Again I called out, "Now tell me who you are and look to it that you take off!" Still he continued, as if he didn't hear me. For a while I watched him, thinking, "As long as he doesn't come near me..." Then I got up again and tiptoed toward him thinking, "Now I'll see if I can hold onto him." Again, nothing there!

At this point I knew nothing. I was confused. Was I still all right in the head? Then I lay down again, but couldn't fall asleep, simply couldn't! The next day I quickly went over to my Priest and told him what had happened. "I don't know what happened to me last night. Have I gone mad?" To this he said, "Why should you have gone mad? If it was to happen again, do not ask, 'Who are you?', but rather ask, 'What is it that you need from me?' It could be a Poor Soul." I responded, "If he comes to me, he must be a relative." -- "No," responded my Priest, "that does not have to be the case, especially because you have always prayed a lot for them."

The next night, there he was again! This time I did ask, "What is it that you need of me?" The fellow stopped, turned and looked at me saying, "Have three Masses celebrated for me; then I will be delivered." And he disappeared instantly. Then I knew it had been a Poor Soul. I again told my Priest and he said, "Good, if it happens again do tell me about it."

Were you ever afraid?

No, not at all. Even long before that, no; not even as a school child was I ever afraid. Mum used to say, "You're an unusual child. The others are often scared." When Mum said that someone was outside in the dark, I would say, "Give me a light, I'll see who it is."

Maria, now it seems you're quite well-known among praying believers, but in the earlier years you were very secluded. How did it happen that people came to recognize your supernatural experiences as authentic?

First of all, when things that I had said later on turned out to be correct and, furthermore, when I said things that only family members knew. Therefore, by confirmation.

Pardon the sensitive question, but have you been tested by doctors or psychologists?

Yes, I have. Many years ago now a Professor of Theology asked for this, so I went ahead with it. This resulted in six pages of professional papers being made available and they were put together by a Doctor of Psychology in Innsbruck. Copies of these went into archives of the publisher of a little book about my experiences that came out some twenty-five years ago. It was written by my old friend and spiritual director Fr. Alfons Matt and in it are included experiences of mine. [2]

Is there any official recognition by the Church when it comes to your particular experience?

I am obedient to my Priest and to my Bishops who have said that as long as everything is theologically correct, as it has been so far, to continue with my apostolate.

At first Bishop Wechner did have problems with my being able to get answers for other people. He called me in to see him and asked me from where these answers came, so I responded exactly the way I had found out myself when all this started.

Very early on I asked a soul where it was getting the information. I thought perhaps that it would go out into Purgatory to find the other soul and then ask the second what it needed to be delivered. But the one in front of me instead answered, "No, all the information that we bring to you comes from and with the permission of the Mother of Mercy." When the good Bishop heard this he said, "Well, in that case I cannot and will not say anything against it."

Who do you mean by the mother of mercy?

Oh, the Mother of Mercy is one of the many titles given to the Blessed Virgin Mary, the mother of Jesus and therefore the mother of all of us.

Mother of all of us?

Oh, yes! She should be everyone's motherly role-model and guide. And as Jesus' mother, she is also our mother.

How many Bishops have you been under and have they all been equally supportive of you? And what were their names?

There have been three Bishops until now. Their names were Tschann, Wechner and Küng. Bishop Tschann was quietly supportive and simply said that he knew that Fr. Matt was no dreamer and that therefore everything must be all right. Bishop Wechner was actively supportive of me and I am very grateful to God that that was the case.

My present Bishop, Klaus Küng, has so far chosen not to express himself one way or another.

In the beginning it must have been very puzzling to you. Who helped you the most in those earlier years?

Oh, without a question it was my dear friend, Fr. Alfons Matt. He was the Priest here in Sonntag from 1938 until 1978. At his funeral, where forty Priests and a thousand others were present, Bishop Wechner of Feldkirch said the following, "The most beautiful thing one can say about a Priest is that he was a Priest from God's heart. Such a fundamentally good and holy Priest was our Fr. Alphons Matt. May he rest in peace!" I doubt very much whether I could have done God's will as I have tried to do it, without his love and support in the early years of my apostolate for the Poor Souls.

In the beginning, did you expect your experiences to continue as long as they now have?

No, I did not really; but I understood after some time went by that Fr. Matt did expect it to continue.

Are you content with having this experience or is it difficult and painful at times?

I do not find it difficult because I not only help the Poor Souls, I help the living to return to their faith or to find the faith and it is that which brings me much joy.

And when you see the Poor Souls, what do they look like?

They come exactly as they were while here on earth and this I myself can, of course, confirm because many have come who I myself had known well. Yes, with the same clothes -- their working clothes. This is because our duty here is the most important. They always come in their work clothes, not in a bathrobe or Sunday suit. Our daily work is our mission.

How old are they when they appear to you? What I mean is this. If a twenty year-old dies and then, say, ten years later he appears to you; does he then look about thirty or does he still look twenty?

> He still looks twenty to me. They always look the same age as when they died.

What exactly is the difference between your experience and that of spiritists or so-called mediums or channelers?

> **If the public believes only one thing that I say, I would want it to be this. The difference is very simple and very clear, and we MUST hold to it with ALL SERIOUSNESS. What happens with spiritists is that they THINK they are calling the souls of the deceased; but if there is any reaction to their calling them, it is ALWAYS and without exception SATAN and his agents who are responding. Spiritists and channelers are doing something extremely dangerous both to themselves and to the people who go to them for advice. They are living an enormous pack of lies. We are NOT permitted to call the deceased! That is STRICTLY FORBIDDEN! In my case, I NEVER called them, NEVER do and NEVER will. Jesus has permitted this through His Mother.**

> But Satan, of course, can and does copy and fake anything and everything that comes from God. He monkeys God and monkeys everything God does. He can copy the souls' voices, and he can copy their looks, but whatever reaction there is, it's ALWAYS from the Evil One. Don't forget, Satan can even heal, but those healings never last.

> Maria, when you meet someone, how do you determine whether it's a Poor

Soul or a living person who is here on earth at the moment?

> When a Poor Soul comes at night I recognize it immediately as one because of its light. They're as bright as a person is during the day. They do not radiate any light so everything around them remains dark, but they themselves are light and, of course, I recognize that immediately as a Poor Soul.

Do they also come to you during the day?

They do, but when they come during the day it takes until the moment they disappear for me really to know that it was a Poor Soul. Until that happens, I cannot be certain. In either case, if I was to reach for them there would be nothing there.

Has a Poor Soul come to you during the day here in your house and, in that case, how would you be able to tell?

Well, they do not knock at the door as you did and, of course, they do not shake hands. Those would be two signals for me that it was a Poor Soul.

Has one been here lately during the day?

Yes, and recently something unusual happened in this regard. I was sitting here writing and when I looked up; one was sitting right there in that chair. That I had never seen before and I must say it did surprise me a little.

How many Poor Souls come to you during the night as compared to those who come to you during the day?

In the beginning they only came during the night but starting in the Marian year of 1954 they also began coming during the day. These days I would say that almost as many come during the day as do at night.

Maria, can you tell me of another case, other than your own, when deceased souls have been seen in broad daylight?

Yes, it happens often. Two men here in our valley were guiding a horse-drawn cart full of wood and, for some reason, the horses bolted briefly and a lot of wood fell off and onto the dirt road. And as they started to re-stack the wood one of them said, "Goodness, I wish someone would come along and help us, so that we do not end up blocking any other traffic!" Suddenly two other men appeared and started to help them, and within minutes it had all been cleared away, lifted up into the cart and secured. When it was done the first two said "thank you" and the other two left.

Soon thereafter, one of these latter two appeared to me and told me that, had the owners of the wood said "Thanks be to God" rather than merely "Thank you", the second two would have gone to Heaven instantly. Now I needed to pray a little for them to be delivered.

As you know, love here between us on earth is most often based on the smallest of acts, gestures and words. This also holds true for the Poor Souls. Even washing the kitchen floor when one really doesn't feel like it, but one does it anyway out of love for the Poor Souls in general or out of love for a particular Poor Soul, will greatly help them to go on their way. In the case of the kitchen floor, it will help someone who during life neglected to keep the house in good order for the family.

When a Poor Soul visits you, is it conscious of its surroundings or only conscious of you? Is there any evidence that it is conscious of the room and its objects?

Yes, they must be, because when they walk around the room, they do not just walk through a table; and they must know of the chair's existence if one of them, as I've already mentioned, sat down in that chair recently.

When they appear at first, do they walk through the wall and in your direction?

No, they simply appear or they come in through the door closing it again behind them. It varies but they normally awaken me with a knocking or calling; and when I awaken, there they stand at the foot of the bed. That's the most common.

When they're with you, how long does the visit last?

Normally it happens very quickly and they're gone again. Just a couple of seconds. So usually when one comes, I simply say, "What can I do for you?" And that one says, for instance, "I need five Holy Masses." And in that instant it's gone. But if they remain standing there, that's a signal for me, that I may ask questions or pass along names for whom information has been requested. That can take two or three minutes and they rarely answer immediately. Usually that soul then leaves and I have to wait weeks or even months for another to come and to respond to those earlier requests. But on a rare occasion it has happened that they answered immediately.

Have you ever permitted someone to be present on the evenings that you are visited by Poor Souls?

Many people have asked, but the Poor Souls have told me that we should not be curious in these matters, so they really do not want it to happen. But once I was in a town with a woman who had a house full of tourists, and she asked me whether they could be present to experience a visit. Either to see it or to hear it. To this I said, "Well, you might be able to hear something, but I doubt very much if anybody will see anything." I made sure to ask if there were any people around with heart conditions. There were, so I said no. This I asked because if a person with a bad heart sees or hears anything at all and merely thinks it's a Poor Soul, they could very well suffer a heart attack. So my friend then asked whether I would sleep in the room next door to her and just leave the door open. And I agreed thinking that if the Poor Souls do not like it, then they just won't show up. But then a Poor Soul did come afterall, and asked me to pray a Lord's Prayer with it. I prayed it in silence and it was impossible therefore for anybody to hear. But the Poor Soul prayed it in a normal voice and then disappeared. The next day the woman was acting very strangely which made me wonder what was wrong with her. So I asked her, "Are you all right?" -- "Yeah, but let me ask you something. Did a Poor Soul pray a Lord's Prayer with you last night?" -- "Why do you ask?" -- "Well, I have to tell you, I heard a Lord's Prayer being prayed last night and it sounded as if it was coming from the bottom of a deep cave. I was so afraid, I was sweating."

And so I had to tell her that she was the first one in my experience to have heard anything.

You said, "If the Poor Souls don't like this..."

Yes, yes, but that is just a manner of speaking, because it is up to the Mother of Mercy with Jesus' permission when they show up and when they do not.

Has it ever happened that a soul came to you while others, among the living that is, were already with you?

Yes. Once a religious Sister and her brother were here with me and suddenly a soul appeared. I asked it what it needed and did so under my breath so that nobody would notice. I got an answer and it was gone. Then the Sister asked me, "Did you just have a visitor?" -- "Why do you ask?" -- "Well, you seemed a bit distant from us there for a while." -- "Yes, one was just here but I did everything I could for it not to be noticed." -- "Oh yes, but I still felt it," said the Sister.

Now that I've been here with you, does the chance in any way increase that deceased relatives of mine will visit you?

No, it does not. Only your prayers, your efforts and your active love for them will increase the chance that God will permit them to come closer to you or to me. It is ONLY by permission of God that souls come to me. Nothing that anybody does here in any way affects their coming to me or to anybody else.

Has anybody ever taped your communication with the Poor Souls?

It once happened in Vienna that someone had hidden a tape-recorder in my room. But when it was discovered and played, all we heard were the questions and the knocking that had awakened me. But the answers that came, and there were answers that night, were not on it.

Have people ever tried to spy on you while this was going on?

Yes, that happened many years ago when some boys climbed a ladder at night to watch me and listen to me. They were a bit shocked as they watched me taking notes and listened to me asking the soul questions. Plus I was suffering at the time, which touched them even more, but they heard and saw nothing of the soul that was there with me at the moment. When I found out that I'd been watched, but that the boys had seen and heard nothing, I asked a soul how this happens. The conversation that followed was this: "The boys are still alive." -- "Yes, but I am afterall still alive too, yet I still see and hear you." -- "You belong to us. We are in darkness. The path to you is light." -- "But if I didn't accept you?" -- "Through God's mercy we may request it of you, because you belong to us." -- "What does that mean, 'you belong to us?'" -- "Through your vow you gave yourself to the Mother of Mercy in a special way. She gave you to us. This is why the path to you is light for so many souls. You do good to accept us with love and sorrow. In this way you can deliver us more quickly, you suffer less, you are given more graces and merits and can also find out more from us about those you ask for."

"The path to you is light." How do you explain this?

With my vow to the Mother of Mercy, the veil, as some would call it, has been lifted so that I may experience them clearly. And then they may come to me for assistance.

Have you seen every soul that you have asked about?

No, most definitely not. This is because when a soul comes, it can give me responses for up to twenty names at a time. So really I've only seen a small fraction of all the souls I've asked about.

Has a Poor Soul ever shown you any sense of humor?

Well, in one case, it concerned a teacher, and as he was standing in front of me, I asked him, "Where did you live?" He answered, "In a house." And when I took this to my Priest he said, "You see, you should not be too curious."

But other than that, not really a sense of humor. I've never seen them laugh. They tend to have a patient, suffering appearance.

And do humorous things happen between you and others who cannot imagine what you experience? Can you think of one?

Yes, on occasion. It did happen once that an acquaintance came by to see me and she found the front door open; and when she came to this door right here, she just pushed it open a bit without knocking. When I looked up, being so accustomed to my visitors, I just saw the face looking in and I said, "What can I do for you?" Instantly she screamed, "I'm not a Poor Soul! I'm not a Poor Soul!" (laughter)

Other than at the very beginning, have you ever again tried to touch one?

Not really, but this did happen once and I suppose I must have been sleeping especially deeply. A hand going across my face awakened me and I thought, "What's this?" And when I was completely awake, I saw it was a Poor Soul. I most definitely felt it, but when I attempt to touch one, I feel nothing or, at the very least, a little coolness.

Do they only appear by themselves or do they also appear in groups?

On rare occasion they also come in groups, but in those cases they all need the same thing to be delivered.

Have you ever been visited by Poor Souls who were not Central European, who were not Austrian, Swiss or German; and if so, how did you understand them?

Oh, many, many times. I've been visited by Africans and Asians, and when they speak to me, they speak in German, normal German, although sometimes a slightly broken German. So it might be a Japanese who looks entirely Japanese of course, but he speaks German to me. Yes, Americans, Spanish, Hungarians, Polish and many others have visited me.

So, in the case of the Japanese, did their Japanese relatives come to you with the names?

No, in most of the very distant cases they were permitted to come without the family's request. Of course, I've had many foreigners here, but not from Africa or Asia. But I did just recently have a bus of pilgrims from Polynesia come through here and that is certainly very far away!

Maria, do the Poor Souls come to you on any predictable basis? Do you in any way know ahead of time that one will come on, say, Tuesday or Thursday?

No, there's usually no way for me to tell. But what I can be certain of is that one will come on the first Friday and Saturday of every month.

And how often are you being visited lately?

About three times a week, and they come more often than that in the month of November as well as during Lent and Advent.

If we pray for the Poor Souls and then request something of them, does it make any difference whether we ourselves ask it of them or do it through you?

No, not at all. The only difference is when it comes to my asking what precisely they still need to be released from Purgatory. This does seem to be a very clear way to be certain of it. But with regular prayers and all other requests there would not be a difference in their reaction to them whether you ask or I do on your behalf. It comes down to your faith and trust. Also to your ability to observe and listen.

And when we ask them to assist us, is it enough to simply think the request or must we ask it out loud?

They cannot read our minds, but they do know our suffering and in knowing our suffering they also know many of our true needs and therefore they'll step in for us.

Saying it out loud guarantees that they hear it, but be assured that a whisper is enough. They are always around us, but I would not advise you to start talking to them in public. And, of course, Jesus knows our thoughts, so thinking a request of them silently will also be conveyed to them by the Mother of Mercy.

If someone sends you a name and they do not receive an answer for a long time, say, for eight months to a year, what would you prefer the people to think?

If an answer never comes, that does mean the soul is lost and in Hell, but waiting a long time does not dictate this at all. I just cannot start writing letters saying that for such and such no answer has yet come. It is also possible that a soul is already in Heaven when the relative or friend asks about him, and in such a case I would find that out quickly. Still I am very certain that for all souls that were in Purgatory at the moment they were being asked about I have gotten answers. But please, also remember that letters can and sometimes do get lost.

Looking around here, Maria, I see many little drawers and what I am wondering is whether you have thousands upon thousands of names for whom you are awaiting answers?

Oh no, not really. Those drawers hold many papers and other things of mine. Do not forget, a mere 25% of all Priests believes in my experience and testimony, so it only follows that even less than that of even practicing Catholics, not to mention non-Catholics and non-Christians, trust in this. At any one time, until a few years ago that is, there were at most several hundred names, but recently it has exceeded a thousand. But it has never been in the thousands.

Do you ask for anything in return for doing this for people?

> Never! God's special love for people who trust in Him takes care of me.

Can one send Poor Souls to another person?

> No, one cannot. How often would I have liked to be permitted to do that and especially to those who make fun of them or of this phenomenon!

Is it considered a sin not to believe that souls of the deceased visit us?

> No, it isn't a sin, but one may not make fun of these things either. It is not an article of faith and therefore it's not a sin. [3]

What do you think differentiates those people who experience the Poor Souls being nearby from those who do not?

> I think it's the more sensitive and observant who notice them more clearly than the others.

What is there that we can do to experience them more clearly?

> Oh, pray for them a lot and then also keep oneself as clean as possible. By that I mean in a state of grace and keep our bodies as free as possible from anything that interferes with our clarity. A balanced, healthy and moderate diet and, of course, no drugs or excessive alcohol. And fasting too helps a lot in this regard.

Do the Poor Souls do things to shorten the Purgatory of their living relatives?

> Yes, they can pray a lot for us, and the Poor Souls have told me that this is often the case.

What are the different ways that the Poor Souls can show themselves to their living relatives?

> Most common of all is by knocking. A friend of mine also experienced the knocking and counted the knocks to determine how many Masses that particular soul needed. It never repeated itself after he had attended the requested number for that soul. And when it happened again, he knew it was a different one because the knocking was not only a different number, but also at a different spot in the room.

Then they call our names. Sometimes people can recognize the voice exactly and that serves as a reminder to pray for that particular person. Or they can become even more active by causing what is called poltergeist activity. This might be our finding a clock on the floor that was on the wall the evening before, or closed windows and doors being opened. All this is merely to attract our attention and to encourage our prayers for them. These are souls who need very much attention, because they are in the deeper levels of Purgatory. Footsteps in the attic are also heard often. They can also leave behind a precise hint so that we know instantly who it was.

Do they show themselves only to their own family members?

For the most part, yes, but on rarer occasions they show themselves to very close friends or to people such as myself who have been asked by God to spend much time praying for them and helping them. I know that people can speak of very close friends when they were young coming back to them later, after the other has died. They come as a rule to those who had cared a lot for them, to the most sensitive and to the most loving and/or prayerful. But I know of cases where non-related and even non-forgiving people were visited in quite bothersome ways by the Poor Souls.

A farmer I knew was building an addition to his barn and when he came to a certain height while building a wall, it would be found the next day toppled over. Even though he had built many walls in his life, this one was giving him repeated problems. He even called in professional builders to help him with whatever he might be doing wrong and they said he had been doing everything right all along.

Then I was called to come to see him, which I of course did. I asked him a little about his family and farm, and then asked him if he knew of anybody whom he needed to forgive. At first he could not remember, but then I dug a bit deeper and his memory cleared up. Years before he had a neighbor who always said unfriendly things about his wife. This man then died and other people moved in. At first he completely refused to forgive him, saying that all that the other one was getting, he deserved, and no way would he forgive all the nastiness. I then gently explained to him that we all must forgive to come closer to God and that if he didn't he was not only harming everyone else, but most especially guaranteeing that he would suffer much himself later on. Then he understood, and never again did he have the slightest problem with that wall.

How else can they show themselves to us?

Also in dreams, but rarely so and they tend to be unreliable. There too they always ask us for prayers or for something that opens their way on upward. If they do not do this, then it is something else going on.

A controversial yet truly loving, prayerful and very successful psychiatrist in Britain says the Poor Souls do the following when they communicate with their family or friends, and here he's using his technical psychological terms: *"Extraneous unwelcome thoughts enter our subconscious. All thoughts have to have a physical outlet. These may be verbally expressed, acted out or expressed in symptoms of discomfort or malfunction in the appropriate end organ. And then, rather than drugging or giving long-term therapy, we should ask who it is visiting the subconscious with these messages, and it is that other soul then that needs our love, forgiveness and prayers to go on its way to Heaven."* Is this in your opinion correct?

Yes, exactly. That definitely sounds correct. [4]

Other than people whom you personally knew while they were alive, have souls come to you whom you recognized as well-known people?

Famous people have been delivered because their relatives came to me for help in this area. For instance, Marshal Hermann Göring of Nazi infamy appeared to me because his family had come to me for assistance. He is now in Heaven. God loved and still loves him, and we may never judge.

Then others too. Once a man came to me where I immediately knew that he was important by the way he held himself and by his clothes, although I could not tell from where he came or when he had lived. When I asked what it was that he needed from me, he told me and then added, "I am Pope Paul." I first hesitated, thinking this might be a satanic trick. "No, you're not", I said. "I knew Pope Paul and you're NOT Pope Paul!" -- "I am Pope Paul IV, not Pope Paul VI." He'd been in Purgatory since the mid-16th Century because during his Pontificate he could have done a lot more than he did. I also believe that he had ordered the Jews of Rome into ghettos, which certainly was not in God's plan for him to do. But in his case, of course, it was not his descendants who came to me to ask about him. (laughter)

So here we have a renowned Nazi who spent far less time in Purgatory than did a Pope. Some would then say it's better to be a Nazi than a Priest, Bishop or even a Pope.

Goodness no! This difference in the amount of reparation needed, occurred because the Pope had been given much more of the truth about God than Hermann Göring had. And then Fr. Matt told me that Göring had been duped into that horrid situation with relatively few protective weapons at his disposal. God's equally infinite love and justice then balanced these differences out; and now both these men are in Heaven with Him, but certainly not at the same level.

Oh, I'm sorry, but I'll be right back. I've forgotten to feed my chickens today! Just two minutes, I'll be right back.

* * *

In Maria's absence I think on behalf of as many caring, prayerful and interested people as possible, hoping that Maria's forth-coming answer would touch a very large number of them. She returns in two minutes and we continue.

* * *

When I leave, may I give you a famous name about whom I'd like to ask?

Yes, sure.

I am thinking of President Kennedy who, as you know, was very much loved by many Americans and Irish, not to mention millions of others around the entire world.

Oh, never mind doing that!

What do you mean by that?

Oh, he was in Heaven very soon after the assassination. A Poor Soul had told me this even though, here too, no family member of his has ever come to see me about him either.

Wonderful! So, may I instead ask about his brother Robert F. Kennedy who was also assassinated a few years later?

Of course, you may. If I remember correctly, he died with a Rosary in his hands and that will certainly mean that Our Lady was with him and so he's fine, I'm sure. Also, I've been told that his last words were, "Is anyone hurt?" This certainly tells us even more about the love in his soul, but, yes, you may write down his name for me later. [5]

The 16th century!? That just struck me now. Have others also suffered in

Purgatory for that long who then came to you for help?

Yes, I was asked to help an officer who had died in Corinthia in 1660. And there was also a Priest from Cologne who died in the year 555. I had to accept what he needed entirely freely; otherwise he would have been in Purgatory until the very last day. He had participated in the martyrdom of followers of St. Ursula. I can also now remember the years 1740 and 1810, but I've forgotten now who they were.

Have the Poor Souls ever told you anything specific about your future?

Not in any detail, but on several occasions they have said that something very big was at the door, just ahead of all of us now; but whether I will still see that I don't know. As I said before, it will come from God and will be for everyone's conversion. He will make His existence very clear, but even then not all will convert their hearts toward Him. Otherwise only warnings or directions for other people as in the avalanche I spoke about earlier.

Have the Poor Souls through you ever helped solve a crime for the police?

No, not that I can remember. But in several cases my testimony, which was based on what the Poor Souls had told me, helped prove that evil was in the works. But let's not forget, people who come to me are for the most part deeply Christian and thus would rather pray for people than to chase and accuse them.

Have the souls ever told you anything about the future of their visits to you?

No, they have never said anything about that.

When they or you speak of conversion, what precisely is meant by this? Do you mean that everyone should join the Catholic Church?

No, conversion does not mean that. Conversion is changing the heart, the mind and our entire lives toward the existence of God. Although it is true that all divisions among Christians were man-made divisions and that the Catholic Church does hold the most truth as taught by Jesus, we cannot expect that man can erase these many differences. God will bring about the unity of the Churches and I personally think that this too will happen very soon and still under our present Pope, but conversion means to change our lives in such a way that we are always close to God.

If there are spiritually healthier people than others, are there also spiritually healthier areas of the world than others? Have the Poor Souls said anything about this?

Yes, there are. The Poor Souls have told me that Africa is well on its way to conversion and therefore in the best shape. In the worst shape are America and Western Europe. I believe that both of those have much reparation coming to them, and very soon. And for the former Soviet Republics I would say that they are somewhat in between because they did suffer a lot during the many years of oppressive communist rule. Also South America is somewhere in the middle. But it is the USA that we must pray for the most. They have not suffered a war in this century on their own soil and they are swimming in pride, greed, occultism, sects, abortion, divorce, materialism and are just terribly spoiled. What is at the door, as the Poor Souls put it, will dramatically affect the USA.

On the subject of God's justice, what happens when a much loved person dies and many millions of prayers are offered for him as compared to an unknown person who might have lived an even holier life that no one knew about?

Our Lady takes care of that by distributing those extra graces wherever they are needed the most. She NEVER forgets ANY of her children!

Have the Poor Souls said anything about damage to the environment, to nature?

Only that all damage to nature is a very serious sin that, of course, will also need reparation.

Are animals sensitive to the presence of Poor Souls?

Yes, they are and especially horses, dogs and chickens. I know of many cases where horses clearly refused to walk past a particular house and later it was determined that souls were bumping around there and thereby calling attention to themselves.

You say dogs. Well, the Poor Souls must know, of course, that dogs are happy to follow orders. Do you know if the Poor Souls can give a dog an order to, say, go get his master because the barn is in danger?

No, this does not happen because dogs do not have souls.

But when it comes to animals Saint Hildegard of Bingen did say that Satan hates the dog more than all other animals because he is so close to man and in this way he did once attempt to harass me. Suddenly one evening a dog appeared in my room prancing around, barking and making a general nuisance of himself for a couple of minutes until I ordered him away in the name of Jesus Christ the Lord.

If people wish to find out where their loved ones are or what they need to be delivered into Heaven, what is the best way to contact you and what do they need to send you?

The best way is simply this. Just make a list with an inch between the names. Write the complete name, the town in which the person died and the birth and death years on one line. In the space between the names they send me, I will then write the answer that the Poor Souls bring me and return the same sheet to them. Most answers are very short and simple. Do not just wait out of curiosity, pray for them as you wait. That will speed up the process. [6]

Has it ever happened that no answers came at all because the people who asked only did so out of curiosity?

Yes, it has. Many years ago someone came and asked about Hitler and Stalin. I saw no harm in taking the request. A while later an answer came and it was this: "No answer is coming because the one who asked it never had the intention of praying." This was then true for they never came back again.

Well, do you think that even Hitler might have reached Heaven afterall?

From elsewhere I know that he is in Hell. And this because he has identified himself in possessed people as they were being prayed over.

Oh. Does it ever happen that a soul comes to you but without saying a word?

Yes. In such a case I know it needs prayer and, more often than not, it will return later with permission to tell me what it still needs.

Have wrong answers ever come back to you?

Some years ago, I received an answer which I then brought back to the person who gave me the name. When I gave it to him he laughed and said, "Now I know that you are a fraud because the person I asked you about is still very much alive!" This made me so desperate and angry that I ran to my Priest and said I wanted this whole thing to stop if I am getting false answers. He calmed me down and told me not to worry because it was the man's sin which had invited Satan to interfere.

Then I have also found out that a few others had gotten wrong answers while again asking for people who were also still alive. But those were not even courageous enough to confront me with it. People who lie like this invite Satan. Their dishonesty brought on more falsehood and that in the form of Satan disguising himself in order to slander me. So if people come to me with unclean hearts, then it is they who will be caught. And also, since then my discernment has grown greatly.

And to be entirely thorough now in answering to those who doubt me due to wrong answers, I wish to add the following. The souls are never wrong if it concerns something that has happened in the past or something that is happening now; but they can be wrong, so to say, when it concerns something that still lies in the future. The reason for this is that God can and does occasionally change His will.

So it can happen that an answer comes concerning the future that turned out to be different from what finally did occur. This only means that God changed His plans, and this is by no means proof that the souls were wrong or that I am a fraud.

Do you know whether some of the people who tried to trick you, thus exposing themselves as being at the very least insecure if not outright liars, were Priests?

Yes, Priests were among them; but please do not think that this has happened a lot, because it hasn't.

Can you think of any other public figures who according to the souls are also in Heaven? I ask this in the hope that your answer might again put emphasis on Jesus' teaching that we may never judge one another.

Yes, I can and that teaching is of great importance if we really wish to be with Him as soon as at all possible. The two people who come to mind both had to suffer a lot and both had very little if any religious or spiritual guidance in their youth.

About three years ago now the souls told me that Norma Jean Baker, whose stage name was different of course, was already in Heaven. And then just recently I found out that John Lennon was also in Heaven. He was murdered by a fellow who at the time suffered a possession and who later, while in jail, was freed by a good Priest praying a deliverance prayer from outside the walls. In any case, Jesus' mercy toward all three of these people has been very generous, certainly far more so than from most of us here on earth. But in both of these cases a friend of mine had to explain to me who exactly they were, because when I had these names with me I was not at all aware how famous these two had been.

Have you ever received an answer from the souls that might have been dangerous for the one who brought you the question?

Yes, something similar did happen. The souls once confirmed a very evil act and, for his own safety, then also advised that the person who had asked about it not to talk about it any more.

For people who are living in democracies, is it a God-given duty for them to vote for their governmental leaders?

The souls have told me that it is not a God-given duty that we vote.

Have you ever received an answer from the Poor Souls that did or might change the course of history for a large number of people?

Just very recently the souls confirmed something that Melanie, the visionary of La Salette, had already spoken about and here it concerns the true heir to the French Crown. A soul told me that the truth about him and his story would soon be uncovered. [7]

5 -- PRAYER & FASTING

You mention prayer so often that I'd like to ask you about it. Why do you give it such importance?

Prayer is what brings us closer to God. Look at it this way. When we have a friend the first thing we do is give him time and he gives us time. If we neglect to give our friends time, it will not take very long before we find ourselves completely alone and in many ways lost and in the dark. All right, once we give him this time we do two things, we listen and we talk. And if we wish to remain a friend, listening is far more important than talking. True friends, as you know, can gain much strength and support by merely being next to each other in silence. Prayer is most often simply being with God in silence, listening to Him, observing and absorbing Him. There is no one He ignores. And in prayer we are giving time to our very best friend -- the friend who gave us life. Would it not be appropriate to return to Him just some of the time that He created and gave to us? I think it was St. Augustine who said that prayer is man's greatest achievement and God's greatest gift to man.

What do you think is the greatest mistake that people make when it comes to prayer?

It seems to me that they rush to God only when they are in trouble or only when they think they need something. Prayers of petition are fine and are, of course, heard also; but we should be with God always praising and thanking Him for everything that he has given us and everything that He has done with us and for us. People are so ungrateful and in Western society have come to take so much for granted. And taking things for granted quickly permits greed and then hate to take over. The implied teaching, so prevalent in western society today, that all men must have the same chance for a university degree and a big house with two cars is not God's teaching. God gives His biggest secrets and greatest joys to the smallest among us. Satan promises power, influence and success. God promises peace, joy and fulfillment. The shallowest of all prayers is, 'God give me this, God give me that.' Again, back to a merely human friend. How long will he stay with us if all we do is say to him: I need this, give me that? Very small children go through this stage in their social development just when they discover their own individuality. This is when we see them cracking plastic buckets over each other's heads, yanking the shovel away and throwing sand in the other's eyes. At this stage discipline must be taught. Prayers must also include hello, thank you, sorry and I love you.

So prayer has to be developed and learned?

Yes, it does. Developed and learned inside ourselves where God then works the greatest of miracles. Truly prayerful people take nothing for granted and quickly see, hear and touch the greatness of God in the tiniest of things both internally as well as externally. In prayer we bring to Him everything inside us and everything around us. Only in listening does the child then learn how to talk and this talk should also be developed between the child and God. If the child learns that God is always next to him, it will quickly learn that it is always loved and protected. Parents and teachers alone cannot do this fully. Without God a sensitive child can be devastated when it learns that its parents and best friends too make mistakes. Children who know of God find a balance and will be greatly strengthened. They are the ones who learn to communicate in love with all those and everything around them. Children who are denied knowledge of God will grow up in fear, which then leads to the need for power, status and material goods. This way they will never enjoy the peace that God wants for all of them. We cannot blame the condition of the world today on God! Its condition is the fruit of our having gone away from Him. Everything that worries and hurts us today comes from the fact that we have ignored Him. Come back to Him in prayer and the results will be felt immediately. He is our only friend who never, never sleeps.

So if prayer must be learned, does it then follow that we ought to start with small steps as a child does?

Yes, yes, exactly. As long as we remain very conscious of the fact that prayers too may never be judged. There is no such thing as a small one or a big one -- an A grade and an F grade. God remains God, and it is the true saints who humble themselves so completely in front of Him. That is why Mother Teresa could and had to honestly say, "I am a much greater sinner than you."

What would you advise me to do if I have never prayed and want to start by speaking to God this evening?

Turn off the television, ignore ... no, unplug the telephone, go to your room and close the door behind you. Prayer is the ONLY thing in the world with which we may and must be ENTIRELY SELFISH. Then be in silence and tell God that you wish to be near to Him. Do these on a regular basis and do not let Satan pull you away with all his me, me, me chatter. Then learn a little bit about Jesus, His Holy Family and His Disciples. Constant and small steps by yourself in the presence of His Total Love. Then find yourself a picture of Jesus or a Cross to put in the corner of your room where you found that initial peace and quiet. There you will hear Him the clearest. Turn your heart in his direction. Give your heart to Him and only to Him during this time. Start perhaps with fifteen minutes and gently work it up to an hour. If you do this over a month you will be amazed what peace and joy this alone will bring you, but I must warn you now that attempts will be made to distract you from this and from Him. Ignore these gently but firmly, and simply continue with it.

Then, if you find the need to turn your entire life around -- and the world is full of this today -- go to a good Priest or minister and tell him that you have enrolled in God's kindergarten and would like to continue this among others. In relation to God, every one of us is in kindergarten. Conversion means the changing of the heart. Conversion means stopping everything that blocks our way to Jesus.

Then find a Bible and take this too into your selfish little corner. Give everything to God and to His Mum and you will soon arrive in the midst of peace. And there has never been a single human being in the world who somewhere in his heart did not feel the need for peace. The reason for this is that God Himself has said, "Before I formed you in the womb, I knew you" and that experience -- our soul being in God's peace -- is in every soul to some degree. [8]

And the very best and quickest of teachers and guides through whom to reach Him is His Mother who, afterall, was also His teacher and guide. If the Church that you are led to has ignored her or says that she is not necessary, then either ask the Priest there to reinstate her or look further until you find someone who will help you with this.

There are, for instance, Marian Shrines or Medugorje Centers in nearly every state and country today. At these centers you can ask to see her messages and take these home with you. Study them in your quiet time with God, but again, please do not go too fast. One message every three or four days is more than enough to meditate upon. Through what she tells us, come to Jesus slowly, just as all of us grew up slowly. Once you have taken these tiny steps in changing your life you will -- and I promise you this with all of my heart -- VERY soon realize how truly enormous in importance they really are. Do this with your heart and not with your mind. There are plenty of brilliant theologians who have yet to discover God in this simplest and purest of ways.

Have the Poor Souls expressed anything when conversions happen in their families?

Oh, yes! They show great, great joy when that happens and, of course, they themselves assist in the conversion process of their relatives.

In finding a Church, Maria, do you have suggestions for those of us who wish to be with others in God's presence?

Only suggestions so that you can quickly come closer to the entire truth of the Gospel. A Church that does not speak clearly against abortion must be avoided. Also Churches that are led by one overlytrained and thus powerful individual, Churches that attack the Vatican and those that bring social entertainment into them. Also any church that teaches that Satan does not exist must, at all costs, be avoided. And avoid all "churches" that ask you to participate in any mental exercises claiming that they bring you closer to God. This is very dangerous. Don't forget Jesus is always with us and we do NOT need to do any mental exercises to reach Him!

And seek a Church that believes in the Nicene or Apostle's Creed or, at least, in a very close variation on them.

Is there any particular type of prayer that is better than any other?

No. God knows us infinitely better than we know Him. All of us are put together in so many different ways so the best prayer for you is the way you pray best. And don't forget that God knows what is best for us, for others and for the whole world so it is very good to pray a lot for God's will to come about in any situation. And with prayer it would be very helpful to follow Jesus' advice in the Gospel to also start fasting.

Fasting helps our prayer life immensely, and prayer will help us to fast. There are many good books on fasting. With the combination of prayer and fasting we quickly come much closer to God and his Mother in Heaven. Be children and throw yourselves at them with complete trust. With them you will find peace and true joy in being alive.

What, in your opinion, is the correct definition of fasting?

Fasting, as done and taught by Jesus hand in hand with His praying, is a spiritual discipline to be reached for initially in our consumption of food. Our Lady teaches the ideal in this regard as being bread and water on at least one day of the week, preferably Friday, if not two or three days. But this too should be done slowly and gently and never contrary, for instance, to our doctors' instructions. Always wisely and gently as God would want it to be.

Fasting also means holding back from things, from situations, from people or from temptations that can easily pull us away from Jesus' wishes for us. Situations where we know that we could be controlled and lose our freedom to do good deeds. The list of these is, of course, endless, due again to the very wide variety of our types. Something that could tempt you cannot tempt me and vice versa. Our hearts know ourselves the best and we must always strive to be honest and clear when it comes to what we do not need. Fasting means holding back to the point where we can tell that God is doing more for us than is the world around us. This is another powerful way of reaching Him and this is so important because each of our souls is much more valuable to Him that the entire universe.

I know of people who have fasted for seven, eight or nine years straight and when it was over they were transformed in ways that would be considered entirely miraculous. God had become involved in ways that cannot be achieved through any worldly methods or teachings.

Fasting makes it much easier for us to pray and prayer also makes it far easier for us to fast. And fasting for the Poor Souls will also bring them great help for which they will be eternally grateful.

Fasting from television is needed very badly today and when people do, they will be helping Poor Souls who neglected their duties or their families. And Purgatory, I know, is full of those. Again there is no limit to the value of it. A tiny fast from something brings very much good, just as a tiny prayer does.

Can you give me an example where a very small prayer made a very big difference?

Yes, every smallest prayer is heard. Let me think. Oh yes, and here again it concerned a Poor Soul who came to me some years ago.

A man appeared one night and after he'd told me what he needed to be delivered, he remained standing in front of me and asked, "Do you know me?" I had to answer no. He then reminded me that many years ago, in 1932, when I was only seventeen he had traveled with me briefly in the same compartment of a train to Hall. Then I certainly did remember. He had complained bitterly about the Church and about religion, and I felt I had to respond to this by telling him that he was not a good person to pull down such holy things. This response surprised and annoyed him, and he told me, "You are still too young for me to let myself be lectured by you." And I just couldn't resist being a bit rude and fired back at him, "Still, I'm smarter than you are!" That was that, he sank his head into his newspaper and didn't say another word. When his station came by and he left the compartment,

I simply prayed under my breath, "Jesus, do not let this soul get lost." And now that he was with me, he told me that that tiny prayer had saved him from getting lost.

Do you have any prayers to which you have a special attachment?

For myself? Not really, but I love watching what happens among people when they discover what prayer really is.

More often than with other prayers, I plead with people to rediscover Jesus in Adoration in front of the Blessed Sacrament. This is an enormous grace and source of healing and of miracles that has been neglected drastically by the so-called modern Church. Adoration two or three times a week would bring peace to entire areas of the world.

I have a special love for the Rosary, that is so very healing in a special way for families.

And I do often advise people about St. Bridget's prayers. St. Bridget of Sweden received two sets of prayers from Our Lord and another set from Our Lady. The one set from Our Lord we pray for one year [9], while the other set, which she received from Our Lady, we pray for twelve years. (See page 265) Then from Our Lady she received the daily devotion to her Seven Sorrows. (See page 268) Our Lord and his mother promised so very much through St. Bridget to the souls who pray these, and they simply must become much more well known than they are today.

The promises He made for those who pray the set for twelve years are these. I remember them because there are only five, yet the enormity of these five should be obvious. To all who pray these He promises:

1) The soul who prays them suffers no Purgatory.

2) The soul who prays them will be accepted among the Martyrs as though he had spilled his blood for his faith.

3) The soul who prays them can chose three others whom Jesus will then keep in a state of grace sufficient to become holy.

4) No one in the four successive generations of the soul who prays them will be lost.

5) The soul who prays them will be made conscious of his death one month in advance.

But here too, I'd like to warn people, do not think that one can continue living as one wishes and that this is a guarantee to go straight to Heaven. One must with all sincerity live with God at the same time as one prays these and from then onward. If not, the soul that thinks it can outsmart the Light of God will have a very uncomfortable surprise when it is time for it to go on its way.

Do souls ask for things other than prayer from their relatives?

On occasion, yes. It can happen that a soul who shortened his life due to excessive smoking would come to ask of a relative to stop smoking for a while. So that would be a fast, of course.

Is it valid and good to pray for or to pray over animals?

Yes, it is good and certainly valid to pray over sick animals because animals do have spirits although they do not possess a soul. We most certainly can pray for their peace and their health. And we should bless them also because Satan hates anything that is close and helpful to us.

What is the spiritual significance or importance of folding one's hands flat while praying?

If we fold our hands flat while praying God gives us more graces, and here again this is what the souls told me.

How much should people pray for others versus praying for themselves?

Oh, people should pray MUCH MORE for others than they should for themselves. Again the rule holds that we should do and make the least of us while giving as much as at all possible to others. That is what God wants of us.

6 -- HEAVEN

Are there days on which more souls are delivered from Purgatory into Heaven than on others?

Yes, it is at Christmas that the most souls are delivered, but again this depends on how much was prayed or done for them. It is

Christmas because Christmas is the greatest of all days for graces. And then also on Good Friday, Ascension Day and All Soul's Day many are released.

What advice do you have for those who wish to become holy while here on earth?

Be humble. That's the answer. Make nothing of yourself and never forget for one moment that you are no better than ANYBODY else is. ONLY Jesus and his Mother were not poor sinners while they were here among us in the flesh.

Maria, are there ways for the average person to tell when a soul he has been praying for has been delivered into Heaven?

We all have such different sensitivities, but often people have felt such a deep joy while praying that they were certain beyond any doubt that it was a signal for this. But discerning this precisely is never something to worry about. If we pray for someone who is already in Heaven the Blessed Mother takes these prayers and applies them elsewhere where they are badly needed. Not the smallest of prayers ever goes to waste.

What is the fastest way for us to go to Heaven?

Again deep humility. Satan can never get near it, and it is the quickest way to get to Heaven. Then good deeds towards our neighbors and toward the Poor Souls. Acts of charity in deep humility. Look at Mother Teresa's life. For these attributes she became one of the most loved people on earth. She chose to work in the hell of Calcutta, serving the lowest, dirtiest and sickest, and that brought her to God instantly, I am sure.

Are all souls in Heaven at the same and equal level?

No. The levels in Heaven are many. All the souls there are in total joy and they know that they did not earn more and thus do not want any more. Some souls there are more glorious and more luminous than others are, and this beauty depends on our good deeds while here on earth. So with greater efforts here we can go higher up in Heaven.

Does a growing process of any sort still go on in Heaven?

Theology alone cannot answer this, but I know that one of the visionaries of Međugorje has described seeing her own mother with Our Lady at different times, and that over the years her mother has become increasingly beautiful. This will have to remain a mystery to us until we witness it ourselves.

Do people who have never set foot inside a church go to Heaven?

Oh, certainly they do, and I'm sure many more than we think because all of us have some pride in us. But because they never had access to the truth, their Purgatory is much lighter than that of faithful church-goers. But their level of Holiness will not be the same either because they did not receive or accept the same graces.

A woman appeared to me once holding a bucket and said, "This bucket is my salvation." I asked her what she meant by that, and she explained, "I hardly ever prayed and never went to church, but once I voluntarily and without charge cleaned up the house for an old lady before Christmas. It was that one loving act with this bucket that saved me." Here again we see how valuable acts of love are. The person who never goes to church and never prays, because no one ever guided them there, has the same chance as all others do to act in God's will.

Have you been shown Heaven?

No, I haven't; but many visionaries throughout history have been given glimpses of it. Some of the children of both Fatima and Međugorje saw Heaven as well as Purgatory and Hell.

And do you believe them when they say that?

Yes, and with certainty. There were discerning and careful Priests around who tested them separately from one another. They were not telling stories and were actually missing for twenty minutes or so.

What we know of Heaven is, of course, minuscule but the glorious light, the joy and the praising of God, who is at the center of everything, are always emphasized.

Do koala bears, clematis vines, Impressionist Paintings and the 'Chorus of the Slaves' from Verdi's Opera 'Nabucco' exist in Heaven?

Ah! In Heaven, the souls tell me, all our deepest wishes are fulfilled. And concerning that piece of Verdi's, one of Our Lady's most beloved Priests once said, "Now, that is already a proof of God's existence."

7 -- ANGELS

Many say we all have an angel. Is that true?

Yes, we all have a Guardian Angel.

And when we die, does this angel get another job down here?

No, no, he comes with us into Purgatory. Yet while there, the souls do not get to see their Guardian Angel all the time.

Oh, so has it ever happened that while you saw a Poor Soul that you also saw his Guardian Angel?

No, that has not happened to me, but they are always there.

And when a soul reaches Heaven what does his angel do then?

His angel stays in Heaven with him. Guardian Angels only get the assignment to accompany one of us here onto earth once.

Do all Guardian Angels look the same?

No, they do not. A credible visionary of the angels tells me that some are fiery and others quieter. These quieter ones are the ones who accompany suffering souls. Their apparel is reddish and they wear a band around their heads, somewhat like a diadem. Others wear white, are jollier and wear a crown. These serve those whom they protect more than the others do. The poor sinners' angels wear deep red, their heads are crowned and they hold their hands across their chests while looking up toward Heaven with a pleading appearance.

What is the relationship between a Poor Soul and its Guardian Angel?

On occasion they are very close to one another. The Poor Soul then sees its Guardian Angel, and the Guardian Angel consoles and protects the soul from attacks and also guides and teaches it.

Do people here among us also sometimes see and communicate with their Guardian Angels?

> Yes, this happens far more often than is realized and must be accepted and nurtured as an enormous grace. All of us, when we pray a lot, can get to know our Guardian Angel.

When people experience, say, a car accident where they're certain that something extraordinary happened to their benefit; they, more often than not, say it was their Guardian Angel. Could it have been a Poor Soul instead? And how could one tell the difference?

> Yes, it could have been a Poor Soul, but there is an easy way to tell who it was. If it was a Poor Soul, that soul would at the very same moment in some way request of the individual to pray or do something for it. See, it is always a two-way communication with the souls. With an angel it is not. The angel needs no assistance from us while God only permits the Poor Souls to show themselves when they may ask for our help on their journey. So without this the chances are high that it was an angel.

So, if someone does not pray for the Poor Souls, the chances are high that it was an angel. Therefore anybody caring to have extra protection should certainly pray for his or her deceased relatives?

> Yes, yes! And if one does, one can be very certain of their response because they so badly want to get into Heaven with Jesus. A Poor Soul told me that if everyone were to pray quickly for protection from the Poor Souls and his Guardian Angel and would use holy water regularly before driving off in his car, 80% of all car accidents would NOT happen. 80%! That would put many insurance companies out of business and drop medical costs everywhere. And an equal percentage of all other accidents is also caused by evil.

Do the angels also protect us more when we ask them to, than when we do not?

> Yes, most definitely. We alone, without calling for their assistance, cannot possibly handle the unseen assaults upon us. We must call upon them and firmly ignore the teachings that imply or say outright that angels do not exist. Even that has been said in the modern Church!

Also, much dangerous nonsense is being sold these days concerning the Angels, and much of it is occult.

Do black angels exist and, if so, who are they?

Yes, they do. They are angels who fell with Satan.

There is so much talk about and media attention given these days to UFOs. Do people confuse angels with UFOs or vice versa?

No, I don't think so. Let me put it this way. Just recently a friend of mine asked me to ask a Poor Soul if there was intelligent life on other planets. The answer came a few weeks later. The Poor Soul said, "No." So there is no intelligent life on other planets. But this does NOT mean that all those sightings and stories of abductions are not true. So many people would not wish to lie about this, but it does mean something else. If there is no other intelligent life elsewhere in our universe, and here I'd like to add that anyone with a deeper knowledge and faith in the Holy Bible would conclude the same, then all of those sightings are Satan's work. Satan wants us to be very curious and what better way is there than to lead us astray running after little green creatures out into the voids of space? Curiosity has killed far more than merely the cat. And all those films and television shows about civilizations out there can easily lead the young into danger.

Do all people have only one Guardian Angel?

No. The visionary of the angels told me that Priests and Sisters have an extra angel and so do doctors. If the doctors would only seek their angels' assistance, many of us would be in far better shape than we are now. Yes, the Bishops also have more and so does the Pope.

Can our Guardian Angel read our thoughts?

He can guide and protect us by putting thoughts into our minds and he can send away thoughts that Satan put there. People should ask for their Guardian Angel's protection much more than they do and should try to develop a sensitivity toward him in a deeper way.

Who is the most important angel for us and for the Poor Souls?

St. Michael the Archangel. He is the strongest against all evil, and we should often ask him to protect not only us, but also the Poor

Souls. We should ask him every day to protect us and our families, both living and deceased. For this they would be so very grateful!

Yours is a case of private revelation through the Poor Souls, correct?

Yes.

Are there then also cases of private revelation through the angels?

Yes, certainly there are and one of the most well known cases today is a community built around the experiences of an Austrian woman by the name of Mother Bitterlich. The community is called Opus Angelorum or The Work of the Angels, and I am a member of it. But it too is under great attack today just as Međugorje is from certain quarters. The accusations that abuse and mind-control go on at Opus Angelorum are as obscene as the accusation that a particular Priest in Međugorje is writing the messages there himself and that he paid off the Vatican to lean affirmatively toward what is happening there. And as it normally is, the people who have prayed, investigated and discerned the least are the ones who speak the most negatively. The latest insult against Opus Angelorum is that they are being forced to receive Communion in the hand! May God bless those, who impose such things on them, with His wisdom. But Our Lady will soon take care of all of this.

If people experience and sometimes even hear and see their Guardian Angels, can they also get to know them as they do other friends?

Yes, certainly they can. Many people today know their Guardian Angel's name and call upon him every day to guide, protect and assist them. In prayer we can discern our Angel's presence and discuss everything with him. He is thrilled to help us and he never falls asleep on us. And he can walk us right through very difficult and dangerous situations.

Other than St. Michael, who are the other big angels?

As mentioned in the Bible, there are seven Archangels and of these Saints Gabriel and Raphael are the two most well-known. St. Gabriel wears Priestly clothes. He acts especially for those who pray a lot to the Holy Spirit. He is the Angel of Truth and no Priest should let a day go by without asking for St. Gabriel's assistance.

St. Raphael is the Angel of Healing. He especially helps Priests who hear many confessions and the penitents themselves. Married people should also never forget St. Raphael. He wears an apron of sorts and a belt and carries a scepter-like staff in his right hand. We must also engage the assistance of both of these huge Angels for others as often as needed. And today they're both needed more than ever before because the world is swimming in falsehoods and pain due to unconfessed sins.

Then there are the nine Choirs of Angels which form three hierarchies: the Seraphim, the Cherubim and the Thrones; the Dominations, the Virtues and the Powers; and the Principalities, the Archangels and the Angels. [10] Never should we neglect to ask for their intercession as well.

Do neutral spirits of any sort exist? What I mean is; do angels exist which are neither benevolent nor evil, which are neither working for God nor for Satan?

No, neutral angels do not exist. They either stayed with God and are doing good works for Him or they fell with Satan and are doing evil works for him.

8 -- HOLY MASS

What is it that the Poor Souls ask of you the most?

Holy Mass. Most often Masses to be attended and celebrated, but then also praying the Rosary, praying the Way of the Cross and other prayers.

You say they need Masses from us. Why Masses, rather than anything else?

That is because at each Mass it is the renewal of Jesus' sufferings and death on the cross. In each Mass He again prays for us and with us, and offers Himself to the Father for us. Padre Pio, who often suffered Christ's Passion during the Mass, said that the world could exist easier without the sun than without the Holy Mass. This remark should give us much to ponder about and is also, I believe, prophetic. In going to Mass we join Jesus in saving the world from destruction, and in going to Jesus we save ourselves. The Mass is the greatest of all prayers, the greatest of all events in the world, and yet so very mysterious and so small and humble. In bringing the Poor Souls to Mass we assist them in countless ways that we will only really comprehend in Heaven when we are all together and around Jesus.

Does each Mass that we attend or have celebrated for the Poor Souls help them the same way?

No. How much it helps the soul for whom it is offered depends on how much the soul, if he was a Christian during life, loved the Mass during his life. Yet, if the soul was not a Christian during its life, and therefore knew nothing about it, attending a Mass will help that soul a great deal more.

Does the Mass we attend or have celebrated for a living person help as much as doing so for a Poor Soul?

Attending or having a Mass celebrated for a living person helps him a lot more than doing so later.

Why?

Because here we can still receive graces and that is no longer the case once we are in Purgatory. And also, here among us it helps greatly in protecting that other person from any danger.

Is there any physical proof that Jesus is actually in the Consecrated Host?

Of course, there are many proofs for this. You can read a lot about Eucharistic miracles throughout the history of the Church.

Just as an example, Therese Neumann of Konnersreuth consumed only Holy Communion and water for some thirty-six years, yet she still gained weight as she grew older. (11) And today there's a woman somewhere in northern France who has been consuming nothing but the Consecrated Host for some fifty or sixty years and a while ago her Bishop had her locked into a hospital room for two weeks to test her. And she came out as healthy as she was before. The Bishop was only doing his duty by insisting on this and the woman was doing hers by being obedient. Jesus allows such miracles to show humanity that He truly is the Bread of Life.

Then you can read about the miracle of Lanciano, Italy where several centuries ago a host turned into a piece of flesh and blood during the words of the Consecration. It was tested as recently as the 1970s, and it proved to be a piece of fresh human heart muscle.

One of my favorite Eucharistic miracles happened in Langewiese, Germany after some hosts had been stolen from a church. The thief, despite being a Christian, had let himself be bribed with a small amount of money to remove the hosts and turned them over to the others so that they could blaspheme them. And it was while this was happening that the hosts suddenly started bleeding. The participants' shock as well as their fear of worldly justice made them hurriedly wrap up the hosts in a cloth and then bury them in a woods near the town of Langewiese. Soon a Polish aristocrat happened to be traveling on the road near these woods with his coach drawn by four horses when suddenly his horses stopped abruptly and knelt down. None of the men's efforts could make them get up and move. Not even the whips could make them get up! At that point the aristocrat started looking around and came upon the linen containing the bloody hosts. Quickly the news spread throughout the area, and the Priest from Langewiese led a procession to the spot and lifted the hosts out of the ground and returned them to his church while the bells rang out.

Over the centuries there have been thousands of proofs for Jesus being literally and physically in the Consecrated Host, but Lanciano is just one of the most famous ones.

Did you personally know Therese Neumann?

I just barely missed Resl by two weeks. But I visited her at her grave, and I was quite ill at the time, yet upon leaving her I was perfectly healthy again.

Is it possible that in towns where there is much prayer and many Masses that the Poor Souls would congregate more there than in a town where there is less prayer?

Yes, definitely. They would come nearer to their relatives now that the living are praying so much, in hope that some of it will be to their benefit. Mostly the faithful would hear them and sometimes also see them. This is where Priests and others in positions of leadership must advise their people that it is normal to hear from their families and close friends who have moved on. In this so secularized world more often than not 'hearing voices' very often mistakenly implies mental illness, and this is clearly Satan's doing. Of course, some voices are mental illness and others are evil, but then again many are good and thus a great gift. But the often heard idea that 'hearing voices' means exclusively mental illness is blatantly exaggerated and thus causes tremendous wrong to be done to many very sensitive and good people. Both discernment and experience are needed to assist in these cases and the vast majority of doctors today are not versed in such matters sufficiently. It is they who should go to Mass and pray a lot to learn more about these God-given matters.

In your opinion, do people today celebrate and attend enough Masses for their deceased relatives and friends who are probably in Purgatory?

No, not at all, and a central part of my apostolate is to plead with people to do so far more often than they do today. Far more Masses should be attended and celebrated for them. It should happen on a regular basis -- on their birthday, name day, wedding anniversary, and the day of death. Also whenever one finds oneself thinking a lot about them. There is always a reason for that to happen, and one should act upon it quickly. We must do all we can for them, and offering a Mass for them is the greatest of gifts we can give them.

What do you mean by "name day"?

Oh, I'm sorry. Some would call it their Saint's day. The day that the Church sets aside especially for the saint after whom you were named. Yours, of course, would be December 6, the feast of Saint Nicholas. If children today were taught about their Saints rather than merely drowning them in material gifts on their birthdays, would that not help them a great deal in preparing them for their lives? Birthdays are also important but the emphasis should be on the children being the gifts from God rather than on more and more material. Their Saints' days will also show and teach them just a little about a wonderful role model. We should say to them that this gift is from Jesus and Mary, but also from their Saint who cares for them in a very special way, and this is not merely pretty talk, it is the truth. That would make them curious and eager to learn more.

So do you mean giving a Christian name also helps the child and not giving one can hurt, or rather, weaken the child during its life?

Yes, that's true in a way. The Saint after whom the child is named will automatically, very lovingly, powerfully and protectively step in for the child. This is then lost if a child is named -- whatever -- Glowing Bird. Now, of course, this does not diminish God's love for it but it then does have fewer intercessors for it, and today we must seek and reach for as many intercessors for us as at all possible. I am certain that it saddens God if we deny a child a strong intercessor. In all ways possible, we must bring our children everything for their happiness, guidance and fulfillment.

Maria, there exists today a type of Mass referred to as a "Healing the Family Tree Mass". These are suggested by the British psychiatrist I referred to earlier and by the many followers he has around the world, both religious and lay. In these Masses, done differently from the regular ones where the Penitential Rite flies by in a minute or two, the Priest stops and permits the people to pray and confess during this Rite, whispering it to another person on behalf of his or her deceased relatives. Do you know if the Poor Souls prefer this to other less specific Masses?

It is the sincerity and depth of the prayer for the deceased that counts. It is so important to step in for them specifically, because it heals on both ends, among the deceased as well as the living. Forgiveness must be a two-way street for all of us to be free, as Jesus wants us to be. We must apologize to Jesus for what they carried with them. By asking forgiveness for them also, we are doing them much more good than by merely asking for forgiveness for ourselves. How can we ask for forgiveness for ourselves, if we do not ask for the same mercy for others, be they alive or dead? "Forgive us our trespasses as we forgive those who trespass against us." And what relative never hurt us? It is precisely they whom we must forgive the most and do the most for.

Yet I see a small danger in calling them "healing" Masses because doing so might attract people who merely want to witness a miracle but really have no intention of praying. This, in turn, can lead some to hold them secretly which is not in Jesus' wishes either because He does NOT wish to exclude anybody. This would only be understandable when people might suffer terribly such as under the communists for celebrating a Mass at all. Then it would be understandable. But offering Masses for the dead is not some magical formula as some people might hope it is. EVERY Holy Mass heals in ways that we can simply NOT imagine! At every Mass we should at least briefly intercede for the dead as we do in the Penitential Rite; but what makes the true difference is doing so with the heart throughout our daily prayerlife all year long.

Are there things that the Poor Souls have told you about regular Masses today that they do not like and that make them unhappy?

Oh yes, and there is so much of it too. The so-called sign of peace and the holding of hands during the Lord's Prayer are just two such things. They come right after the Consecration and precisely while we ought to be concentrating on the Lord and on Him ONLY. It is just then that He is closest to us and there people go, looking around and searching for hands to grasp rather than being uninterrupted in the deepest prayer possible WITH HIM, and NOT with one's often unfamiliar neighbor. This again is bringing social ritual into the church, rather than bringing Jesus more deeply to the people. I say "often unfamiliar neighbor" because let us never put our guard down! It is precisely the most holy of places that are infiltrated the MOST by Satan worshippers. And physical contact greatly strengthens the curses they spread around. How happy it makes them to hold hands or even hug people just when they've been distracted from Jesus! Danger often lurks behind false familiarity or a forced unity. This then combined with the lack of confession makes Masses today a successful hunt for those among us who have chosen to torment Christ's people. Pray the Lord's Prayer ONLY with the One who gave us that GREATEST of all prayers. And go shake and hold hands outside later when you have the time and choice as well as the discernment with whom to do it.

Being truly prayerful and cautious does not mean being unsociable or judgmental.

And then there is, of course, clapping which is the worst by far. Churches are for praying. Jesus is there in the tabernacle and we take time off for applauding just another man for saying or doing something that happens to be popular, correct or strong?! No! This endangers the Priest or whoever said the popular thing, by lifting his ego rather than assisting him in his humbling mission of bringing Jesus to us. This is so wrong. Again, very much against the devotion that we MUST teach everyone and especially the young today. They all hold hands and clap at school, and we must show them that churches are only for them to meet with God the Father, God the Holy Spirit, God the Son, Jesus, and Mary and for NOTHING else.

Was it the souls themselves who said that the sign of peace and the holding of hands were problems?

Yes, it was.

Have the souls said anything about Eucharistic ministers?

Yes. Under normal conditions, only the consecrated hands of Priests may distribute Communion. The Law of the Church states that this must be held to unless there are 'extraordinary circumstances' such as the Priest being bed-ridden. [12] 'Extraordinary' does not mean the difference between the congregation waiting two minutes to receive or waiting ten minutes. We must always prepare in prayer to receive Jesus, and people who insist on getting everything over as quickly as possible have no idea how enormous a privilege and source of graces and protection receiving our Jesus is for us.

If anybody needs evidence that Eucharistic ministers, the way they are pushed today, are not within God's wishes I can tell the following story about something that happened near here recently.

A woman who distributed Communion, and who led many other women to do the same, died recently. I knew her briefly and heard a lot about her. Before the funeral, the casket was open for family and friends to say their good-byes. Then at a certain prearranged time it was closed. But within less than an hour a close relative arrived late and begged the Priest in charge to please open it again briefly so that the loved one could also see the deceased as the others had. The Priest agreed and with one or two other witnesses on hand lifted the cover and looked in. The small group saw something that was not the case just a very short time before. The woman's hands had turned pitch black. This was to me, as well as to others, God confirming to us that unconsecrated hands may not distribute Jesus at Communion.

Then there's the so-called 'People's Altar' the inception of which also delighted Satan. Jesus is in the tabernacle that should AT ALL TIMES be in the center of the church. By turning the altar around it caused a series of things to happen. To begin with the congregation's concentration upon Jesus was badly broken by now having the face of the Priest in between and the face is, of course, as anybody knows the strongest point of communication between people. It is ONLY during the homily that the people should concentrate upon the Priest, his words and his face. In turning the altar around Jesus was given a back seat which in turn led to his being pushed off to the side and then finally, as it is already in many modern churches, off into a separate wing if not an entirely separate room. And it is precisely this that Satan had in mind all along -- to get rid of Jesus!

Have other cases of private revelation also expressed complaints about these matters similar to what the souls have told you?

A Marian apparition that I heard described by someone reliable who was present certainly confirms what the souls say. This apparition took place during a Mass a few minutes after the Consecration. Our Lady came as she always does to the visionary present at the preset time. Yet on this occasion she neither prayed with nor spoke to the visionary and left after a few seconds having only blessed the small group. When the visionary was later asked by the others present why it happened so very quickly her answer -- with a move of her hand -- was, "Because Jesus was standing here."

So, if Our Lady does not find it all right to communicate with someone while Our Lord is present in body and blood, how dare anyone else interrupt our communicating with Him?!

And it was publicized lately that Communion in the hand was the fourth warning given to the Sister who saw Our Lady in Akita, Japan. Hearing this made me very happy.

How often should, in your opinion, people attend Mass?

Every day. You're surprised; don't be. To come nearer to God we must first, with a tiny bit of discipline, MAKE TIME FOR HIM. Did He not give us this life and this time? It is therefore not too much to expect to give a part of each day back to Him. I am fully aware that today's society has most people geared to rush about with innumerable excuses to neglect the third of our beings that consists of the spiritual. Man needs food for his body, his mind and for his spiritual life. If any one of these is ignored the person can never achieve his balance and fullness, and thus he remains behind. He loses out and God never wants anybody to fall back. I promise you with all my heart that once you give Jesus this time, you will soon be entirely puzzled how you ever existed before. He brings us such peace, such strength and such joy. Jesus is not just another psychological crutch. He is God and thus our one and only very best friend.

Mentioning Mass every day reminded me of a woman in Purgatory who appeared to me. When I asked the usual question, she responded: "Go tell my children that I will be delivered when they offer seventyfive weekday Masses for me. I am in Purgatory because I failed to teach them the value of weekday Masses." So I called upon this family and told them what their mother had instructed. They were not a poor family, and one of the next generation said, "Fine, we'll pay for seventy-five Masses, and that's that." -- "No," I told them firmly, "that will not do, because the reason she is still in Purgatory is her having failed to teach you the value of weekday Masses. Together you will attend seventy-five Masses and carry your good mother in your hearts as the sole intention. THAT is what she wants of you." After a grumble or two they agreed and proceeded to take care of it.

D'you see, God had an even greater plan for them. Since I brought this news to them I can fairly say that they continue to go to Holy Mass almost every day long after reaching the requested seventy-five Masses; and so, what they received was ten-fold more than simply the knowledge that their mother was in Heaven. Perhaps they even saved some money. (laughter)

So, a careful balance of the three parts of which we consist is very important for us to be fulfilled in this life?

Yes, and very much so. If the secular world says that the spiritual is no longer needed in this world of science and psychology, it is in direct contradiction to the facts. Then why do thousands of people fly off to India to sit and chant on the banks of the Ganges and why do the sects and cults of today enjoy overfilled halls in every city? The spiritual side of people must be taken care of with food and drink just as the other two parts must.

There is much ignorance and confusion today when the secularized world is confronted with spiritually gifted people. They have no problem with physically gifted people and actually put them on thrones of money and glory and that especially in the eyes of the young. Then come the mentally gifted people who do most of the thinking for the masses. Yet when a spiritually gifted person comes along they get confused very easily because here even more discernment and love are necessary to tell if it is from God or not.

Most people have at least heard that demon-possessed people have on occasion extraordinary physical abilities and strengths. Far fewer know that Satan was the most intelligent of all angels and can thus participate easily with those whom the world today calls its most intelligent. And when it happens that a person comes along with unusually refined spiritual traits we far too often delegate them to the madhouse unless, of course, they offer things that we people so easily fall for such as success, money, power, fake love, and on and on.

When we look for the most loved and truly respected people among all three of these areas, it is always those who with their special gifts also bring along humility because they have recognized that what they have is only a gift from God and thus they are merely a humble vehicle for His greatness.

The physically gifted person must certainly also take good care of his mind and his soul, and the mentally gifted must by all means also take good care of his body and his soul. So it also follows that the spiritually gifted must also actively engage the other two parts. God always wants humility and balance in everything we do. Balance is so very important. It is here in the Holy Mass when all three come together in perfection for us: Jesus' actual presence for the soul, the Gospel and other teachings for the mind and the bread and wine for the body.

What happens or how are people weakened when the spiritual third is neglected?

If that so very important element of them stays inactive, the person will subconsciously seek a crutch -- a dependency upon which to lean to make up for this. It is here that people fall so easily into drugs, alcohol, sex, into a total dependency on seeking money, power or social status or run off to some sect which promises them peace and fulfillment, while not telling them that their leaders are in Communion with evil spirits.

And it is the Mass, you say, that fills this need more than anything else?

Unequivocally yes! It is the most powerful way for us to reach God; it is the most powerful prayer that God has given us. His love for us, His total sacrifice for us comes through the Mass in ways that we can never measure.

What then is the most thorough thing for us to do for departed souls when it comes to offering a Mass for them?

The quickest, least loving and laziest thing for us to do is merely to make a small offering and have the Priest put it into his book. It is far better -- and there is evidence supporting that more healing and releasing occurs when there is a relative or good friend in the penitent position than when there is not -- to attend a Mass for the individual. The best of all is if the soul has its name written in the book, and in addition someone is there to intercede for him. This is complete, thorough, pure and the most loving of all.

On the subject of writing the names into the book at a church, it is also best that only one name be given to Jesus in each Mass. I am fully aware that today due to the severe lack of Priests, and therefore lack of scheduled Masses, this sometimes will be impossible. Three names are very common today, but then what stops them from putting thirty names into one Mass? Especially when they need the funds so badly most of the time. It should be only one. I send all of my Masses to the

Carmelite Monastery in Fatima which not only promises that only one name is taken into each Mass but also is in bad need of the funds.

If we wish to be thorough and do both, please remember that time and space plays no role at all, and therefore it is not necessary to attend the very same Masses where the name is registered. Keeping this in mind can alleviate conflicting schedules or legitimate limits set on people's time or ability to travel.

Again when it comes to time and space, please remember that God is God. Often I have seen it happen that healings occurred well before the Mass was actually celebrated. Here I mean, not only releases into Heaven for the Poor Souls, but also burdens among the living that vanished when it was agreed that the Mass was needed. God knows in those cases that the intention is good and will be followed through, and he NEVER wants anybody to suffer one second longer than needed.

Can you tell me of an incident where a soul made it very clear that attending extra Masses for them is necessary and good?

Yes. I knew a young woman who wished to do more for the souls and when she asked her mother what she should do for them the mother suggested going to two Masses every Sunday rather than only one. And so she did this for while. But soon the Priest noticed that she was going twice each Sunday and asked her why she was doing this to which, of course, the young woman answered that she was doing it for the souls. The Priest could not understand this and went so far as to tell her that the second Mass would not be valid and that she was wasting her time. Heart-broken and puzzled the woman stopped doing what she had started and again went only once every Sunday. Then not all too much later the Priest died and appeared from Purgatory to this same young woman and told her that he would not be delivered until she had attended all the Masses that he had blocked by advising her so poorly. Advice such as this, so very common today, will later on be regretted dearly!

Earlier on you mentioned science. Have the Poor Souls ever told you anything that, let's say, corrects something held to be the truth by scientists today?

Right now I can only think of one such case. It concerned someone asking about the location and the number of years since Eve had lived. Some scientists in the U.S. and elsewhere believe, based on some terribly sophisticated studies, that she lived some 250,000 years ago in Northern Africa or Asia Minor and I asked the souls whether this was approximately the truth. The answer they gave me was that it was not true, so those good scientists still have some work ahead of them!

9 -- SAINTS

Do any Saints play important roles for the Poor Souls?

Saint Joseph can help us greatly in avoiding Purgatory entirely, and we should often ask our favorite Saints to pray a lot for our loved ones in Purgatory. The Saints' prayers for them assist them a great deal. And officially the Patron Saint of the Poor Souls is St. Nicholas of Tolentino.

Do the Poor Souls ever mention the Saints?

No, so far they haven't mentioned them in any specific way to me but they do mention the angels and most especially St. Michael who is so very important.

How would you respond to Christians who question the importance of the Saints?

Ignoring them is a great loss. By reading about them our faith is greatly strengthened. I promise you many of their stories make contemporary writings in any media seem pathetic. God has put Saints into man's history with good reason. And praying for their intercession on our behalf or that of others is also very necessary and fruitful. With them we then have very strong advocates in front of the Throne of God.

Are there any saints alive today?

Oh, very many. In times as sinful, dangerous and volatile as these, God's graces abound and that results in many saints. They rarely make the headlines because for the most part they remain hidden until they too have gone to Heaven. This is because for the greatest part it is their humility and obedience that makes them saints and the humble will never want to be seen or heard. As we all know so well, bad news travels fast and is sold for a lot of money. Good news travels far more slowly and does not keep the media going. It does not sell papers.

Who would you consider as being a saint in this century?

Padre Pio. Pope John Paul I who was murdered for his goodness and for his recognizing Satan among the Freemasons who have strongly penetrated the walls of the Vatican. [13]

Then Maximilian Kolbe and the other more recent Polish Priest, what was his name? The one who was tortured, tied up with wire and drowned by the Secret Police -- Popolisko? Something like that. He has appeared standing next to Jesus and dressed in martyrs' colors of red and white. [14] I could come up with more, but I know that some of the greatest are still among us, yet hidden and protected.

For instance, in northern Italy there is a Priest where the Sisters had to close the windows high up in the church before his Masses. Do you know why? Because during the Consecration he was in such a deep ecstasy and so very close to Jesus that he lifted off the ground and floated upward. The Sisters didn't want to lose him! Soon his Bishop stopped his Masses in public because they understandably caused a commotion among the people. Just imagine how he must suffer here with the world as it is today! What fanciful labels would non-believing Psychiatrists attach to him!? That I'd like to know.

Yes, there are certainly very many saints today but understandably the Church has to be very careful and discerning in dealing with them and, therefore, the process for their potential beatification may only begin once they too have gone on their heavenly way.

What are the greatest misconceptions people have today about saints?

Misconceptions? I feel that the most common one is for people to think and say that those others have received graces that they have not, and so they cannot be as holy as those others either. To say "Thank God I wasn't chosen to become a saint." is putting the cart in front of the horse and is a weak excuse. Had the ones who say such things acted as well as those others, then they too would have received more and greater graces. God's justice lies deeply in the fact that every one of us is given the same opportunity to become holy.

Do saints get angry?

Yes, certainly they do; and most especially when they sense, hear or see acts against honoring God or against honoring love, no matter what the circumstances. Feeling anger and being angry is not a sin, but what one does when angry is what gets weighed carefully. But righteous anger is definitely permitted and in God's will. Wasn't Jesus Himself angry when He chased the merchants from the Temple? He most certainly was! And He still is today when people make money from a holy place or situation.

Knowing, of course, that all Saints are entirely different; what, in your opinion, are the most common personality traits among Saints other than humility?

Loving all people, no matter who they are. Seeing good in everyone, no matter who they are. Forgiveness toward anybody and readiness to do anything for God and any of His people no matter how difficult it might seem to be.

I would also include that Saints always seem to have an especially deep respect and love for the very young as well as the very old.

Do you feel that you personally have met some saints?

Yes, I do. A woman down there in the valley, for instance, in the town of Schnifis was one such person. She was bed-ridden for a very long time with crippled legs and, I think, in constant terrible pain. Every time I visited her she was beaming and I finally asked her how she could be so joyful all the time. Her answer was that she knew that she was saving so many souls for God and that she saw it as a privilege to be permitted to do so for Him. She, I think, was a true saint.

Would you tell me the names of some living saints you know?

No. That would bring them unnecessary suffering and also endanger and weaken their deep humility.

10 -- CHURCH TEACHING & BIBLE

Who in the history of the Church would you consider to be the strongest in confirming what you are telling us here concerning Purgatory?

Jesus.

In Matthew He says, "You will not come out from it until you have paid every penny." And it, of course, is sin. Then, a little further on, concerning sins against the Holy Spirit He says that such a sin "will not be forgiven, either in this age or in the age to come." [15] Here He clearly says that there are sins that will be forgiven in the next world. Because Hell is final and Heaven is without any sin or any effect of sin at all, this "next world", this in-between world, has for a very long time now been called Purgatory.

And in much more recent times I would name Pope Pius X, a very great Pope in the eyes of many. During his time they already wanted to bring in many modernizations, but he refused it and stood up to it all.

Then also St. Augustine, St. Thomas Aquinas, St. Bridget and many others. I should also mention Padre Pio, Therese Neumann, Maria Anna Lindmayr, Anna Katharina Emmerich, the Curé of Ars and Cardinal Journet, and with a little research you'll be able to find many more.

And are there other people who experienced the same as you do?

Yes, there are several well-known ones and many unknown ones. Padre Pio saw the Poor Souls often and you can easily find many books about his life. [16]

Then also St. Catherine of Genoa, John Bosco, Christina of Belgium and again St. Bridget.

Those are all Saints! You are in the company of many Saints. Are you a saint?

Goodness no, and far, far from it! The Poor Souls themselves have told me that many would have handled this far better than I have. It is not experiences such as mine or any type of private revelation that makes saints. For that matter, I know of a woman who had the very same charism as mine and because over the years pride had slipped in, her soul was lost.

Every one of us has the very same chance to become holy here on earth, including those many among us who do not receive any private revelation at all. Because I have been given this experience it is much more difficult for me to become holy, because I have been given so very much more than many. I always try, but I, like anyone, often fail.

Before you told me that the souls could read. Would it then be a good and loving gesture to keep a Bible open for them to read, say, Matthew's Gospel?

Yes, it is, but only because it is a good, loving and a very charming, trusting and faith-filled gesture will it help the Poor Souls, but that they actually gain from it by reading its information, having already seen the light of God themselves, that I doubt very much. No, the Gospel is only for the living.

Have the Poor Souls said anything about married men wanting to become Priests? Is that all right?

Yes, the Poor Souls have said it is; but only as long as the wife is willing to go along, and what is meant by that is that she must be willing to live in her own quarters. However, it is not permitted, the souls say, for already ordained Priests to get married and then to remain Priests.

Jesus said that it is difficult for the rich to enter the Kingdom of God. What might you have learned from the Poor Souls about this?

This again depends on love of neighbor. If the rich do many good deeds for the poor, of course, they too will go to Heaven and go there as quickly as anyone else. It is more difficult however to do God's will when burdened down with too many of the world's riches and the ensuing need to protect and manage them. More rich people worry about their material goods than those who always have to be careful and dependent on giving and accepting help all the time. And fewer rich people can be found at church -- that is for sure. When Jesus said this, He also meant God's Kingdom here on earth, because His Kingdom is also here. We can include ourselves in His Kingdom while still alive just as we can include ourselves in Hell here on earth. He is thereby inviting us to listen to Him rather than to Caesar or to Satan. He wants us in Heaven with Him so very badly and this is one of thousands of invitations to walk free of all the stuff that drags us down so easily.

Of the two men who were also crucified with Jesus, what did the good one do to get into Heaven?

He reprimanded the other who was still mocking the Savior. He said, where we two deserve our suffering, He accepted them without any fault whatsoever. Simply because he said 'yes' to God's will and acknowledged Jesus' innocence.

In the teaching of the Church during these last generations, which do you think were the greatest mistakes that resulted in so very many people leaving the Church or leaving their faith?

It is not the teaching of the Church that is at fault. The people in positions of authority neglected to teach their young that Jesus is all good, all positive and all loving. They preached too many threats and too little about love. They taught almost nothing about the immense beauty of prayer and of fasting. They pushed aside Our Lady and St. Michael the Archangel, and when that happens, the two greatest intercessors for us are neglected and then turmoil is always the result. So, in short, I would say that due to the lack of these: love, prayer, fasting, penance, Our Lady and St. Michael; Satan was permitted to gain ground on all fronts.

Is there a story in the Bible that you feel confirms what happens when we pray for the dead?

Much is to be found in the Bible concerning this, but the clearest and probably the most complete is the story of Lazarus coming alive. When it concerns praying for the deceased there are virtually hundreds of references that tell about the need and the goodness of doing so. In the Second Letter to Timothy, St. Paul prays for the deceased. And even in the Old Testament Judas Machabeus sends funds to Jerusalem to have sacrifices offered for the sins of the dead. [17]

I have heard Christians say that without Jesus we are only dirt. And some say that the closer people come to Jesus the more they become His marionettes. How would you respond to these remarks?

Christians say these things? Hmm.

The first sounds as though it is merely an overly enthusiastic remark possibly referring to their no longer realizing how it was possible to live life without calling on Him every day. But in truth this is not the case at all. People are always far more than dirt because whether they are close to God in their lives or not, God's love for them never changes. His love for them always remains infinite and that love alone makes every human on earth infinitely more than dirt. Padre Pio said God values every soul far more than the entire universe!

And as for Christians becoming God's marionettes, that is the furthest from the truth you can get. The closer people get to God, the freer they become, not the opposite. Marionette implies losing our freedom to do good. Our freedom to do good deeds is one of God's greatest gifts to us, and can, over time, only be taken away to a great degree by Satan. Possession means being owned by Satan.

These Christians you refer to here should pray a lot that God will show them what real Divine love is all about.

Have the Poor Souls requested anything of us that is, for the lack of a better word, more worldly, but that also comes from Church teaching as such?

Well, they've often asked me to tell everyone to give more to the world missions. I've always refused these donations because they should go directly to your parish for this purpose. It is so important to help spread the word of Jesus to the ends of the world. This also helps people here and erases many of their sins and thereby speeds up their journey to Heaven. These gifts must, however, be given in silence if the people wish to receive all the graces that God is ready to give them for this. If a gift is given with grand announcements to anybody, the graces will be far less.

I have heard Christians say that they cannot change others and can only change themselves. By what you've told me this seems only to be partially true. What are your thoughts on this?

It is certainly the truth that God's first wish for us is to strive every day to come closer and closer to Him. His justice can be found in this very easily. Every person on earth has an equal chance to better himself, but what God has given us does not stop there. He gave us very powerful intercessors in Mary, the Angels, the Saints, the Poor Souls and in each other. When we enlist these, it is certainly true that we can cause changes in the circumstances of others that, in the end-result, will change how they are. This is also our responsibility. It only shows love toward our fellow man especially when God wants us to love and enlist intercessors for our enemies.

We can love our enemies into another behavior merely by recognizing our own sinful state and by asking God and those in His Kingdom to step in for them. Have a little faith, persist in loving, call upon His friends here and beyond and I assure you that many of the loveless of the world WILL change their ways.

Is it not true that many of the things that the Poor Souls have complained to you about, are things that came out of Vatican II? How do you then feel about Vatican II?

Yes, many of these modern matters did come out at the time of the Council, so to say, but these changes had nothing to do with the spirit of the Council itself. At the core of Vatican II, there was so much good and most definitely the Holy Spirit was working strongly there. For instance, it was very good that we began recognizing God more clearly in the other denominations; and that ecumenical love was a strong subject there. However, as always happens with holy places, people or events, Satan is lurking right outside the wall and attacks, divides and causes turmoil wherever possible on the periphery in an attempt to weaken what is at that core. And to be more precise than that Satan's agents are far more organized and persistent than most Catholics. I have been told by at least three very reliable sources that the Freemasons met as early as in 1925 to start pushing through Communion in the hand. [18] It took them a while but they certainly succeeded!

As for all those other modernizations that people so erroneously think were a God-given fruit of the Council, I can assure you they were NOT [19] and that the Freemasons within the Vatican organized them way in advance with the sole intention of strengthening Satan's grasp upon the Church. When all the Bishops of the world were asked to vote on hand Communion, the strong majority voted against it. Also, no where in the documents of Vatican II can one find hand Communion mentioned even once, and Pope Paul VI himself said after the Council that the smoke of Satan had penetrated the temple of God with the intention of suffocating the fruits of the Council. How right he was!

And as a good example of something very good coming out of the Council that then also became too modern is the Charismatic Renewal. It was very good in its early years; but, then again, without Our Lady there just is no renewal! Today that movement is badly fragmented and can only be pulled together again if all its leaders were to call in the Blessed Mother into all of their activities. Do not forget for a minute that Our Lady was there in the Upper Room as the Holy Spirit descended! The Renewal's modernization has permitted Satan to fragment it so efficiently.

And over all, when we look at the Councils throughout history, it becomes clear that after every Council there came a time of confusion, and this Council was the largest to date, was it not? All these things, however, will soon settle down again.

It sure was the largest, but back to the Renewal for a moment. Do you have any advice for those who are involved in the Renewal?

Yes, they should talk less and be far more humble and prayerful. Sensation and faith do not blend.

Have the souls ever responded to a question that you or someone else posed of them where an answer did come, but where the answer seemed to be beyond accepted Theology?

Well, perhaps and here I look forward to hearing from reputable theologians if they care to respond. It did happen that someone asked whether it was only aborted or stillborn babies and the very young that, due to the lack of any prayers, went to Limbo rather than to Purgatory or straight to Heaven? To this a soul answered: "Among the very young there are also some adults." To this I have to admit that I do not know what the circumstances are that would allow this to happen.

Does this then mean that Priests and we laity should occasionally offer a Mass or other prayers for those in Limbo?

Yes, it seems that we should, but again it takes very little effort on our part to have Jesus pull them on over into Heaven. One Mass will certainly account for a very large number to be allowed into the VERY BEST of all places.

11 -- BISHOPS & POPE

Maria, have any Bishops appeared to you?

> Oh yes, several. An Italian and an American whose names I did not find out appeared to me. Then a soul informed me about a German Cardinal who was quite near to us here. The German and the Italian must remain in Purgatory until the day that Communion in the hand is forbidden in their dioceses and the American must remain there until it is forbidden in the entire USA and Communion on the tongue is reinstated. Later on I again asked to find out the names of the other two but again no names were given.

> Concerning the German Cardinal, I found out from Fr. Matt that from his death-bed he had said that he had made a big mistake by pushing for Communion in the hand. As is often the case, facts such as this are never publicized, and thus the damage was done.

> For all of them we can alleviate Purgatory, but not yet deliver them from it.

Have the Poor Souls said anything else about Bishops?

> Especially in these times when so many of them have, one can say, become so modern; I must advise them, due to what the Poor Souls have said, to change their ways or their Purgatory will be exceedingly painful, deep and long. The movement among them to allow women to become Priests, as the Church of England just has, is one of the most worrisome things today as is the movement to neutralize the language in the liturgy to satisfy the feminists within the Church. I really must beg them to stop this and to listen to their Holy Father; otherwise they will come to regret it so very dearly. And possibly you know that the Pope just repeated his strong 'no' on this very subject.

> Also the many other movements of the same nature such as the Priests who feel that they too should be permitted to marry only prove to me that they spend far too little time praying and listening to God.

What would you say to the many well-meaning and prayerful women who today say that they too should have the right to become Priests?

First I would ask of them to pray a lot to the Holy Spirit for enlightenment on this matter; and then I would ask them to respond to wellmeaning men who might say that they too should have the right to conceive, carry, give birth, feed and nurture one of God's greatest gifts to us, our children. Both of these wishes are confused and thus not in God's plan.

Had Jesus wished that women too become Priests, Mary, the holiest of all women, would certainly have been at the Last Supper, and even she was not!

Jesus did not set things up in ways other than in which He did; and again, God knows far better than we do what is the best for us. Anything contrary to His ways brings confusion, and confusion is one of Satan's most obvious products.

Are some of the Cardinals and Bishops who you say pushed Communion in the hand past the Pope in Hell?

Yes, some are; but I will not say that they were lost purely due to that. I know that other things were also involved which, in combination with this, caused this to happen. But I cannot say that it was that act alone which caused the loss of their souls.

Before you mentioned the Freemasons in the Vatican. Of the many Cardinals surrounding the Pope, how many of them are Freemasons?

I do not know the exact number, but many of the Cardinals were when he became our Pope. In the meantime this Holy Father has appointed so many new Cardinals, who certainly are not Freemasons, so it is less today, but still some who are remain there, and also very near to the Holy Father.

What have the Poor Souls told you about the present Pope?

They have told me that people must pray very much for him because he is constantly in very great danger. But to that I may also add that many Poor Souls are protecting him.

Also, he has already undertaken measures that protect a holy transition to his successor's Papacy. [20]

Maria, does the present Pope know about you, your experiences and your apostolate?

Yes, he does.

Knowing now what importance you give humility and obedience, and, in a special way, to your spiritual directors and your Bishops, may I presume that while you continue with your apostolate for the Souls in Purgatory that you are also in obedience, at all times, to the present Holy Father, Pope John Paul II?

Yes, I am! If not, I would be a big hypocrite. Of course I am obedient to him!

Seeing his great potential for holiness, Our Lady raised him and picked him. And to these enormous graces that she gave him, he responded by so publicly choosing his motto to be TOTUS TUUS. I have a deep love and respect for him and pray for him often. Yet even if I felt and knew otherwise about him, I would always be obedient to him because that is what God wants of us; because he and only he is the true successor of Saint Peter, the Rock upon which Jesus built His Church.

So you, your experiences and your apostolate have the blessing of our present Holy Father, Pope John Paul II?

Yes, I have his blessing to continue with my apostolate.

Have you ever been visited by any Cardinals, Bishops or any other wellknown men of the clergy from Rome?

Yes, two -- a Bishop and an Archbishop -- have been here to visit me in the last few years. Both love Mary, both love the Church, both are strong supporters of Međugorje and both are close to the Holy Father. But, in order to protect them from unnecessary attacks, I prefer not to mention their names.

Say, it's already 2:30, how about a break? Fresh springtime air would be nice, wouldn't you think?

INTERMISSION:

As we get up, Maria expresses her wish to show me her little vegetable garden some seventy-five yards downhill from her house. Upon leaving her front door she says, "A neighbor has been giving me problems down there. D'you see, the fence around my garden has been damaged, and I have asked him to fix it." We walk down her very steep driveway passing the church to our left and the restaurant to our right and she adds, "He tells me that the damage was done by the snow this last winter and that he has nothing to do with it."

We approach a small patch of reasonably flat earth that is surrounded by an old, rickety and weathered wooden fence. Another neighbor of hers, a woman, is just cleaning out all the dead material left over from the previous summer. After introducing us and chatting a little, Maria says, "Come look here, Nicky. Does this look to you as if the snow had caused it?" She points out a part of the fence where several boards had obviously been pulled or kicked from the posts, the color of the wood showing clearly that it had been spared from the severe elements until very recently. The nails too appeared newly exposed, shiny and clearly bent. I had to agree that it hardly looked like snow damage to me. After chatting with Maria's cheerful neighbor for a few more minutes, we again start uphill toward her house. She is slow and seems to be in some pain because of recent hip problems. As we reach the beginning of Maria's drive, she shakes her head a little and in a mere whisper says, "Ah, it doesn't matter, the sad old grump of a guy! D'you see, what he doesn't know is that a Poor Soul told me that it was not snow damage."

We wander back up to her house and its warm den.

"... will rise to a disciplinary curative time of punishment."

Correct translation
from Aramaic and Greek of both
Matthew 25:46 and John 5:29

Maria Simma at work in her den.

Maria Simma's former house.

Maria Simma's former church and house surrounded by her beloved mountains.

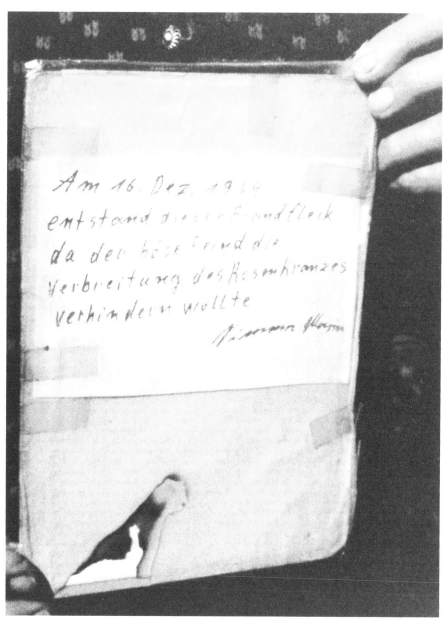

"On December 16, 1964 this burn occurred because Satan wanted to stop the spreading of the Rosary. Maria Simma."

12 -- PRIESTS & SISTERS

Maria, in your experience over this half century, how many Priests did you say believe in your testimony?

Oh, I doubt it's more than a fourth of all Priests. Those are the ones who believe it deeply and, of course, the modern ones do not believe a word of it.

Why do you think the percentage is that low?

The Poor Souls have told me that the Church has never before in its history been in such bad shape as it is today. The sin of apostasy is everywhere, and it is the Priests who will be held the most responsible for this. Instead of praying and teaching the Gospel, they seem to be running about studying psychology, public speaking, accounting or whatever -- learning how to come closer to the public. It is THEY who should show the public how to come closer to Jesus and Mary through prayer and not teach themselves how to adjust to or 'catch up' with this so secularized society. They have certainly forgotten that if they and their people pray, Jesus will arrange for all the other matters to fall into place. Show me a truly prayerful parish where things do not turn out for the best. You can't.

When Priests say that your experiences and those of others cannot be true because they do not occur in the Bible, how do you respond to this?

God is very capable of permitting things that are not specifically described in the Bible. Just because your name, or that mountain out there, is not to be found specifically in the Bible does not mean that He doesn't love you infinitely and find your soul more important than the entire universe, and does not mean that that mountain is not in His plans. Also, many things in the Church, such as the Rosary, the Sacred Heart and the Scapular, all came about due to private revelation, and are therefore not mentioned in the Bible.

Jesus himself told us about Purgatory and the Bible is full of references concerning the need to pray for the deceased. [21] Anything that teaches against or stops love between people, and this includes people who have died, is not from God.

Often people ask why we should go to Mary or why we should go to the Saints when we can go 'first class' and go straight to Jesus? Priests and Sisters are among them too. What do you respond to them?

God put all of us here to help each other through this life, and if others by their good example can teach us something about the innumerable ways of getting into Heaven with Jesus, why should we not accept their assistance as well? By throwing Mary and the Saints out, the other denominations have hardly gained; but, rather, lost the greatest intercessors for them in front of the Throne of God. No one who, at the same time, does not listen to his fellow man as well as help that fellow man, is worthy of life. I see going 'first class' with only Jesus as badly disguised pride. Just as a child grows in this life with its brothers and sisters, cousins, uncles and aunts; so does a Christian grow by studying and getting assistance from the Saints whose lives are well documented and from the holy people who are around us today.

For those who dare say that they have no need for the Blessed Virgin Mary, I ask, what was it that Jesus Himself said to Saint John and to His Mother just moments before His last breath on the Cross? "Woman, behold, your son. Son, behold your mother." [22] Will Jesus even let us go 'first class' if we ignore the mother who bore Him, raised Him and taught Him? I challenge them to say that they really know Him if they do not listen to THOSE words at the very moment that He was dying for EVERY one of them! Hearing them speak against Mary hurts me terribly. So just imagine what that does to Jesus!! But she is just now, in these years, making a very powerful comeback throughout the entire world. She is leading an immense number of people back to her Son through her apparitions that seem to be occurring in every corner of this distressed world.

Have the Poor Souls said anything about modern Priests and their role and behavior out in public?

Yes, they have. What they like the least is when they leave their habits behind in order to blend into the public. The same has been said about religious Sisters. This waters down the necessary respect that the public should show toward them. They have made vows to serve Jesus and not vows to be like everyone else.

Are there Priests in Purgatory and what, in general, puts them there the most often?

Yes, very many Priests are there. Of course I cannot tell you the exact percentage or the order of frequency of particular sins, but what comes to mind the quickest are disobedience to the Holy Father, lack of love for the Holy Mass, lack of love for prayer and fasting, not reading their breviary and, again, Communion in the hand.

You probably know better than I do that the subject of Communion in the hand is highly controversial. Why is this?

The public has not been told the entire story about this and must inform itself well. The Law of the Church is that a part of the Communion railing must remain for those who wish to receive, kneeling and on the tongue. These were the words of Pope Paul VI. So every church without it is already in disobedience. The Poor Souls have told me that NOT ONE POPE TO DATE has personally been for it, but that it was pushed through politically by a group of Cardinals and Bishops. The older Priests and Bishops know this and, for the most part, have not told the public about it; and therefore it is they who carry the greatest responsibility. All the Popes, in turn, knew full well that Communion in the hand was against the reverence of the Holiest of Holies, and our present Pope does not distribute Communion into people's hands.

Of course, under these conditions, it is not a sin for the communicant to receive it on the hand, but I beg the people to listen to our Popes. Also it has permitted so much more sacrilege to occur. Please be aware that witches pay a lot of money to hurt Jesus directly with the Consecrated Hosts that are often secretly removed from the churches. We must stop giving them such easy access to the Holiest of Holies. This is a very serious matter. Were all the Priests to pray to the Holy Spirit and pray the Rosary, then none of them would go astray in these matters as they do so easily and frequently today.

If the older Bishops and Priests were to ask all their parishioners over the age of, say, forty whether they preferred to receive Communion kneeling, they would with their love for their brothers and sisters accept and allow that the vast majority would prefer to do so.

Nobody can say that two generations ago there was less prayer than today because the very opposite is true. And by going back to more humility and prayer the young would quickly learn the value of the humble, penitent position in front of the Holiest of Holies. I've even seen kneeling communicants being skipped over simply because they were kneeling! Then I've also seen children receiving First Communion being told to stand even though their parents and grandparents suffered because of this. All this is Satan's doing and saddens me terribly. And when people then say that they will be a part of the crowd out of brotherly love, I say no; because when brotherly love is contrary to our humble reverence toward the Holiest of Holies and the Divine Love of God, then this weak permissiveness is not from God.

I also remember when the German Bishops participated in pushing this past the Pope; it was the Americans who at first said they would not agree with it because it was against the wishes of the Pope. But just look what has happened now! And how many Priests did we lose because their conscience could not carry this? Many.

On the subject of Communion in the hand, something interesting happened a while back in Munich while I was giving a talk there. It came to this subject, and suddenly I noticed that it really got quite a few people excited. Three people were trying to talk against what I was saying, and they did so virtually all at the same time. I silently asked God for help. As the room became quite loud and agitated, a good-looking forty-year-old woman in a long black dress off to the side of the room, rose and with great gentleness, but also with evenhanded authority, spoke to the room and in a minute or two had everyone calm again. I was impressed by her knowledge and equally impressed by how she conveyed it with such love. As the talk came to an end, I went to the organizers to ask to speak to this woman and to say thank you for her help. In a way I thought she was a part of the group of people who had invited me to speak about Purgatory. They, however, thought she was a friend of mine whom I had brought along. We were both wrong. She couldn't be found, and we even went to the front door to ask the people who had stayed at the doors during the entire talk because the talk had been by invitation only. These told us that no such woman had either entered or left through those doors and the hall had no other entrances. She was gone.

Was she a Poor Soul?

Most likely, yes. And some of us did then pray for her.

Some people say that because Jesus distributed the bread into the hands of His Disciples at the Last Supper, therefore it's all right for the Priest to do the same today. What might you say to this?

Not true! Both Katharina Emmerich as well as Therese Neumann, possibly the two greatest German mystics ever, were both permitted to see the Last Supper; and in both cases Jesus distributed the consecrated bread into the mouths of His Apostles.

And please; now understand and trust. I am far from the only one saying this! Precisely this subject, among many other related ones, is being discussed today at the highest levels of the Church, and I know here too Jesus will prevail no matter how chaotic things have yet to become.

But, allow me, what you say Katharina Emmerich was shown is again private revelation...

Yes, it is; and every time throughout history it has been through private revelation that God has set things straight. And as any one of us can confirm, if we research the well-known cases throughout history, the fruits of those were enormous, with a huge number of conversions around them. Just look at Rue de Bac, Lourdes and Fatima, or Therese Neumann, not to mention the many millions of conversions that have occurred in the last fifteen years around the happenings in that undistinguished little village in the middle of the most volatile part of all of Europe. Here, of course, I again mean Međugorje.

Now that I am again thinking of Međugorje, here is another perspective concerning Communion in the hand...

Yes. What may that be? And please, Maria, let me hear all the possible angles you know of because so many good people, I know, are looking for the correct answer to this.

In apparition towns such as Međugorje, Schio, Garabandal and the others where Our Lady has chosen to appear, she often does or did so outside. Take Međugorje, merely as one example. There she has often appeared and still does so on one or the other of the two mountains. (See photo page 132) At those apparitions you can find anywhere from a small handful of people in the dead of winter all the way to, say, 5,000 on big Feast Days during the warmer seasons. Without the slightest hesitation everyone up there, and no matter what the weather, will jostle and crunch down into the mud and upon the sharp rocks while getting poked by thorn bushes to kneel while she is with them. That comes very naturally to everyone, and it should; BUT just two or three hours earlier down in the Church while Jesus Himself is being received in the Holy Host, nearly everyone stands proud as soldiers! Is this what Our Lady wants of us? To kneel in front of her and not in front of her Divine Son! NO, IT IS NOT!!

Please, the good people must listen to and follow their own consciences and not do things merely because others do.

Yes, and here is another confirmation for you on this matter. It might not be as shocking as the earlier one concerning the woman's blackened hands and no harm done if we consider it amusing; but it certainly is as persuasive to me as any other story.

I personally know a very good and very prayerful woman who also had problems with this, and she simply prayed about it and then asked Jesus Himself to send her a signal quickly to finally clarify matters for her. He did! The very next time she went to receive Communion the Priest, as he had until then, put the host into her palm. As soon as he had put it there, it lifted off her palm, sailed away and disappeared in thin air. This little miracle too had several witnesses.

Maria, you are convincing!

And Mother Teresa also preferred communicants to receive kneeling and on the tongue, and therefore that form is the only one allowed inside her Communities.

D'you see, Communion in the hand is, from the Church perspective only a tolerance, but it is NOT what the Church really wants.

When Priests in Purgatory have come to you, who then takes care of the prayers or whatever else is needed for them to be delivered?

Priests must then take care of the prayers they require; but if there is anything else, I take it upon myself.

How often should Priests celebrate Holy Mass?

No less than once a day, and the most Masses that are allowed by the Law of the Church are two, if the second one is a funeral or wedding. But God certainly understands extraordinary conditions that allow Priests to celebrate more Masses, such as when another Priest is unavailable. This is because celebrating Holy Mass is the very core of their work. It is their greatest duty and should become their greatest love toward God to whom they took their vows.

Can we presume that Sisters too are in Purgatory?

Yes, and for them it is mostly the lack of humility, lack of modesty, and disobedience that put them there.

And what about Priests going to Hell?

Just a short while ago I had a Priest here with me who had recently been very ill. Over several decades he had been in and out of hospitals and three times came very near to death. During his latest illness he came very close to death, and there in his agony he had a vision of Priests falling into Hell like snowflakes. This shocked him so badly and caused him to cry for weeks. It took a long time for him to recover from this vision alone.

May I ask why he had come to visit you?

Oh, I knew him briefly many years ago, and after this experience he came back to me to thank me for what I had told him and had helped him with back then. It was merely a courtesy call that now carried much importance to him.

Have concerned relatives or friends of deceased Priests come to you to find out whether or not they were saved due to their, how should I say, perhaps different and worrisome behavior?

Yes, that happened a while back.

A couple from the Alsace part of France came to me because of a Priest they had come to know. He had been badly disturbed for quite a while, and one day in a rage he threw a Sacred Heart of Jesus statue out of his church smashing it. Soon thereafter he committed suicide, and these understandably worried people came to me to find out where he had ended up. It turned out that he was saved afterall but in very deep Purgatory, not yet to be delivered.

Many people say that Priests are out of touch with the world. How do you feel about this?

That sounds to me like much of the proud propaganda going around today. I would want to tell them that the most learned of men on this earth often need Jesus far more urgently than the simplest of folk. The remark that Priests are out of touch is not true if the Priests pray. Only if they do not will the graces be limited. I think that that particular criticism is badly misguided. One can be and should be critical about the lack of prayer, but not about the lack of being in tune with the rest of us. Every one of us shares in the human and thus sinful experience and, again, no seeking of or listening to a Doctorate in Psychology, Philosophy, or whatever will ever change this. If anything, the modern Priests are distant from Jesus and not distant from other men.

How many Priests and Bishops were you permitted to deliver into Heaven since Vatican II with your prayers, Masses or sufferings?

Well, I cannot tell you exactly but I am certain it is between forty and fifty.

And of those forty to fifty, how many were in Purgatory due to these modernizations around the Mass?

Almost all of them. And of those, the majority was there because they pushed Communion in the hand.

If very few Priests today believe in your testimony, does it then follow that very few ask for the assistance of the Poor Souls today?

Yes, I'm afraid it does mean that. Very few do.

Can you tell me of a case where a Priest did get assistance from them?

Yes, I can. A Priest near Budapest, Hungary recently wanted to renovate his church and build a small monastery for it. So he first went to his Bishop to ask for help. The Bishop told him to do what he wanted, but he told the Priest that his own coffers would not be helping in this project. So then the good Priest prayed, and said he would depend on Our Lady to help him through the Poor Souls. Soon he came here, and I quickly agreed to go with him to his parish, as well as others in that area, to speak on this subject. Within two weeks of my returning here from that weekend, he received $100,000 for his church and monastery. The Poor Souls quickly responded for him.

That's quite a few duck feathers!

No, no, (laughter) it wasn't with the duck feathers! But God does very quickly help those who trust in Our Lady and in the help from the Poor Souls.

I am sure you know better than most that many seminaries today stand empty. What causes this and how could it be remedied?

The remedy for this would be if they returned to emphasizing the spirit of prayer, sacrifice and penance. Then the men would come again in waves. The souls who feel themselves called to serve God in this way know clearly that prayer is their path and when that is not nurtured, then for what, finally, are there seminaries?! Were they to do this, a wave of applicants would result and then, just a little bit further down the road, it would no longer be necessary to allow unconsecrated laymen's' hands to distribute Holy Communion. This alone within the seminaries would strengthen everyone's active faith and keep Satan at a much greater distance.

You've put great emphasis in trusting the Virgin Mary to lead people to Jesus. Have you seen any difference, therefore, between Marian Priests and those who have become, as you say, modern and have thereby left her out of the picture?

Oh yes! I can discern a Marian Priest quickly. They are far more gentle, humble, penitential, loving and protective than the others are. In their humility they become strong, and in their strength their fruits become far clearer than those Priests who operate without her. They also have many fewer problems with celibacy and with Our Lady at their side, come to experience the enormous graces that come with celibacy. It is she who with our help steps on Satan's head. This, again, is not mere symbolism; it is fact. Satan runs from her and from her Priests. Marian Priests and the Marian Army of lay people around them will, in the end, save humanity and nothing short of that!

And this will happen with the Triumph of the Immaculate Heart of Mary. [23]

So here the world has an openly Marian Pope and a Marian Army of Priests and laity who will be leading this army through the Triumph of the Immaculate Heart of Mary. If people wish to join the Holy Father and his Marian army, what is the best way for them to do this? How could people do the most for the Triumph of the Immaculate Heart?

By starting to pray, by starting to live the messages of Međugorje and by consecrating themselves and their families to the Immaculate Heart of Mary.

13 -- CHURCHES

When the Poor Souls have warned you about the present condition of the Church, have they also said anything about church buildings today?

Yes, that too. Many things that we would associate with modern churches bother them very much. Churches are ONLY for praying and for meeting with Jesus and Mary. The Poor Souls say they want there to be no sophisticated equipment, no plush carpeting and nothing to make things as comfortable as a wealthy living room. The churches are there for you and Jesus to be alone together. Decorations that serve no other function but to decorate have to go, because they distract. And the Poor Souls have also mentioned that much of the socalled modern art horrifies them. Much of it is gruesomely ugly, not to mention historically incorrect. And Mary should again be given a prominent place.

More important than anything else, however, is that all tabernacles MUST, by all means, MUST be in the center! In the center of the church and not off to the side or even in another room, ONLY in the center. If Jesus is no longer the center of things, then He too will soon be carried out. Then all we are left with is a second town hall! Believe me, every time that someone looks at the tabernacle with love, Jesus then elevates his place in Heaven.

Then the Priests should also return to using the pulpits. Bringing the Priests down to the level of the parishioners was yet another of Satan's tricks. Up in the pulpit they would gain far more respect.

No social functions should be arranged in churches, only holy functions. Bring back the Saints too, at least St. Joseph, St. Michael the Archangel and the Saint after whom the church was named. And I've mentioned the Communion railing already. All these things that are missing and all the comforts that have been added in the last decades separate us from our Jesus, and thus make Satan very happy. I know of coffee being served, animals on people's laps and televisions being set up in churches. I've seen churches without Holy Water at the doors and without kneelers. None of this is good, and none of it is within Jesus' wishes.

So they're simply not happy with modern churches, is that it?

No, I have seen several modern churches where everything was all right. One, for instance, in Lienz, Tyrol is very modern but also very prayerful and done correctly. So, ugly, non-prayerful and incomplete does not need to equate with modern, but modern is, in most of the cases, ugly, non-prayerful and incomplete.

What about holy functions that the modern churches might have forgotten?

Yes, that too. They miss.... The Poor Souls miss processions that are the same as small pilgrimages. Processions for Our Lady or processions for the Saints that were such an integral part of spiritual life before. We give parades to sports teams and politicians. Then why do we no longer hold processions for Jesus, His Mother and Their Saints? Things of this nature bring Jesus and His Saints out into the world as it should be, and not the other way around by bringing the world into Jesus' houses, as happens so often today.

Then also in many parts of the world the Priests no longer go out to bless every home at least once a year. This too weakens the faith and weakens the love and respect that must stay intact between the Priests and the laity. It also makes the houses much easier to enter for Satan and his demons.

The loss of such holy functions makes Satan perfectly happy. Yes, and also First Saturday devotions have been forgotten in so many parts of the world. They too must be brought back! For matters of this nature we were given Priests to begin with. We need them, and they need us to remind them again of their responsibilities.

Can you tell me how Mass is celebrated in your own church here in Sonntag and whether the souls are happy with how things are done here?

Yes, they are satisfied with the way we have kept it here.

The Communion railing was never removed and Holy Communion is given only on the tongue. There are never any women around the altar and that includes during the readings and having only altar boys serve. Jesus in the tabernacle is in the center and Our Lady and some Saints are prominent in several paintings and statuary. Confessions can be heard every week, and the people take advantage of this regularly. Adoration of the Blessed Sacrament and the Rosary are attended regularly also.

All our children are in front during the entirety of the Mass where I keep them until the adults have left the church. This is only to keep order and silence and to avoid having them run and dodge between the legs of the adults.

14 -- CONFESSION

What, if anything, have the Poor Souls told you about the Sacrament of Reconciliation or Confession?

Oh, yes, they have often mentioned it. They are very saddened that it has become so unpopular, so neglected. It is SUCH a great gift from God that ONLY Satan would want to destroy it. And, again, I'm afraid that he's done a very good job at this.

Confession, as it ought to be called, is something to run for with joy and NOT, as Satan wishes, something of which one need be in the slightest of ways afraid. Do not worry, there is nothing that you could possibly tell a good Priest that he hasn't yet heard about. A good Priest knows full well that he, with all that he has learned and experienced, is a far greater sinner than you are. It is a BIG joy for Jesus and everyone else in Heaven when we bring our woundedness and weaknesses to Him.

The Poor Souls have told me that 60% of all depressions in the world would not be if people took advantage of this great gift. Again, many doctors, drug companies and agencies would be out of business if everyone went to Confession regularly. Our Lord can save and heal everybody and everything of His choice, if people would only call on Him! Our Lady has said, and I think this was in Međugorje, that monthly Confession would heal the West.

Confession is greatly misunderstood. For most people it is not hard to discern bad from good, but it becomes much more interesting and far more challenging when the question is the difference between good and better. Confession is not only there for us to confess that we robbed a bank, where in actuality very few of us rob banks. It is there for the greatest part for us to seek ways of becoming better and better in the eyes of God. What was there in the last month that I could have gone about in a holier way? That's what we must ask ourselves and I challenge anybody to say that they did everything this last month the way that Jesus would have done it.

Humility brings us the greatest of graces. Jesus gives the greatest things to the small at heart. Confession reminds us repeatedly of the smallness that He wishes for us SO THAT He can give us enormous gifts.

How would you respond to those many people who say, and do so with sincerity, that they do not need a Priest to go to Confession? That they do not need to tell everything to another person, but can go straight to God themselves?

If this were true, again, the psychiatrists and psychologists would not be enjoying such a booming business. Both the smartest and the simplest could go to the same Priest, and both would be equally amazed at the fruits, at the graces that will flow out of that short and free meeting with Jesus. Every human being has the same need to confess guilt and all those long-lasting, long-winded and very expensive therapies and group encounters would not in any way be necessary if the people would only come to Jesus! On top of that, the great graces do not come from there, they do not come from doctors or from other secular laymen, they come from Jesus and ONLY from Jesus! People are led to cheat themselves so easily.

Don't you think that the One who gave us life to start with, is ALSO capable of giving us infinitely more than the 'how to cope' chatter of the majority of psychologists? God bless them! Most of them do not dare address the reality of sin, and then how could they possibly address the reality of forgiveness? They have to live on repeat business, and our not going to Confession then guarantees them their next big car. They thrive on our sins while Jesus died for us to conquer and erase them forever!

And to the retort that Jesus never taught that we must go into a confessional to confess?

That is true, so I suggest they confess to a Priest out loud, but in public. The point is it has to be out loud. Jesus said repent and in doing so He carries the sins away, and only then does Satan no longer know of them. He can no longer attach himself to it or attack the person through that weak or broken link between God and us.

But it's a Priest in the confessional, it's not Jesus.

Are you so sure?

An Italian grandmother wanted to take her eight-year-old grandson to Padre Pio for his first Confession. She was understandably very excited when she arrived in his church. So then the boy went to Confession and came out beaming with joy. The grandmother knew what Padre Pio looked like. He was short, plump, and balding, with very dark eyes and then about sixty-five years old; but still she went ahead and asked the boy, "Tell me, what did he look like?" Very calmly and in detail the boy answered, "Oh, he was tall and well-built, with chestnut eyes, had long brown hair and was about thirty years old."

You're kidding!

No, things like that happen often in very prayerful and holy settings.

Let me give you a hypothetical case and then ask you about it. We have two families. Both live reasonably good and healthy lives. One family goes to Confession on a reasonably regular basis while the other one does not. Will there be differences among their descendants and, if so, what might they be?

The first family will have a sound basis to come closer and closer to Jesus over the generations, while the second family will then carry many burdens that they would not have, had the initial parents gone to Confession on a regular basis. These burdens will include illnesses and weaknesses that could have been avoided. The balanced and constantly penitent attitude of the first family will show itself in the strength and joy of their descendants, while those of the other family will be far more open to Satan's attacks upon them.

So are you then saying that people who are constantly reminded of their sinful state end up being healthier than those who are not?

Oh yes! With the humility of Confession, prayer, and the constant love of God that comes from that, a strength and balance grow that very much result in healthier people. And that means healthier emotionally, mentally and physically. This then also extends down through the generations.

So we can with our love, prayer and confession guarantee better health of our children, grand-children and great grand-children?

Yes, exactly. Far, far too much of today's medicine is limited to repairing damage. Were the good doctors of today, in all areas, to concentrate the same time and energy on prevention, prevention as asked of us with the Ten Commandments, the world would have just a fraction of the illnesses it has today. Preventive medicine costs us nothing, and on top of that, we come to realize much clearer the immensity of God's love for us. This is no game of His; He is full of joy when we are full of peace and its resulting joy. He ONLY wants us to be happy, free and healthy!

Could you then explain the role of contrition and repentance at the moment of death?

With a good Confession, with heartfelt contrition and total honesty, all guilt is then removed, but there is still reparation to be taken care of. One is not yet completely released from those sins. Then also to gain total absolution, the soul must be free of all dependencies.

So, was a mother to die who has many small children, she would need to let go to such a degree that she can truly say, "God, I give everything to you, only Your will be done." This can be very, very difficult.

Freedom through total payment of every penny, as Jesus says, is between God and us, between us and others, with extra reparation, and a complete freedom from all dependencies on matters other than God himself.

So to be entirely free of all sins, it is really a three-legged process. Is that right?

Yes. First atonement between ourselves and God, then atonement between us and the person whom we hurt which always also means ourselves, and finally reparation in the form of prayer and good deeds. The sin not only has to be wiped away but it also has to be made up for.

Should non-Catholics and non-Christians also go to Confession?

Oh, yes! No good Priest who wishes to do what Jesus has asked him to do would ever send anybody away. Yet was it to happen that someone is sent away, then I advise the person to simply look a bit further and to pray for the Priest who turned him away. No matter who the penitent is, how he was brought up or where he is from, all that is needed is a deep sorrow for everything the person did wrong. Soon that penitent will find a Priest for Jesus' wish. I can promise him that. Although non-Catholics cannot receive the Sacrament of Confession, going to an informal Confession will do their souls so much good! This I can promise them and were a non-Catholic to do so, the graces given him or her by God will be very, very great.

15 -- THE ROSARY

How do you feel about the Rosary?

Oh, it's so important! Yes! The Rosary is so very healing and such a great source of peace, and in a special way for families who pray it together. Satan truly hates the Rosary for that very reason!

The following happened on December 16, 1964. In a minute you'll understand why I even remember the exact date. On that day I came home tired, but saw that there was a big pile of mail that had arrived. I said to myself I would quickly look through it, but answer only the two most urgent letters. I picked the two and discerned that what was necessary in both families was a family Rosary, and that it would eliminate the distress that both families were experiencing.

So I sat down and pulled out my folder of stationery and envelopes. I put it in the center of the table here, opened it and removed two sheets of paper and two envelopes. As is my habit, I started to address the envelopes before writing the letters. Suddenly there was a very shrill whistle, and Satan was standing over here to my right. He was in the form of a somewhat dark good-looking thirty-year-old man, and he was glaring at me with a vicious and boiling hate. I ignored him and continued addressing the envelope. Then I smelled smoke, and that got me by surprise. I even looked inside the folder and to the open window. Nothing. Then I thought, "I haven't lit anything yet today, it must be at the neighbor's." Then I looked to the right again, and Satan had taken the two sheets of paper, pulled them to the edge of the table and laid his hand on them. There was a perfectly black, burned area on the sheet where he had just placed his hand, and it was that which I had smelled. I ordered him now in the name of Jesus Christ the Lord to depart, which he then quickly did. I then finished my two letters and at first wanted to throw away the burned sheets. But I noticed that only the top one of the two was burnt away and the bottom one was merely darkened. So, I thought, I'd better show this to my Priest; and he was very grateful that I hadn't thrown it away because he wanted to have a physics laboratory in Innsbruck study it. This because, in his opinion, it was a physical impossibility to burn only the top one of the two sheets without also burning away the bottom one. So he sent the sheets to them, asking them if they could do the same. After three months they returned them saying that it was impossible to do and that he must have been mistaken about the second sheet having been under the burned one. No, I had not been mistaken.

The original was lost when my house was burned, but there was already a photo of it that we have kept. The photo shows it only once the bottom sheet had broken away. (See photo page 76) Well, in short, THAT is how much Satan hates the Rosary!

What do you say to those who find the Rosary boring and useless due to its repetitiveness?

Humility dictates that when we speak, we should only do so about things we have experienced. Those who say this have not prayed the Rosary. Meditating on the mysteries, meditating on the life of Jesus brings us so much peace and joy that Satan goes wild. Mary made many promises to those who pray it, and she did so through St. Dominic.

I know of a woman who bought a new Rosary only about a hundred yards or so from the church that she was heading for in order to pray it with a large group of pilgrims. As she knelt down in the pew, she reached for it in her purse and found that all she had left was a handful of single beads and many small bits of wire. Satan had flattened out all those tiny wires merely to block her from praying it! Satan hates peace and hates healing, and the Rosary is extremely healing and a very powerful weapon against him.

Has a Poor Soul ever appeared to you asking that you pray a Rosary with him or her?

Yes, that happens. One time I can remember now was in the '50s, as I was taking a train from Bludenz. It was a day when many people were traveling so I chose, as I often do anyway, the last car of the train. I got in and soon found a compartment with only one woman sitting in it, and so I joined her. I had not even settled in yet when she proceeded to pull a Rosary out of her bag saying, "Now, here is somebody who will pray a Rosary with me." My very first thought was, "If you do this with everybody, it's no wonder that you're sitting all alone." But, of course, I was happy to pray it with her and, while we did, no one else entered our compartment. Upon finishing it, she said, "Thanks be to God", and was gone instantly. So there I was sitting alone in the empty compartment with many people milling around everywhere else. Not for a second until then did I have an inkling that she had been a Poor Soul.

16 -- SACRAMENTALS

What are the Sacramentals, and are they important to us and to the Poor Souls?

Very much so. We should always use them and the Poor Souls love the Sacramentals which are holy water, oil, salt, medals, candles and so forth. I know a wonderful and a very interesting story about just that.

I knew of a woman who had made the Poor Souls the promise to light a blessed candle for them every Saturday. On one such Saturday her husband said, "Oh stop that, you don't have to do that. It's old-fashioned, and the dead are happy. They hardly need that, and I don't care what you promised them." The woman, of course, was saddened but still wanted to go ahead with it, but without being disobedient to her husband. So she thought, "All right, I'll just stick it in the wood stove where George won't see it. He hasn't lost anything in there." So she went ahead and put it in there, closing the little door that, by the way, had a small window in it. Then she left the house and soon her husband returned. As he was about to throw something away he glanced over to the stove and to his surprise saw some light inside. This puzzled him, and he opened the little door to look inside. To his great astonishment, turning somewhat pale, he not only saw the burning candle, but around it six pairs of perfectly folded hands. He closed the door and waited for his wife to return. When she did, he said, "Why put your candle inside the stove? You might as well put it out here on the table."

Here you speak about blessed light. Do they also like particular music?

Yes, they like holy music and, in a special way, the sound of blessed church bells that call their families to prayer. So is it a surprise that some in the secular world claim that church bells are an invasion upon their privacy? There's one more point for Satan if the towns are so spiritually dead as to react to these wishes.

How might holy water help us and the Poor Souls?

> Holy water should certainly be kept on hand in every house or apartment. It should be used on a regular basis. If anything disturbing or any great sin occurs there, the space should be sprinkled with it. It is great protection from Satan. The Poor Souls want it at every grave and they congregate and help us wherever it is used often. Also, to discern whether some activity is demonic or not, holy water will very quickly answer that question for us. Demons run from it and peace returns when it is used.

> Also there are studies today that prove that holy water is also protection against dangerous radiation.

How else might our having something blessed by a Priest help protect us in everyday life?

> Priests should return to blessing as much as possible. This should include the blessing of homes, crops, cars and all enterprises. One good idea would be blessing all the salt that is used in winter to keep the roads free of ice. Doing that would dramatically lower the number of accidents and thus be helpful to everyone.

17 -- OTHER RELIGIONS

Have you been visited by the souls of Jews or of Moslems?

> Yes, and they are happy when they appear to me, understanding things now much better than they did before. It is the case that by being in the Catholic Church one can do the most for Heaven. But those who were brought up differently and thus believe differently, and do so conscientiously, will also, of course, become holy.

> I must warn all Christians that there are many saints also to be found outside our churches. Just one of these Our Lady mentioned recently to one of her visionaries. When the visionary asked her who the holiest person was in the town she was living in at the time, Our Lady answered that it was a Moslem woman.

Are there religions that are not good for souls?

There are so many religions and most certainly there are some that are not good. Today even witch covens and mind-control cults and seminars will call themselves religions; and especially the latter will, without batting an eye, call themselves Christians. But their leaders are only power-hungry mind-controllers and are often possessed.

It is the Orthodox and the Protestants who are the closest to the Catholics. They believe in God and in the Ten Commandments. Yet the Protestants do not have a devotion for Our Lady, or at least not officially, although I know that many today do pray the Rosary. Excluding the ones that clearly serve Satan, it is the question of how much truth the various churches teach. And because God measures how full the cup is and not how empty it is, every group that acknowledges and celebrates a good, saving and freeing God is also good in His eyes. It is unquestionably the most difficult for Catholics to become holy in the eyes of God. That is because they have access to the greatest amount of truth, even if the Church today is in such drastic shape. We carry the greatest responsibility to bring Jesus to others, and at the same time we can do the most for them in silence and prayer because we have so much help with which to do that. The most is expected from those who have been given the most. [24]

Are there any people in Heaven who during their lives never entered a church of any sort?

Of course there are! If a person lives by his clean conscience, trying always to love and attend to his neighbor, he will be with God in Heaven. God loves and blesses those who never had access to Him while they were here but who still loved and protected life, the greatest of His gifts.

What should people of other religions, who have never learned the prayers that you have mentioned today, do to help the Poor Souls in their families?

It is not a question of memorizing recognized prayers of the Catholic Church; it is a matter of the heart. They should actively extend their love and total forgiveness to them and do good things for them.

Merely with the Lord's Prayer and the Hail Mary, they will be able to do great things for their relatives in Purgatory and thereby also receive help from them in return. Remember that the only prayer that Jesus gave us was the Lord's Prayer. In it is everything that the Love of God requests of us to do. As simple and short as it is, how many people in the world today do what it asks? With a little time, I suggest they should also slowly look at the other prayers. These are only sketches, one might say, for what should come out of our hearts for our fellow men and for our deceased friends and relatives.

Again, ALL this is not a question of the mind but of the heart. Love comes from the heart and not from the mind. Lack of intelligence by itself has never killed anybody, but lack of love kills every minute of the day and night. Life does not become holy, and healings do not happen with our brains but with our love.

Are there as many healings during the Masses or services of the other denominations as there are in Roman Catholic Masses?

That will depend purely on whether those present believe that it is Jesus Himself in the Consecrated Bread, or whether to them it is merely symbolic. If there are healings, even if they only consider Communion symbolic, those healings will be imitations and will never last. Satan never stops wanting to confuse and trick us away from our true Jesus.

Then there are other denominations where the ritual has been so watered down that some consider it Communion with Jesus at every meal when they break any piece of bread. Are there also healings there, and does it really matter if the ritual remains the same as the Roman Catholic one?

It does matter. I feel it should be the Catholic ritual, but I am equally certain of Jesus' immeasurable love; and therefore, I would never dare question whether healings happen in those other Communions or not. Still it is the Catholic Mass, when taken to heart seriously and in any depth, that is the most balanced and healing for the soul, mind and body.

Have Poor Souls who during their lives were non-Christian said anything to you about the Pope?

Yes, they have. They've told me that they now recognize the Holy Father as the absolute spiritual leader of all of humanity.

Non-Christians have said this?!

Yes, souls of people who were non-Christians while they were here among us on earth have said precisely that to me.

What happens to people who join a sect or a cult?

That depends greatly on why and how they arrived there. If they were born into a family where that was the accepted place to go, then they will be judged very gently. It was not of their own doing, they did not know better. But if a Catholic or Christian of another higher denomination goes there, he will suffer a lot for it. In such a case the person would have to return to his true belief before he dies in order to be freed of it.

I have heard many in my generation in the U.S., and this also among secular doctors, use the expression "recovering Catholic". What do you say to this?

Oh, how sad and angry this idea makes me! When this has happened, it is ONLY Satan's doing. When God's Divine Love is not taught, and the parents, Priests and teachers use only threats and projected guilt, then spiritual wounds can easily happen. Jesus never, never but NEVER accuses anybody, for He knows the human condition far better than anybody does here. Only Satan tricks us with threats. Threats have chased many away from the Church, and Our Lady says repeatedly that we must pray much for those who have yet to feel the love of God and who have therefore gone elsewhere. Those who have caused this among their young will have much to answer for. When this is the case, the Lord will give the victim of the threats much mercy because He will know from where and from whom the threats came.

18 -- PROTECTION & GUIDANCE

Maria, do the Poor Souls ever give any guidance, instructions or advice to their living family members?

Oh yes, that happens. It happened a lot through me in 1954 when souls would come giving their date of death and the town. They would ask me to tell the family to correct something. Often it was an inheritance that was unfairly distributed or against the wishes of the deceased.

In another case that comes to mind right now, a soul told me to tell his son, a Priest who lives just across the valley down there, to put back his Communion railing. So first I took the instruction to an acquaintance of his, but he said, "Oh, you tell him yourself; he'll believe you more than he'll believe me." So I did that and wrote to him. But until today the man has not followed the advice. I believe the Priest is a good man, but he's simply afraid to act upon it.

Will they also guide us in the same manner if we step in and pray and do good deeds for them?

Yes. Just trust and make the first move to help them.

Have any agencies or groups, say, government agencies, social groups or fraternal societies, ever tried to weaken your testimony or attack or block you in any way?

Well even if they tried, they could not achieve anything. Yes, for instance, once it did happen but I only heard about it later. For a while we had a policeman in this area who was a bit difficult. He had heard some talk going around the bars and it concerned a woman up there in the mountains who said that she sees and speaks with many ghosts and does so all the time. And talk like that he did not want to hear in his bars! So he and another decided to visit her in order to tell her to be quiet. So off they went in their big car wearing their most impressive uniforms. They drove up here and stopped down there at the restaurant, walking the rest of the way to my door. Or at least almost to my door, because about ten feet in front of it they suddenly came to a stop. They simply could not move any further! They tried a second time with their broad shoulders lowered, and again they were blocked by something they couldn't see. They gave up quickly, went back down into the pub of the restaurant, ordered a tall beer, never to mention the subject again! It was a neighbor of mine who saw them and only the next day said, "Maria, I saw you had some important guests yester day." -- "Who? I had no guests yesterday." Then I found out what exactly had happened.

What instructions, if any, have you personally been given by the Poor Souls?

> They have asked me not to leave home for more than five days at a time, because of all the mail I get.

Has it happened that people have come to you with shady intentions; and, if so, how do you handle them or have you been warned in advance?

> I try to receive everyone but yes, I have been warned in cases that I should not give a long testimony. If they only come out of pure curiosity, then I won't talk a lot. It's happened that I had people with questionable intentions with me and then my voice-box simply would not function. I simply couldn't talk freely as we're doing right now. Then they would say, "Why do you not tell us more?" And all I can say is, "Why do you not ask me more questions?" That has happened on quite a few occasions.

Well, I am certainly delighted and very grateful that you now have been speaking with me for so many hours! Did you ask a Poor Soul before I came whether my intentions were clean?

> No, I did not; but had they not been, you would have been awfully bored! (laughter)

Is it true that we take with us everything we learn here on earth?

> Yes, it is.

If that is the case, is there any evidence that the Poor Souls help us with what they have learned while here? So, if a seamstress needs help with her work, would it do her more good were she to specifically ask seamstresses in Purgatory to help her?

> Yes, there is evidence for that. Were we to be assisted quickly during a potential car accident the chances are very good that the helper knew something about cars rather than about knitting.
> I know of a man who often had to smuggle things across the borders here during the war. He always asked Custom's Officers in Purgatory to help get across without getting caught. He wasn't even

caught once in many years of doing it. But what he was smuggling was for God's people in the form of Bibles and other religious articles. A drug, money or weapons smuggler should not try to get the Poor Souls' help for his work. They NEVER help us with bad endeavors.

How else could the Poor Souls guide us?

We can ask a Poor Soul to guide us spiritually, and this would be especially helpful if a time comes when we do not have access to a good Priest and feel lonely in that regard. They will help us with this. In the cases, however, that I knew of where this was happening I never really heard how it was happening, but the Poor Souls have said that it does. [25]

Can the Poor Souls act protectively for us in ways that actually slow down the free will?

Yes, in a way, but only positively so. They could step in and block us from grabbing for the bottle, from driving too fast or anything else that could endanger us. They certainly could help smokers quit far more easily than were they to try to do so without their assistance.

Perhaps this is a good moment for me to say a bit about the idea of free will. When they help block a negative habit, our will becomes freer and not more limited. We are never acting freely when we are so weak as to sin or to bow to a dependency. In choosing something that binds or controls us, we have to at first twist and polish it so that we can lie to ourselves saying that it is, afterall, all right and good. This distortion makes us not free. Only in Heaven will we be free to concentrate purely on the absolute Good, our God.

Can you give me an example of how a Poor Soul freed or protected someone?

Yes, but it was another form of it.

A young man was looking for a good and holy wife. He had a woman in mind and visited her on occasion. Yet every time that he went to her house, there was a man off to the side somewhere who called over to him, "Don't go there, you will not be happy with her." The first few times he ignored it and went on. But then the third or fourth time he stopped and took a closer look at this man. It was his own father who had died many years before. He then certainly paid attention and went hunting elsewhere. So here he was freed and protected from future troubles.

Then, yes, another case. I knew a young woman who tried repeatedly to enter a convent. But for different reasons she was always refused. Then she got into the habit of sitting in a pretty spot by a lake in order to find her peace with God. One day she was heading that way and suddenly heard a voice very close by saying, "Stop, come back." She ignored it and continued. Again the voice said, "Come back!" Still she continued until suddenly she felt two hands push her back. To this she then responded and did not go any further. Later on she told a believing psychologist about what happened, and he said to her, "I understand it completely, because in the state you were in, you would have easily been mesmerized by the water and could have easily fallen or jumped in without even knowing it and possibly drowned."

And here is a fun story about protection of property again. A fellow near here by the name of Hans was awakened one night by a voice telling him to go out to the barn. He turned over and ignored it. Again, "Go out to the barn." The third time perhaps he finally did so. He went out and looked around. Everything was fine, and he thought, "Strange, what should I do? I'll just sit down and wait a bit." Within a few moments, the door opened and a stranger walked in. Hans stayed silent and hidden. The stranger walked straight over to the pigsty, climbed in and picked up two of Hans' young piglets. Now he understood very well. D'you see, it had been his father's voice. Hans jumped up and chased the man, and, in doing so, caused the thief to drop the piglets as he dashed out the door. Another case where the Poor Souls protected property and thus freed him from a loss.

They know our world and our situation in it exactly, and so our requests of them should be as broad as our lives are.

You say that they always protect us somewhat, but do they protect us more when we pray for them often?

Oh, yes. Much more! One could say that they then get our address. When we start praying for them the news must go around very quickly. They need our attention so very badly that they will do a lot in order for us to realize that it is they who are calling. When I ask them for specific help for something, I say, "Help me with this or that and I will give you an extra Mass next week; and if you don't, I won't." You might think that this is making deals with God or challenging Him; but I don't think it is for the simple reason that time or space does not bind prayer. If the intention to do so is honest, then their activity and the timing of it cannot be measured from our point of view in this element of time. Try it, you will notice that they become very active.

Can they return lost things to us?

That too, and I have a great example of this. Two years ago a Sister went on a speaking tour in France with Vicka, one of the Međugorje visionaries. Of course the trip was fast and hectic, and as they went, the Sister found herself carrying a flight bag with a lot of money in it. This money had been collected to pay for the rent of the rooms where Vicka was scheduled to speak. They often shared the same bedroom, and early one morning, just minutes before they had to dash off to their next meeting, the bag was not to be found. Sister knew precisely where it had been the day before but, of course, could not delay their departure because many thousands of people were waiting to see and hear Vicka, and so off they went without it. Before leaving though she asked the landlady to turn the room upside down and then, if need be, the entire house, because it was a lot of money and it was already owed elsewhere. The trip continued, and the bag was nowhere in the house. Vicka then continued on her way to Germany, and the Sister traveled back to Međugorje, still very desperate about the loss. Understandably, she felt very responsible. Upon arriving in Međugorje, she called out to the Poor Souls, "Find that bag for us, and I will give you a Novena of Masses."

Only three days later a letter arrived in Međugorje, and it was from the landlady of the house in France where they had slept that night. It said: "Just now we found the bag, and all the funds are in it with nothing missing. It was at the very spot that you told us you had seen it the day before you left!"

This does not surprise me in the slightest. A Novena of Masses certainly takes many souls up into Heaven. I found out about this only when that Sister visited me and left the question for me to ask a Poor

Soul, "Did a Poor Soul return the lost bag of money during the Vicka trip to France?" A month or so later I was given the answer, "Yes."

Now, is it possible that the bag one evening, so to say, floated on its own back to that very spot?

With God, everything is possible, but I would think that the Poor Souls chattered into the subconscious of the thief to return the bag. And it was this pressure on his conscience, which is formed within our subconscious mind, that the 'good thief' found intolerable. But did he re-enter the house secretly to return it exactly to where he had found it? That is quite mysterious, I must admit. Or did he have free access to the house anyway? No matter what, the Poor Souls received nine Masses from the Sister, and they will never neglect to pray and to act for her.

Do you know of a similar case of protection that would be meaningful to a greater number of people?

To a greater number of people? Yes. This should be very meaningful to the entire world. The Poor Souls told me that they had helped extinguish the fire at the Chernobyl nuclear power station and more recently I also found out that they helped shorten the Gulf War. These things they did because so many people were praying.

There is nothing where they cannot step in for us! They saved a good part of the next village uphill from here in 1954, which was a terrible year up here for avalanches. Across this valley we had more than seventy-five people lose their lives because of the huge amounts of snow. Blons was nearly entirely destroyed, but up there in the village of Fontanella the souls stepped in because there had been a bedridden woman who for thirty years offered all her prayers and sufferings for the good of that Parish. So one can say it was she who really saved all those houses and certainly many lives. When the snow experts looked at it the next morning, all they noticed was that something very powerful, of course more powerful than even the avalanche itself, had stopped it in its tracks.

That's what they can do, so not asking them every day for their protection is a great loss. Please, never forget them!

If we can ask them to protect us here, can we ask the souls in the highest of the three levels to go down into the lowest level to protect the souls down there?

No, not that. The reason for this is that they only know and act for what is ahead of them. They seek and yearn for the Light of God and aim only in His direction. We must ask St. Michael and the other angels to protect and help those in the bottom levels.

How else can they help us?

I believe it is only limited by our imagination as long as our imagination stays holy and good. They will never help us to accomplish something that is contrary to God's wish. And please do not lose hope if, on occasion, the help is not clearly evident. Do not forget that for everything they do they do need to get permission from Jesus through His Blessed Mother. And as we all know, Jesus' plan for us is not always in line with our wishes even if they are good ones. Also their work often remains unnoticed because the peace resulting from their protection is so often silent and invisible.

For instance, you are walking across an intersection with a green light. As you do so a car is heading for the same intersection, but what you do not know is that the driver has dozed off. A Poor Soul can quickly awaken him, and thus the car stops without your ever noticing anything. Your life was saved and still you never knew a thing about it. So often they work for us, and we don't notice anything.

Can you tell me another story that concerns, say, general assistance rather than spiritual or bodily protection?

The following happened in France. A woman had made the promise to make a Mass offering for the Poor Souls every month. She was a modest and pious woman whose work it was to be a domestic in larger houses. Then it happened that she lost her job and was out of work for longer than she had expected. Her money was almost gone, but one day, leaving Mass, she realized that she had not yet made her offering for the Mass that month. But now she had a true problem. Was she to make that month's offering for the Mass, she would be completely penniless in just a few short days, and so she hesitated. But she quickly trusted in Jesus and knew that He would not abandon her in a pinch. She went to the Priest and, as usual, went ahead and made the offering for one Mass for the souls in Purgatory. Then she headed home. As she left the church a well-dressed good-looking man of stature walked up to her and said that he had heard she was in need of a new job. She acknowledged this but still wondered how he could have possibly known. He was gentle but convincing and told her to take a particular road and to knock at the third house on the right. And off she went, still a little bit puzzled. She found the house quickly and liked what she saw immediately. She went up to the door and knocked on it. A very friendly old woman came to the door, and let her in with joy when she heard of this woman's need for work and that her experience was that of a domestic. It did not take long for them to agree on the work that was necessary, and both were so happy and relieved to have found what they each had needed quite badly. As the new-comer walked around the large and quite elegant living room, she noticed a framed photograph on the mantelpiece above the fireplace. It was the man who just minutes before had addressed her outside her church! "Madame," she asked, "who is the gentleman in this photograph?" -- "Oh," said the old woman, "that's my son, Henri, who died four years ago."

If we know of someone, for example, who as a child suffered much at the hands of its parents or society, can a Poor Soul protect that person from Satan's constant attacks through these wounds that are, of course, still open until, say, that person can acknowledge and address the wounds by going to an appropriate Priest or doctor?

Most definitely and the Poor Soul can also guide the person to the appropriate man. I know of cases where precisely that happened, and only later did the Poor Souls tell me that it had been they who had stepped in and helped.

What happens if someone asks them to help with something that is not entirely holy? You said earlier that they do not help in those cases.

No, no! If someone asks for their help with bad intentions, it is never they who help if any help comes at all. Only Satan will help someone with bad intentions, but he can, of course, also fake their activities.

Do you know of a case where they appeared to someone who then asked them to help him with something improper?

Well, yes. During a bad car accident once, three souls appeared to the driver, saying to him, "And now you will help us." They had clearly held him in place because the car had flipped end over end at least once, and he walked away from it without a scratch. When it became clear to him that they had protected him from certain death, he wanted more help from them with the insurance papers. Now, he did attend Masses for them but thought that they would also help with this. After quite a while it became very clear to him that they were not helping with this because the man did not get a penny for the wrecked car. He was angry with this and seemed not to understand why they hadn't helped there as well. But what had happened was that he had not told the entire truth to the insurance company, claiming some falsehoods about the accident. That dishonesty earned him nothing but more troubles.

19 -- LIMBO

What happens to stillborn or aborted children, where do they go?

The Poor Souls tell me that they do not go to Heaven, but because they were innocents they do not, of course, go to Purgatory. They go to a place that is in between. One can call it Limbo, but sometimes we call it 'Children's Heaven'. The word Limbo comes from LIMBUS that is the space between the print on a page and the edge of the paper itself. The souls of babies there do not know that there is something better. They do not know that they are not in Heaven, and it is our responsibility to lift them up into Heaven. And that, of course, does not take a lot because they never had a chance to sin. We can do that with a 'Baptism for the Unborn' or with a Requiem Mass. Stillborn and aborted children should also be given a name and accepted into the family. This enters them into the Book of Life.

I knew a nurse working in a hospital in Vienna who always baptized the stillborn and aborted babies in that hospital. She did so twice a day, in the morning for those who had died that night and in the evenings for those who had died during the day. While dying herself she called out, "Oh, here come all the children, so many children!" The Priest at her bedside answered, "Why sure, you baptized so many, and here they are to help you now." And these children then assisted her on her way.

Do babies in Limbo also appear or come very close to their relatives here?

Yes, they do. Especially their siblings are often conscious of another child being close by, even if they know nothing of the stillbirth or abortion.

I have heard that highly sensitive children have often seen their stillborn or aborted siblings, but that when they do, they see them growing older as time passes at the same rate as the living ones. Does this not contradict your saying that the souls always appear to you the same age as when they died?

No, I do not think it does because God always knows us the best and shows us things the way we can understand them the best. So when children show themselves as getting older, as you just described it, it only means that God wishes to make it as clear as possible to the very sensitive and loving child who exactly is visiting it. Children pray much more easily and freely than adults do and are more readily believed by their parents than others are, so this experience will certainly bring quick results if the loving parents jump in and take care of matters as they should, on behalf of all their children. Jesus Himself said, "Let the children come to me, do not hinder them." (26) And this also includes all stillbirths and abortions.

How do you feel about abortion?

Abortion is the greatest war and greatest horror of all time. Satan has been permitted by this so crippled society to kill the innocent by the millions just like another swarm of flies. The reparation for this will be enormous! I do not wish to say more than that.

If a woman then has admitted that her abortion was a great sin, what must she do so that she can be sure that Jesus has erased everything? Can you answer this, or should I change the subject?

> No, that's all right.

> The woman must immediately confess it to a Priest and truly ask Jesus for forgiveness. Then the woman must do deep and heartfelt penance for this in a way that truly brings peace back to her. Then the child must be given a name in order for it to find acceptance and love in the family that it so definitely belongs to and for it to be entered into the Book of Life. She must ask forgiveness from that child. And finally she ought to have it baptized and give it a Mass as I explained earlier. If all this is done and done with a humble and penitent heart, then it will be enough.

After all this is done, do any effects of it still remain behind?

> Besides the mother never forgetting it, the Poor Souls have told me that she will see in Heaven the spot where her child should have been after having lived a full life, but that spot will then be empty. But because Heaven is Heaven there will be no pain there of any sort concerning this.

Will all abortions be punished in the same way?

> No, because it does often happen that youngsters today are forced by parents or society to have it done, and in those cases the far greater responsibility will be carried by the adults who forced them to have it done. The media and governmental Laws that lower the conscience of society, and the doctors who make profits and who lie or conceal the well-known negative consequences that come upon the mothers later on will be punished severely. Also the medical and cosmetic industries that use fetus by-products to develop products will find out the immensity of their sins. We must pray a lot for them all.

Many women in the USA, the rest of the West, as well as in the East I suppose, say that they may do as they choose with their bodies and that which is within it. How do you answer them?

> How dare they do to a helpless child something which they themselves would never permit another to do to them while they as adults are hardly as helpless to protect themselves?! How quick they are to

run to court when a branch from a neighbor's tree breaks off and damages some of their property, but when they take a life, it remains their right, and no one else may dare to try to intervene for that life! These are very poor people who need our prayers every day to be freed from this selfishness, arrogance and confusion.

20 -- THE OCCULT

What can you tell me about the occult?

The word 'occult' means hidden or in darkness and is given to all practices that, recognized as such or not, are in communion with Satan. Today there are far too many for any one person to list thoroughly, and every part of the world has different practices that, of course, have entirely different names. Satan is THE expert disguise artist. [27]

But what is most powerful and destructive today is the pure and simple evil within the huge number of people who curse others, send spells and enchantments upon others. Black magic in all its forms is rampant today like never, never before.

What is the effect upon people who are the targets of such spiritual assaults?

Every such assault can at least cause confusion and fear and just as often lead people into depression, oppression, agony, confusion, divorce, hate, demonic possession and finally an agonizing death if they are not very well protected by a good life and by the protection of the angels as well as the Poor Souls.

And for the people who practice in the occult, what will the effect be on them if they do not cease immediately?

The effects of these contacts, whether conscious, ignorant, active or passive, with ANY of these will be the same on them and WILL ALSO run down upon the following generations. The effects of these sins will always run their course unless the people involved actively and persistently call upon Jesus, Mary and St. Michael the Archangel to intercede and block the attacks from continuing.

What ought people do if they have been active in any of these practices and wish to stop now that you have said this?

First, stop it immediately and stop seeing anybody you got to know through these practices and do this WITHOUT announcing it to anybody. Burn to ashes all materials that you have collected while participating in these practices. Just leave silently and then find safety among Christians. Once there, find a good and experienced Priest or layman who has experience in these matters. Leaving silently is very important because if you announce it to anyone, the news of your potential conversion might very easily travel up the hierarchy in whatever system you've been, and if it arrives up there, they can and will attack you. In all these arrangements there are witches or wizards who can and will attack you with the demons under their control.

Maria, this sounds extreme!

Satan is extreme and will stop at nothing to hurt and discredit those who leave his clutches. Leave silently!

Do you know of cases where people trying to leave evil practices were harmed because they did not stay silent as you advise?

Yes, I do. A name was brought to me once to find out whether this person was alive and then whether or not he had been murdered. The answers I received from the souls confirmed that he had been murdered because of his conversion. Unfortunately he had not listened to advice the Christians around him had given him not to return to his former surroundings. They somehow sensed that his earlier acquaintances had plenty to hide and would not be happy with his sudden and deep conversion. His neglecting this sound advice then did cost him his life; but then again we were able to have him delivered very quickly and he is now in Heaven with Jesus.

How else can witches and wizards hurt us?

Oh, in endless ways. They can cause divorces. They can send illnesses upon people or burn houses down leaving no slightest trace of the source. They can terrorize people at night. If there is enough power in, for instance, a group of covens they can easily murder without ever leaving their houses. A Priest in .... was murdered by them a while ago and, on top of it all, they were perverse enough to do it on Christmas Eve! They can listen in on conversations at great distances without any mechanical means and then later slander those listened in upon. They can cause car accidents and such. And they can do all this at any distance. Yes, all they need is a name, an address, a photograph or something like clothing from the person to proceed with their evil. Yet, any negative results from black magic always have to be permitted by God. Good Christians have nothing to worry about for if they stay humble, in a state of grace and in prayer then this protection is far stronger than anything that the demons can do.

Do black masses exist?

Yes, and more today than ever before in history. It is at these that they torture Jesus by doing horrendous things to Consecrated Hosts, innocent babies and children. Babies are conceived, and then born without Birth Certificates so that they can then do this to them. [28] They also sacrifice virgins, have orgies, drink blood and eat body parts to gain the power that is promised to them if they do. Satan stops at nothing! Many of these organizations will, after people have achieved a particular level, tell them that they can never leave. This is a lie. One can always leave. Jesus even forgives people who have led black masses.

Where in society do witches tend to concentrate?

Oh, that depends, but very often among children in schools. Also in hospitals where blood and drugs are easily available. Then inside churches and prayer groups to cause division. Also among the police and the legal profession so that they have insiders who can divert attention from the activities of the others. They are very well organized and at every level of society, often hiding behind entirely normal business suits and uniforms. They all seek as much power as at all possible.

If someone suspects a witch, are there any particular traits to look for to confirm it?

They can only thrive on attention and will do anything to gain control over others. They often lack any spontaneity for every move of theirs is planned in advance to fool someone, and when around churches will show an exaggerated and thus false piety. They will brag about their religious and spiritual knowledge and abilities and often prove to be using a false name.

But please never, never let your suspicions be known and keep them entirely to yourself for you will never know if your suspicions will be carried back to them, plus if you make your suspicions known, demons can warn them that you know what is going on. Go your own way in silence and pray for those people every day. Only prayer will free them, whereas our words about them will only end up hurting us.

At least in the USA, there is a hot debate going on today between Priests and lay counselors on one side saying that satanic ritual abuse is rampant and another group that says that these stories are pure inventions being put into the minds of their highly suggestible patients. Do you have any thoughts on this?

Satanic abuse of babies and children is definitely rampant today. I would carefully consider whether those who say it is an invention are not gaining something themselves. Why should they themselves not in some way be representing the very same people who are doing it? What do they gain by accusing those who are helping for having too much power while at the same time making the victims feel that they are crazy? To say such stupidities and lies, they must be gaining something.

Why would people choose to hurt others and choose to have more and more power?

It always starts with them initially being abused themselves, and then they seek more and more retribution and power over others. Both the paths to holiness and to Hell are slow and steady progressions. All babies are born innocent, but not all babies are born un-abused and in peace. The path to Hell can often start well before the baby is born. If the parents fight, take drugs, practice the occult, watch horror movies, go to discos or just sit in front of television all day and all night, the unborn baby receives everything they watch, hear or participate in into its subconscious and is deeply affected by it all.

It is no "old wives' tale" that pregnant women should not look at an ugly picture. In the days when that was still said they were, of course, referring only to paintings and perhaps photographs; so just imagine what happens to the tiny babies who today are exposed to hour after hour of the most detailed horror movies! Even unknowingly people sin horribly upon their children today before they are even born!

You say that the baby takes it all in from both parents. Also from the father?

Of course! The mother can be at home with the tiny embryo inside her while the father can be at war in the Persian Gulf, and the baby experiences everything that he does. So suffering and reparation for that war has already begun at home many miles away. Then if the father sins badly by, for instance, having sex outside marriage during these nine months, the child will very easily carry a subconscious wound resulting in resistance against the other sex and then turn out homosexual. That is why so many of them honestly say that they were born this way. Their anger, pain, frustration and lack of fulfillment are reparation for the sins of their parents. Satan makes people sick, and this illness, these wounds can only be healed with much prayer and especially with the help of St. Michael who is the strongest to fight off Satan's temptations.

Has a soul come to you that during its life had participated in a black mass?

That has not yet happened, but please do not presume that they are in every case lost. I myself have known people who had participated in black masses but then left that and changed their whole lives. And so, of course, they're not lost.

So there's no depth from which Jesus will or cannot pull us?

Correct. If people want Him to, God can always conquer Satan. It always comes down to our wish to be and to do good deeds and that even in the very last moments of our lives. God's mercy is huge!

Maria, can lost souls do damage to living people?

Yes, they attack people on earth and most especially their own families. Much of that is going on today. Some say that Hell is nearly empty now because Satan's army is running all over the world. I work, pray and go on pilgrimage quite often with an exorcist who has often blocked lost souls from attacking their descendants. That is one clear explanation for criminal families that certainly do exist. A lost grandfather, with all the hate that he has within him, will easily push his grandson into the same type of life. Only a strong exorcist can stop this chain from continuing. Jail will not stop it, and the death penalty will not either; for that matter, it probably, more often than not, insures that the chain will continue.

Which of all the occult practices is the most dangerous for people to participate in?

Freemasonry. It easily leads to divorce and finally to suicide, but then again other occult involvements do too. However, the Freemasons' entire goal is to kill off the Church.

The Poor Souls have told me that our last Pope, John Paul I, was murdered, and it was the Freemasons who did it. [29] And when a Cardinal who had held a very important position had also died, a spiritually gifted woman in Carinthia wanted to pray for him. She prayed and was blocked. She tried repeatedly, but simply couldn't. One day this same Cardinal himself appeared to her in a fiery state and said, "You cannot pray for me because I am lost due to my Freemasonry. And I have Popes on my conscience." Then she and her spiritual director, and it was he who came here and told me this, took this to the Vatican and again to the highest Officials of the Church. There one of them, who acknowledged having been at the former one's deathbed where he had witnessed piercing screams, said that he did not want to die like that and went to confess to the present Holy Father.

So you say that the Freemasons killed Pope John Paul I. Have other Popes or other men high up in the Church been murdered in recent times?

Yes.

And you believe this woman in Carinthia and her spiritual director?

With no doubt at all.

Can you tell me, Maria, how in most cases you deal with Satan?

When he bothers me and usually it's with little things, I simply do this. Recently I was sitting here praying the Rosary but for some reason had to leave the room. I hung the Rosary on the chair like this and went outside. When I returned only a few minutes later, it was lying here on the table instead and was hopelessly knotted up. I could not undo it. So I sternly said to Satan, "You stupid idiot! Undo this Rosary or I will take ten souls away from you!" In front of my eyes the Rosary loosened itself, and I continued to pray on it. If anything happens that I discern as interference by him, I just command him in the name of Jesus Christ the Lord to depart, and he always does.

Can you think of anything else that would strengthen our protection against evil these days?

Yes. In the last decades the Exorcism Prayer has been watered down, if not entirely left out of the Baptismal Rite. That too is a big mistake and leaves the door open for evil to affect the child more easily. This too is something where these modern times have led the Priests astray. The Exorcism Prayer must remain there, and in its entirety, for full protection.

Also the prayer to St. Michael, that used to be prayed at the end of every Mass, must be reinstated. The lack of it today also drastically weakens the people's protection when they leave the church. I beg the Priests to be courageous and trusting in St. Michael and to put this prayer back for greater protection for their parishioners.

21 -- HELL & SATAN

Maria, why does Satan exist?

God wanted to test His angels and when He did some of them led by Lucifer, another of his names, said 'no' to Him with pride. He was the most beautiful and most intelligent of all the angels and wanted to have things his way and not God's way.

Does Hell, as the older generation speaks about it, really exist?

Yes, it does. [30]

What attitudes of the heart can lead us to a definite loss of our soul?

The stubborn, arrogant and proud refusal to accept the graces and the love given to us, and to do so to the very last moment. And here I mean, not only the love of God but also the love from other people.

For people who are active in any of the occult practices that you mentioned earlier, what are the consequences? How severe a punishment awaits them after death?

Again, that all depends. There's a great difference between their knowing that it's all from Satan or their doing it out of naiveté, ignorance or immaturity. If they are doing it consciously and knowingly, the consequences will be enormous; but if they do it only out of ignorance, they will be less severe. Yet in either case, it must quickly be confessed and therein be denounced specifically and by name. The deeper the involvement was, the more experienced the Priest must be. But I am also afraid that today many Priests are completely ignorant about such matters, and some are themselves even involved with the occult. The consequences for them in particular will be unspeakable, because they carry a much greater responsibility.

Has Satan, disguising himself as a Poor Soul, ever fooled you?

Yes, that has happened. My Priest always said, "Accept every soul, even if it needs great suffering. The Lord will always give you the strength for it. Never turn a soul away." But once a soul came and told me not to accept the next one. So I asked, "Why not?" -- "It needs so much suffering that you will not be able to withstand it." -- "Then why would the Lord allow it to come to me?" Then it said very strictly, "Then God will test if you are obedient or not!" This confused and worried me and when that happens I call upon the Holy Spirit. It then dawned on me that this could be the Evil One. I sprinkled holy water and commanded, "If you are Satan, I order you in the name of Jesus Christ the Lord to be gone." And he vanished.

Has he also appeared to you at other times in a disguised way?

Yes, quite often and always to confuse matters. Once as a Priest, another time as the Mother Superior of the convent in Hall. In both those cases he tried to tell me to retract my vow to Our Lady. Especially hard was the Holy Week before Easter in 1954. All that week he almost convinced me that I was in Hell, with flames and explosions in my room. Then for a day that following December I felt burning wounds and an awful fear of Hell with complete loneliness, but I noticed no souls near me. Then it all suddenly disappeared.

Once this happened. On days that we have a funeral service at our church at nine o'clock, we can receive Communion at seven. On this particular morning I arrived at 6:45 and was the only one there. Suddenly my Priest hurries into the church, neglects to genuflect, rushes up to me and says, "Today you may not receive Holy Communion." And away he rushed out of the church, again neglecting to genuflect in front of the tabernacle, slamming the door behind him. This was not at all like him and I wondered what was going on. At three minutes to seven he comes in again, walks through the church genuflecting as he normally does every time he goes into the sacristy. I looked around again thinking that he would not go to the sacristy if I, who was not allowed to receive Communion that day, was the only one in the church. No, I was still the only one there. So I got up and also went to the sacristy, knocked on the door and slipped in to see him. "Why, Father, may I not receive Communion today?" I asked him. "Who told you that?" -- "Well, you did only ten minutes ago when you came into the church the first time." -- "Of course you may receive Holy Communion today. I did not enter the church before right now. Don't worry, Satan's only playing his games again."

And what else might he try to do against you?

Oh, anything he can. It's happened that I have left for a series of talks with a fever of 104° (40°C) but I knew that I had not caught it anywhere else. I just ignored it, and when the talk was about to start, I felt as good as ever.

How powerful is Satan and to what degrees are we protected from him by our own good behavior and by our Guardian Angel?

Oh, that protection is very strong. Without it Satan would kill us all very quickly. Let me tell you what happened to a very holy Priest in a monastery near here in Bludenz, and perhaps you would call this assistance by the souls in solving a crime. This man was the oldest there and also the superior of the monastery. He prayed so much and did so much good that he was often the brunt of jealousy and teasing by the younger and less prayerful Priests.

One evening two of the younger men were on their way to their rooms when they passed by one of the main buildings and saw a light on in the basement. Because it was already very late, this light puzzled them, and they went to see who was down there. They entered the basement room and to their horror found this old and much loved Priest there dead. He was found hanging from a doorknob by the neck. His legs stretched out as if sitting, but he was still a few inches off the floor. The Police were called and for weeks, of course, turned the monastery inside out. As holy as he was, nobody could imagine suicide. All the other Priests were, of course, questioned because it was common knowledge that they often kidded him about his proximity to God in his constant very deep prayer life and never-ending good deeds. The lengthy investigation brought no results, and the whole area was left baffled by this.

Then the sad story was brought to me, and I agreed to ask a Poor Soul about it. An answer came back very quickly because so many were praying for him and because the entire monastery was, of course, in a state of shock because of it. The answer was this, "Our Lady had appeared to this Priest and had asked him if he would accept Satan's ability to kill him. And that if he did, it would be in reparation for many souls that had sold themselves to him. This he had accepted."

With this answer I went down to the monastery where everyone, including the police, had been called together. In front of everyone there I read this answer out loud. In the silence that followed, one Priest in the back of the room sighed deeply, and I asked him what was the matter. He came forward in tears and pulled a piece of paper out of his pocket. He explained that he had found it in the pocket of the Priest the evening that he and the other one had found him. He unfolded it, showed the entire room that it was in the hand-writing of the old Priest and then read it to us. It said, "Our Lady appeared to me and asked me if I would accept Satan's ability to kill me; and that if I did, it would be in reparation for many souls who had sold themselves to him. I have accepted."

So he agreed to give his life for people he never knew and who had become involved in occult practices?!

Exactly.

When did this happen, and will you tell me this extraordinary man's name?

Certainly. This happened only in the late 80's, and his name was Fr. Joseph Kalosans. A man as good and courageous as this is surely a very powerful intercessor for us.

What is it that tricks people today into the direction of the occult?

Well, there is always an attractive and seemingly innocent vehicle at first that opens people to any of these activities. Television today is responsible for much of it. It has become the altar in the center of 95% of living rooms today in western homes. There the children are incessantly bombarded with the temptations of money, materialism, sex, violence and power. And so often among these programs, occult practices are shown as games and innocent fun with great promises attached to them. The music today is also a vehicle for this process to begin.

Parents who allow their children to sit in front of this altar of sin all day and all evening are handing their children to Satan very quickly and efficiently. But do not misunderstand me, not all television is bad; but it quickly turns bad when the parents do not control it very tightly.

Do you own a television?

No, I don't; I wouldn't dream of it. I see enough things as it is! (laughter) And any important news comes to me by way of the local paper, the radio, my many guests or my handful of neighbors.

Is there any sin that Jesus does not forgive?

Yes, there is one. It is blaspheming the Holy Spirit. That He will not forgive. But, of course, that means saying 'no' to Him, saying 'no' to His Light, Love, Mercy and Forgiveness repeatedly all the way through to the very end. With God's infinite Mercy, people can ALWAYS get out of this if they want to, but they must want to. Nobody else can or will do it for them. They have to want to. God does not manipulate our will. The souls have told me that every person has the same opportunity at death to say 'yes' in the last moment. Whether it is a long slow illness that takes them or a bullet through the brain, they still all get the same two to three minutes to say 'yes' to God. And ONLY if they hold on to their 'no' all the way through are they then lost and must suffer Hell eternally. God will not force us to change our 'no', and Satan can never change our 'yes'. This is another reason that we may never judge someone or guess about where they ended up. We never see exactly what happens between the soul and God in those moments, even though we can witness relative peace or the lack of it at the deathbed.

Oh, now I'm reminded of a case that demonstrates this necessary caution.

Once a young boy was badly abused by a Priest. This horrible wound caused him to run from all Priests and from the Church. Many around him tried to step in and help him as he grew older but, no, he just kept far away, often attacking the Church and everything that had anything to do with it. Then he became very ill and died cursing the Church to the very end. A caring and prayerful man who had known the entire story then took this fellow's case to Therese Neumann who also could find out where souls went.

When she found out, she said that the boy was saved but still in Purgatory. This surprised the man who asked for him and most especially because the fellow had died cursing the Church to the very last moment. The explanation was this. Although Satan had blocked his way to the truth when he was still a highly sensitive and impressionable youngster, he had always silently continued his search for the true God; and because he had always retained this need in his heart, God's Mercy pulled him up toward Him. Again, this is enormous proof for God's mercy and proof that we may never jump to conclusions, even if we heard or saw for ourselves what seemed to be aimed in the other direction.

Maria, is there ever any way to tell if someone is lost? Do the Poor Souls ever say that a soul is lost?

No, they never say that because they are only conscious of what is ahead of them. But to the first part of your question -- yes, one can with much experience and discernment come to this conclusion. If a family experiences much division and other serious attacks, and one can follow it back up to a particular person, a Solemn Exorcism Prayer should be prayed by someone authorized, experienced and in a state of grace to do so over both that soul and the one here who seems to be under especially drastic attack. If peace then settles in, we can, I'm afraid, come to the conclusion that the earlier soul is lost. I also know a man who can feel the presence of souls when they are still in Purgatory. So, here again, if he says that a soul is not there and in addition we know that the family is obviously under terrible attack and that, because of it, the family has been pulled away from God, away from the Church and away from all prayer; he can say that their ancestor is lost and thus this most powerful of all prayers is necessary to free his descendants from his grasp. Peace and prayerful lives have often come back to these families after this had been taken care of.

What can you tell me about Satan and his activities these days?

Satan has never before been as strong and as active as today.

And why do you think that is the case?

The 20th century can be compared to no other century when it comes to apostasy, murder, greed for money and power, hate, non-forgiveness and lack of prayer. It has been HIS century! His high level of activity is also because he knows that a big event is ahead of us that will be for the conversion of humanity. He knows his game will soon be greatly weakened and he always screams the loudest before he is conquered.

Tell me, how can God, and then we as well, be happy in Heaven when souls that were very dear to us both are lost in Hell forever?

In Heaven everything, but EVERYTHING, is concentrated upon God, and such things are simply no longer near to us there. Everything in Heaven is pure joy, pure praise and pure beauty. There is nothing less than that there, and such sorrows, worries or losses have no room there. God's presence is so strong there, that everything else is left behind and entirely cut away.

When souls are lost, what then happens to their Guardian Angels?

Oh, they also, as do the angels of souls in Purgatory, return to Heaven and only get one such assignment from God.

You've said that both Heaven and Purgatory have many different levels. Does Hell then also have different levels?

Yes, it does. It has an infinite number of levels. The worst is at the bottom.

Maria, you must be very unpopular with Satan. Is this the case?

I suppose it is. I am more or less constantly under attack. The worst thing that happened was that I lost my family's four hundredyear-old house. It was destroyed by fire on June 10, 1986, and was most definitely Satan's doing. It happened like this. I was downstairs at 12:30 because they were delivering the chicken food. Upstairs I heard steps and someone jumping. By the time I got there the place was already in flames. The fire engines came and simply could not put it out. The walls remained but everything else was gone. Only one room did not burn, and when I got to it the best things in it, linens and such, had disappeared too. Stolen. The police saw no use in trying to retrieve the things, and the Poor Souls told me not to worry, that everything would be replaced. And exactly that happened. You see, this house was then built for me when relatives and friends made a collection after the fire. Everything here was given to me. Another woman in Italy, who also sees the souls, had exactly the same happen to her, with the same loss, the same promises and results.

Only later did I realize that I had been warned about it by people who had told me that my house would burn, and then a soul had even said that the fire would not be my fault; but I guess I was still not ready for it and had not taken the warnings seriously enough.

Yet Satan is also very frustrated with me. During an exorcism, I believe it was in Frankfurt, the Priest present asked the voice coming out of the possessed man, "Do you also attack Maria Simma down in Vorarlberg?" The voice answered, "No, because when I try, I lose too many souls."

Hmm. What else has he done to you?

Well...

What is it, Maria?

There was a serious plan in the works to have me murdered.

What?! Will you tell me more about that?

A weekend of talks was planned for me in northern Germany in the Spring of 1974 and I was supposed to leave, as it often happens, on a Friday. But a few nights before a soul came and simply said: "Do not go on this trip." This astonished me greatly because years before they had told me to accept every invitation I was to be given.

First I thought it might be a train strike so I listened to the radio, and, no, the trains were operating normally. Then I spoke with my Priest, who said if the souls say not to go then I should trust in that for there will be a good reason. So I sent an express letter to the organizers of the talks and simply conveyed to them that the souls had told me to stay home on this particular weekend.

Two days later another soul came and told me that a murder plan had been in the works. It had to have been in Cologne because the train from here in Bludenz all the way to Cologne was to be a sleeper, and only there would I have had to change trains late at night. I remembered from before that in Cologne's train station there are long dark corridors that I would have had to walk through and had always considered dangerous.

Earlier I had also sent them a letter telling them on which train and at what time to expect me. That letter, however, never arrived and had fallen into the wrong hands. On the day of my first talk, a soul came and told me that there had been three involved in this plan and that they had found out why I had not come.

You see, the talks were never canceled, I was merely replaced by audio cassettes so that the people would not be all too disappointed. So all went along as previously arranged and the three had gone to the lecture to listen anyway and because of it two of them converted. I also found out that they had succeeded in previous assassinations that had never been solved.

So aren't the souls wonderful? They saved a life and converted two misguided people without ever naming, judging or accusing anybody of anything. THAT is our Christian duty.

If God forgives murderers, then what are the sins that earn us the most time in Purgatory?

All sins except for blaspheming the Holy Spirit can be forgiven, but the sins that earn us the most suffering in Purgatory are, in general, the sins against love, meaning hostility, hard-heartedness and divorce. Also the lack of active faith, when one simply does not want to believe and acts contrary to it. And then immorality. In the past it was clearly lack of faith that earned people the most suffering in Purgatory, but in these times it has changed to immorality.

When a house is, so to say, haunted, how do we tell quickly whether it is the Poor Souls or something demonic, satanic?

If it can be identified as being in any way related with someone who lived there before, then it is a Poor Soul who is requesting prayer. If, however, it is really nasty, violent, dark or even smelly, then an exorcism prayer ought to be prayed in or over the place. In both cases exorcised, blessed and consecrated water should be taken there to send off anything evil. If it then still continues, it is certainly a Poor Soul needing a Mass, prayers and good deeds for it to move on.

Does Satan have permission to attack us during death?

Yes, on occasion he does; but we also receive the grace to withstand it. If a man does not wish to let him in, then Satan can do nothing.

Is hopelessness then a sin?

Yes, it can be, if one has no hope or trust whatsoever. D'you see, God always wishes to give us hope, but then it is up to us to accept it.

At the very beginning you told me that Satan could no longer attack the souls in the higher levels of Purgatory. Yet even the holiest among us here are still tempted and attacked by Satan until the moment of death. Can you explain this difference in greater detail?

Once the stains of sin on the souls in Purgatory are overtaken by light due to the souls' suffering and our good deeds for them, the darkness can no longer come back. Any darkness in Purgatory is always defeated by light whereas, here on earth, light can still be overtaken by darkness. Satan makes use of the smallest stains in order for us to slip back into darkness. The size of the stains is relative to the graces we were given by God; and Saints, of course, were given enormous graces.

Satan seems often so very powerful that people might ask what differences are there between Satan and God?

I understand. Each one of us can choose at every moment to be an agent for Satan or an agent for God. We must call and reach for God in all we do. And we can do much to secure ourselves from Satan's grasp. Where God knows our thoughts, Satan does not except for those that he himself put into our minds. Satan makes great progress, moreover, through hearing our words and seeing our acts, and later attacks those weaknesses he has discovered due to them. Silence always does us good. Remaining always conscious of our sinfulness and, therefore, remaining humble and quiet is one of God's wishes. And it happens that in learning the greatness of silence, we come quickly to listen to God. Silence with God alone in itself is a great prayer.

Only confession blocks Satan's knowledge of our sins. If during an exorcism any one of those praying against the demons has unconfessed sins, the voices will often accuse the one in question and do so correctly, to the great embarrassment of all. Yet if they are in a state of grace, the demons can never say anything. It is correct to say that it is we who give Satan his rights. God is humble, quiet and gentle. Satan is proud, loud and harsh. Remember always that we have been made in God's image, so we must consciously and constantly fight to be what He wants us to be -- with Him.

One of the greatest lies of the times we are in is that Satan does not exist. Even some Priests say that today. It is said by some of them that the possessions in the Bible are today recognized illnesses of the body or of the mind. So, symptoms can be studied, analyzed, named, controlled and -- Bingo! -- they're no longer Satan's doing?! How very naïve, shallow, stupid and arrogant these gentlemen can be. Satan laughs himself silly, and again the hospital beds fill up. Bring holy

Priests or holy and experienced laymen to them and just watch the release from those over-studied symptoms. Satan conquers after he divides. God leads us in freedom and peace to a heavenly unity.

Maria, where in modern western society has Satan made strong inroads that might still be relatively unknown to many among us?

Satan is everywhere today -- in the Church, in the law, in medicine, in science, in the press and in the arts. But there is an area where he is for the greatest part running the entire show and that is in the banks. The West's greed has permitted this, and only God is now strong enough to stop it.

Earlier you mentioned that animals also need our prayers. So, tell me, are there animals that Satan hates more than others?

Because he's been, as we say, 'man's best friend' for so long now, Satan hates the dog the most. But, then again, he hates any creature that ever comes close to our hearts. He is pure hatred and will try all he can to pull us from anything that brings us warmth, support or protection; and certainly animals are a great gift for this from God, as well as anything else.

If Satan hates it so much when we pray, what, in your opinion, is his most common way of keeping people from praying?

For that he again uses a person's pride. Someone who has never prayed and, therefore, knows nothing about prayer will feel insulted when someone says to them: I will pray for you. They will have been misled to think that they are all right and, therefore, need no-one's prayers. This is a trick on the mind and a huge lie. There is not a single person on earth who does not have the dire need of the intercession of others. Prayer brings God to them even when they do not know that it is happening. The power of prayer is enormous and praying is the best thing any human can do for another.

We're both tired now, Maria. Is there anything I can help you with considering that I have a car with me?

Yes, I'm tired too. It would be good to go outside a bit, it's sunny; but, no, I don't think there's anything that I need help with.

Are you sure? How about going to the store or the Post Office?

Well, perhaps. I do have something that needs to be returned to the store. It would be good if we could go up there.

Of course, and I'll just leave these things here until we continue tomorrow.

INTERMISSION:

As Maria puts on her heavy coat, my heart and mind are running. This little old woman is adorable. She's so very humble, but speaks with a clarity that cannot be shaken. She suffers silently, yet always keeps a joy and a humor very much alive within her. She takes my arm as we descend the steep steps.

In the car she is so small she can hardly see over the dashboard. Scarf tightly bound around her head and hands folded peacefully on her lap, she seems so at home and completely at peace although I am still a virtual stranger to her. We drive down past the church and further down to the main road and the store is a hundred and fifty yards up that main road. As we walk across the parking lot, I feel a little awkward but cannot resist watching her every step to see whether she speaks with someone invisible to me. It does not seem to occur, yet she has had plenty of years to learn how to hide it was it to happen now, as she had tried to hide it from that visiting Sister. We walk in silence. With the locals in the store, her particular 'Vorarlberger' dialect again becomes strong. Nobody treats her any differently than just another one of his or her own. Yet if what she says is happening, then she is most definitely very much on her own. Still in no way at all does she seem affected or forced, hysterical or suspicious, controlling or self-righteous. She asks for nothing and gives her entire life. By now my fondness and respect for her leave no room for any doubt in my mind as to her being completely real, honest and truthful. It is very doubtful whether I have ever met a purer embodiment of Christian virtues. She is such a darling and in a kind and childish way I would really love to kidnap her and take her from Sunday to "show and tell" on Monday. Leaving the store, she thanks me for this tiny gesture as if we had been on a vacation and is truly happy that this is now taken care of. I drive her back home and agree to meet with her again the next morning. I let her out and as she approaches her door she turns and for the second time calls out, "Vergelt's Gott und bis morgen." (Thanks be to God and until tomorrow.)

We are to meet again at 9:30 the next morning. I drive off and find a room in the house of a friend of Maria's some hundred yards down-hill from the church.

"... will rise to a disciplinary curative time of punishment."

Correct translation
from Aramaic and Greek of both
Matthew 25:46 and John 5:29

Our Mother of Mercy.

*Sight where the Medugorje apparitions started on
June 25, 1981.*

*Evening Mass celebrated in Medugorje on the
15th Anniversary of the Apparitions, June 25, 1996.*

Five Međugorje visionaries, late June 1981:
Mirjana, Vicka, Ivanka, Jakov and Marija.

More recently. Clockwise from top left: Marija Pavlović-Lunetti, Jakov »olo, Ivan
Dragićević and Vicka Ivanković.

Maria Simma and the author at work, 1993.

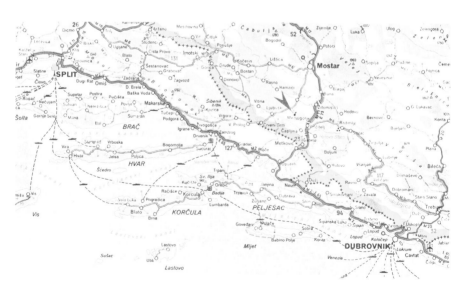

Medugorje, Bosnia and Herzegovina and surroundings.

22 -- ILLNESS

Good morning, come on in Nicky, how was your room at Mrs. Schwarz-mann's house? We've been friends nearly all of our lives, and she often helps me with addressing envelopes and such. And did she say how she was feeling?

> Oh, the room was wonderful, Maria, so much friendlier than at some hotel. Thank you, that was a good idea for me to go there. She said she was well but had to be careful because her heart was no longer the strongest. But she seemed happy to me.
> So, let us continue.

Speaking of physical weaknesses or disabilities, Maria, have souls come to you whom you knew and who were disabled in any way during their lives?

> Yes, many. When they then appeared to me they were completely healed of it. Wheelchairs are gone. Deformations and scars are gone.
> Once, however, a soul came with a large goiter. Yet this was only so that the family would believe me when I told them that their relative had appeared to me with such and such an instruction for them. See, they asked me what he looked like, and so when I mentioned the goiter, they believed me and thus listened to the instruction.
> Now I remember one who was mute during his life and who, of course, spoke perfectly when he appeared to me. He showed joy at being able to speak to me, but I never found out why he could not speak while alive. If they were in wheelchairs in life, those are then gone and they walk perfectly. All minor as well as major imperfections are then gone. But please remember that I see only those in the higher level of Purgatory. I say this now because others have seen sufferings and wounds on the souls. But these are not the same ones that were there during their lives. These are then sufferings of the soul and not of the body, for they no longer have a physical body. I think the closest I have seen to this, was when a Priest came to me and after he told me what he needed, I was given the chance to ask him why his right hand was so black, dirty and painful looking. His answer was, "Tell all the Priests to bless people, homes and religious objects all

the time. I neglected to do this often, and therefore I must now suffer in my right hand."

Is AIDS a punishment from God?

Yes, it is, but I prefer calling it reparation and that for people's immorality. If this shocks people, claiming that God then is not a loving God, punishment and reparation are also loving. And as for the innocent who are now also suffering from AIDS, that accounts for additional and necessary reparation. God's mercy is infinite, but His justice is also total. I say if we knew of His Justice now as we will in Heaven, many of us would die under the strain of our own sins.

Do you think they will find a cure for AIDS?

We already have the cure today, but because it will not make any money for anybody and because it is very unpopular, people will still for a while longer be blind to it. The cure is Jesus and the Ten Commandments. He did not give us those to control us, but ONLY to protect, strengthen and free us.

That would be a preventive cure. How about a reparative cure, a healing of it once it has already been contracted?

That too has already happened in very prayerful places.

Where?

I've heard of a place in Italy but the name escapes me now, and then also in Međugorje that has happened. The importance, however, is not the exact place, but rather the amount of prayer.

When people come into very prayerful places with great burdens and have already been checked by physicians, psychiatrists and Priests and their conditions seem to worsen there rather than improve, can this be caused by some Poor Souls in their background?

Yes, that can be the case; but if so it is caused by souls that are very deep in Purgatory. In these cases a good exorcist will be able to stop the deceased from pressuring the living.

Maria, can you tell me of an incident where non-forgiveness led to an illness?

Oh, that is so very often the cause of illness. Yes, I remember a case in Innsbruck where a young woman could simply not forgive her father. The situation was this. When the father was alive he never gave any joy to his children, and in her case, when a good position came along he refused to let her take it. It was a job that included a good amount of education, and his forbidding it caused her to wander through life without proper schooling. And it was this that she simply could not forgive. A short while after he died, he appeared to her -- not once but three times -- begging her to forgive him. No, the daughter just couldn't. Then the woman fell ill, and during this time it suddenly dawned on her that she should forgive him. She did and did so deeply, with all her heart. The illness quickly left her.

I cannot remember now exactly what illness it was, but it did become clear to her that this was due to her long-term refusal to forgive. We cannot always forget things, but we must forgive. Non-forgiveness is the cause of the greatest burdens and limitations that we put on ourselves during our lives. If we go to God with it all, we become so much freer and fuller. And then also with forgiveness comes a much deeper understanding of what really happened. That also is a huge and very important grace.

Yes, here is another case. It concerned an ugly and itching skin condition that a woman had for some twenty or more years. All modern medicine could do was give her a very expensive cream to reduce the itching. Then she went on a pilgrimage and met with a prayerful and experienced person who one day during dinner turned to her and her husband and simply said, "Let's ask Jesus to tell us what causes that on your hands and your right leg from the knee downward." The instant he did, he had an internal vision showing a woman bending down with her right knee on the ground and with her hands stretched out toward a girl. The girl was this same woman as a child, and the woman in the vision was her mother. That mother had neglected to hold her children and especially this one, now grown up; and she, in turn, had never forgiven her for this. When this was explained, the husband turned to his wife and said, "That's right, that's so right. You have never forgiven her for this." With tears in her eyes, she had to admit it. She took this intention into prayer and into Mass for just two or three days, and the condition receded to just a fraction of what it had been. Then they returned home, and the fellow who had the vision never really heard whether it disappeared completely or not, but the itching and ugliness did go away nearly immediately. One cannot expect total forgiveness within the person to occur overnight, but Jesus surely showed the three who were present that evening where the problem was to be found.

So again the illness happened in a way that could have reminded the living of the sin of the ancestor; and in this way, the soul still in Purgatory made itself known and was begging for forgiveness before which it could not be delivered. Now I am certain that soul, whose name I never did hear, is in Heaven and her daughter is free of a condition that hurt, bothered her and cost much money for several decades.

Earlier, Maria, you mentioned that Satan sends illnesses upon people through witches with demons under their control. How does one discern whether an illness is caused by them or by something else?

By praying with the person or over the person. If it comes from elsewhere, the exorcism or deliverance prayer will show no results, but when it does come from demons, it will. It will at first try hide or to fight back, but with a little perseverance, it will then depart. And in hospitals today the term 'virus' should be a possible warning signal for this. This term is often used by doctors when they come upon something they cannot explain. In such a case get a Priest or another powerful intercessor to them and get friends and relatives to pray quickly for the intercession of Our Lady and of Saint Michael. The Priest should also take along exorcised, blessed and consecrated water, or better yet, oil.

Can you give me an example or two of illnesses sent upon someone demonically?

At the moment I can think of three cases. One was pneumonia, another leukemia and the third was a short but horridly painful case of back pains.

This last case I know the most about, because it happened to a friend of mine who for many months volunteered to work alongside one of the most respected Priests in Europe. My friend suffered from a slightly pinched nerve between the third and fourth vertebras. This was at first treated with injections of a muscle relaxant but these did not help at all, and it only became worse. By this time the pain was terrible.

He then suspected that this might be demonic and he called for two Priests. The first one came but doubted this suspicion of his. After a long and fruitless discussion, the Priest did finally go ahead and pray against it. At the moment that he did the pains exploded and went running up and down my friend's right shoulder, arm and thigh. It was as if a fork was ripping through his muscles and then stopping to grind into his joints. It raced up and down as the Priest prayed, and then after three or four minutes it receded dramatically. During this, however, my friend almost lost consciousness between spasms, cries and screams. When it was over the Priest was in tears and acknowledged finally that the suspicion had been correct afterall. Then six hours later, my friend having slept a little, the second Priest, the one for whom he was working, came to him as well, and he too started to pray against it. This time it only fought back to about a third of what it had before and then calmed down entirely. The next morning he was up again after five days in bed and could resume with his work as before.

Two weeks later he visited here and brought the situation to my exorcist friend. This man then prayed away the very small part that was still present and found out that it had been sent upon my friend by someone in that first town. My friend did not know the person there, but for the Priest to have such a loyal and persevering assistant was enough to make the other one furious.

Did the unknown person need to know or see that there was a weak link, so to say, in your friend's back?

Certainly the demons under the power of this poor person knew of this weak link; but also considering how well known the Priest is, my friend was exposed to much spiritual warfare.

Do prayers for healing and for deliverance help from a distance if the person is not open yet to being prayed with?

Yes, definitely, and far too many people including Priests do not have a faith strong enough to believe this and thus do not put it into practice. In the Bible Jesus healed the Centurion's servant at a distance. Then Jesus said to the Centurion, "You may go; as you have believed, it will be done for you." [31] Jesus healed the servant due to his master's faith in Him, but it wasn't the master's faith that did the healing. This often worries people who then think their faith is too weak to help. Jesus is never too weak to help, but we must often wait, for His plan is often different from ours.

But in such cases when the afflicted is at a distance, it does help to have as much information as at all possible when praying against it. Often the demonic influences have to be named specifically before they let go and vanish, and to do so we must pray a lot and do our homework with perseverance and trust that God will supply what we need.

When people come to you with disturbances and you take the names of their deceased relatives, do you then witness the peace that enters the individual, the family or the house in question after the Masses and other prayers?

Yes, almost always depending, of course, on whether they keep in touch. Many people stay in touch for a longer time, and although I am not a psychiatrist or physician with all those involved names on my tongue, I can certainly tell when a distressed child very quickly turns into a peaceful and happy child, and that without any therapy or drugs. It brings me much joy to see these changes repeatedly. Jesus and Mary exclude no one from their Peace and Joy!

Many different areas of medicine today use hypnosis as part of therapies or to find out what happened in the past that may have something to do with the illness involved. Have the souls said anything about hypnosis to you?

The souls have said that hypnosis is dangerous and a sin. No one may delve into our subconscious and even if they do the testimonies that come from there are very unreliable.

Some people who believe in the falsehood of reincarnation base their beliefs on the results of hypnosis. That is just one case where a relatively small sin leads to much confusion.

When people are very sick and suffer great pain, what is permissible by God as far as what the attending doctors may do?

A soul told me once that he had to suffer a great, great deal because he had been a doctor who had shortened the lives of some of his patients with injections to lessen their sufferings. Doctors may NEVER kill a patient, but they are allowed to administer drugs to lessen the pain. Only God gives and removes life. Otherwise it is murder like all other murders.

When a doctor does take the life of a patient, does the soul of the patient then have to suffer the unfinished time that it should have suffered on earth in Purgatory or does the doctor then himself have to carry that suffering later on?

The doctor himself does, and if he does not turn and stop this with confession, penance and reparation on his own accord; then his family, the following generations, will carry the consequences and do so dearly.

Goodness! Do you know of cases where the following generations suffered and how, in what way did they suffer?

Yes, I do. One case I remember now concerned the daughter-inlaw of a doctor who was regularly euthanizing his patients. She had lost many babies yet both mother and father were entirely healthy and the doctors were completely mystified by the many still-births that she had suffered. This suffering carried by the couple in the younger generation was partial reparation that God needed for the sins of that euthanizing doctor. That was God's justice.

Does that then mean that every abortionist and his family will then have to suffer all that which the infants he has killed would have suffered during the entire length of their normal lives, had they been permitted to live their lives as God had planned for them?!

Yes, unless they stop with it immediately and make up for it, it surely DOES mean that!

I've heard it said that the cities of Sarajevo, Mostar and Vukovar were, before the break-up of the former Yugoslavia, the cities where abortions were most easily available in that country. When it comes to God's justice, does it then follow why those cities suffered the most damage during this Balkan war?

It certainly would! Where sins against life are concentrated, God will arrange for His justice in unavoidable ways. May that example be a warning to all the governments, courts and doctors of the East and West!

23 -- DEATH

You have done so very much for the Poor Souls that at your death you will certainly be escorted to Heaven by many thousands of souls and will not have to...

Oh, no! I cannot imagine going to Heaven without any Purgatory, because every fault is added up. God has made me aware of so very much through my contacts with the Poor Souls and therefore my responsibility is so much greater. It is relative to this awareness that we must suffer. Yet I do hope for just a little help in that regard. (laughter)

What happens to people who commit suicide? Have you been visited by any?

Yes, I have, by many. What happens to them depends entirely on why they did it. Many people have come to ask about them, but until now, only one has been lost. In the great majority of cases the more responsible are those others who were possibly guilty of defaming them, or who refused to help them, or who pushed them into a corner; and due to this they short-circuited. In such cases, others are again more responsible. They themselves do, however, regret having done so. And often it is due to illness. If one handles a healthy person correctly, he normally does not do this.

Have you been visited by souls who overdosed on drugs? Are they lost?

I have been visited by some; but again, what happens to them varies. With hard-core addicts they really cannot do anything else unless God steps in very powerfully. In many cases the doctors correctly say,

"It was only the drug." Yet even then they do have to suffer a lot. Hard drugs are definitely satanic, so there again prayers against those demons should certainly be enlisted. More and more of these cases have now been healed without any of those horrible withdrawal symptoms, and when that happens, it is always with Our Lady and St. Michael sending Satan's soldiers on their way. The dealers of these poisons in particular will dearly regret their actions during their atonement and reparation, that is if they're not lost entirely.

Can you tell me of a case in which someone was saved due to his or her dramatic change of heart when at the door of death?

Yes. A man came to me once with two names to find out what had happened to them. When I asked him to tell me a bit about the two lives, he refused and said that he brought them to me to find out whether I was telling the truth. To that I said fine and waited for a Poor Soul to give me the answers in those two cases. A month or so later he returned and asked me if I had the answers already, and I said yes, I did. The man was in the deepest Purgatory and could not yet be delivered from it, while the woman had gone straight to Heaven without any time in Purgatory at all. I handed him the paper on which I had written it the way I had received it, and he was shocked. He then accused me of being a fraud. I asked him how he could say that, and demanded he tell me something about these two people, a man and a woman.

According to my guest, the man had been the most pious of all the Priests in his area. This Priest had always been at Mass half an hour earlier and stayed longer than all others. And he went on and on and praised this Priest to the extreme. Then he told me that the woman had lived a very shabby life, and he listed many of her most grievous sins to convince me of this. Once he was done, I must admit that I had become a bit uncertain myself, and I agreed to ask again and this time for an explanation. Perhaps, I thought, I had written the wrong answer next to the names and thus had them flipped around. So we both waited a bit longer for the second answers. Then they came and, no, they had remained the same. The man was in the deepest of Purgatory, and the woman had gone straight to Heaven!

The explanation was this: The woman who died first did so in front of a train. Not suicide, she must have tripped or slipped and fallen. In the instant that she recognized that her death was unavoidable, she said to God, "It is all right with me that you take me, because at least then I will no longer be able to insult you." This sentence or thought alone erased everything, and she went to Heaven without any Purgatory. The Priest, on the other hand, had been all that this man had said, but at the same time he never ceased criticizing those who did not go to Mass as early as he did, and he even refused to bury this very woman in his cemetery due to her shady reputation among his parishioners. His constant criticism and judgments such as the one concerning this woman earned him the deepest of Purgatory. So we may never, never judge and guess because of what we thought we knew. My visitor recognized the truths here, apologized from his heart and left satisfied with the news for which many were anxiously waiting at home.

In attending a person's death, are there signals that they might have gone to Heaven straight away?

Perhaps, but these too do not always tell the whole story. What is certain, however, is when a person experiences an extremely fearful, angry and sometimes even violent death, this is guaranteed to mean that they needed to suffer a lot, if they were not entirely lost. I say caution with the other extreme as well, because even great Saints -- as I and many millions would call Padre Pio -- did die a peaceful, even joyful death as many others do too; but still he had to spend a short time in Purgatory. Peaceful deaths are beautiful and lead to beauty, and ugly deaths are horrible and lead to much suffering, but to be more precise than this, as I mentioned earlier, is risky.

Does God respond in any particular way if a person gives his life for another?

The Poor Souls have told me that dying for another, either in his place or in the attempt to rescue him, is always a holy death. This means that such an act will erase very much that still needed to be erased.

About twenty years ago now, I knew a young man who did not have the reputation of being particularly devout. I knew him because he and his family were neighbors of mine. Yet one very strong and good personality trait he had was that he always insisted on helping others. Then one especially harsh winter day he heard cries for help outside, and off he went out the door. His mother tried to persuade him to stay because he was always the one to risk anything. She wanted someone else to go this time. But he was unstoppable, and out the door he dashed. As soon as he was out the door, a powder snow avalanche came down and swallowed him up. They found him dead the next day. To this then other boys said, "We would not want to die as he did." -- "What do you mean by that?" I asked them. -- "Well, you do not know all the things he did." -- "Be as fearful as you wish, but dying as he did for someone else will certainly negate any possibility that he is lost. It is always a holy death." Only a couple of days later, he appeared to me and said he needed only three Masses to be delivered. I still expressed some surprise, and he said, "Yes, because I died trying to help another, God took care of all the rest." To which he then added, "Never again in my life would I have been able to experience such a joyful death."

There must then be a difference between somebody dying while attempting to save another, and someone dying because they were reckless.

Oh, yes! If someone dies and does so merely because they put themselves in a very risky situation that does not mean that it was his time to die. If the accident happens without any fault of the deceased, then God did call that one home to Him. Yet if there was fault lying with the deceased, then the person himself caused it to happen.

I know of a young man who died in Vienna on a motorcycle because he was driving it beyond the law. He told me later that had he been more careful, God would have given him another thirty years to live. When I asked him whether he had been ready for eternity, he said no, but that God gives everyone who does not actively scorn Him the chance to regret. And this young man did regret everything.

At the moment of death, does the soul see the light of God clearly and in its fullness?

No, not clearly but enough for the soul to wish to go on toward it. The relative clarity and fullness depend on the condition of the soul at that moment.

When we pray that someone experiences a peaceful death, does this really help achieve this?

> Is God deaf? It even helps if the person we have in our heart died a long time ago. God and prayer are not limited or in any way affected by time. God is still there fifty years ago as He is also already there fifty years from now. He will do for us exactly as much as we trust Him to help us.

But if we can pray for someone who died already to experience a peaceful death, does this not mean that we can save souls from Hell who are already there?

> No, lost is lost; but the graces from such a prayer will then be distributed somewhere else for the same purpose -- to allow someone to experience a peaceful death.

Will God save someone from Hell knowing that someone in the future will be praying for this person?

> Because God's love and mercy are infinite, I see no reason why He wouldn't.

How seriously should we take the last requests of a dying person?

> I find that under three conditions we should take them very seriously and do our absolute best that they be respected and fulfilled. And under these conditions I would call someone's last wishes sacred. This is because in the death process people are permitted by God to see things very differently than when they were living and, in a sense, in control of things. The conditions are these: 1) The person was mentally sound at death. 2) The wish, seen objectively, was not a bad one. 3) The person died in relative peace. If all these were the case, then we must certainly go ahead and fulfill their wishes.

Was someone to hinder another's last wishes, is such a hindrance, which, of course, often equals thievery of the dead, weighed more heavily than the same thievery from a living person?

> Yes, God weighs it far more heavily because the deceased can no longer change anything if their wishes were not carried out correctly.

When someone knows that he is about to die, what is the best way to prepare himself?

To pray and to give God everything. To open oneself completely to His goodness and to trust in Him completely.

And what is the best approach when one is helping a dying person?

Pray with them, of course, and tell them the total truth. Tell them what you can about the light of God and tell them that we are never, never left alone. Suggest with much love a confession, if it has not already happened. Pray with the Blessed Mother for them and ask her to accompany this child of hers on his way. Our Mother will never neglect to respond.

Is it true what people say about seeing a film of one's entire life as one lets go from here?

Yes, one does in a way. The descriptions of this vary only slightly. A Swiss man I knew who believed in little and only thought that we are taught these things so that we live good lives, fell very ill and went into a coma experiencing the agony but did not die. He had not believed in an eternity. When revived, he described himself to me sitting in a room, and on the wall opposite from him was written his whole life and in great detail. At that point he knew that there was an eternity, and he became afraid. The wall slowly disappeared, and behind it there was this indescribable beauty for which he had no words. Then he revived, came back, and woke up. He has now completely changed his entire lifestyle.

I think it would be very wise for people to study just a little bit about the death process and what happens when people are guided by the Christian truth just before their letting go from here. How often have we heard that someone has turned Catholic on his death bed? How often have we heard that a Christian has turned non-Christian at the same moment in their time here on earth? I'll leave the answers to these two questions to you.

Conception and death are the two greatest moments of our lives when God is so very near to us; and both of these are studied far too little. Rather than abusing and blocking conception and going to immoral means to speed up or delay death, why don't we love, protect and study those moments as carefully as all the other times in our lives? Were society to do this, many huge truths would quickly become indisputably clear.

In this film that people are shown at death, you say they see with great clarity the good deeds as well as the sins they committed during their lives. Does this then also include the sins that they had confessed well, the sins they had regretted dearly and repaired with all their hearts? I ask this because it is said, of course, that when we go to Confession Jesus carries the sin away for good and that that then means literally gone, so much so that even Satan no longer knows of it. So if Jesus has truly taken it away, how or rather why are the sins shown to us again at death?

First of all, not everyone sees such a film, and then, even when they do, it should not be considered an attack by Satan. Entirely confessed and repaired sins do not appear there but God does this to show us His absolute justice, and in seeing both sides, the soul, then knows in total clarity and assigns itself to the proper level in Purgatory.

Some people with this knowledge would say that those who only believe in the last moments are in better shape. Are they?

Yes, the stages of holiness come in a thousand variations. (laughter) No, seriously now, they certainly are NOT in better shape because they missed so many chances at doing good. It is for this reason that their spot in Heaven will not be at the level of others who tried to do God's will all of their lives.

You might not be aware of it, but in these last years 'Near Death Experiences' (NDEs) are being studied more deeply and written about more than ever before. One such book in particular comes to mind at the moment. So, Maria, my question to you is this: When these people who have been pulled back to life describe their experiences, are their descriptions always foolproof, always 100% true?

No, certainly not. Because they have not died. Here too one has to be loving but remain wise and very careful. Some of the widespread descriptions do have blatant falsehoods contained in them. Just like apparitions or inner-locutions, very loving, prayerful, discerning and experienced individuals including believing doctors and theologians must closely proof such experiences. In cases where non-praying secular doctors are the only ones surrounding, guiding and naturally, in some way, influencing these good people, it will, by no fault of their own, happen very easily that falsehoods are then spread.

Take my own case. Just because some psychologist can with certainty state that I am balanced, honest and not mentally ill, by no means is sufficient to determine whether all that I have said is the truth. Those other experiences that are not purely supernatural must also be proofed far more broadly as I myself have been and, for example, the 'children' of Međugorje have also been as well.

In the book about which I am thinking, which has recently enjoyed success in the USA, it says that the souls come and choose when and into which body they will go. For this reason, it implies that abortion, despite being against the natural order, is not really so bad because it just means that the soul wished to go elsewhere. What do you say to this?

Dangerous nonsense! This is clearly Satan's influence. We must pray that this person be humble enough to permit himself and his experiences to be proofed, and not merely by secular doctors and psychologists but also by deeply prayerful and discerning individuals who are experts in Christian spiritual truths, before they continue to spread Satan's lies to even larger numbers of people. And duty dictates that I must add that every abortion that results due to that being written will be this person's or his advisor's responsibility before God.

24 -- FUNERALS & GRAVES

Have the Souls told you anything about funerals?

Certainly. The Poor Souls prefer staying in their home for a while and not to be taken to the cool morgue right away. Those places bring about no prayers for them. They need the prayers that are said when they are still at home, and most often they and these needed prayers are neglected when they are taken away too quickly. Then they watch their own funerals, as I mentioned yesterday. They can tell who is praying for them and who is only there for the sake of appearance. They hear what we here say about them. Tears do nothing for them. Tears are for our necessary healing process, but not for theirs. Funerals should remain simple and be done with much heartfelt love.

What might they not like about our funerals today?

They do not like hearing falsehoods spoken about them, even if the truth was not always attractive. Eulogies must be honest if it is our wish to help them on their journey. The family ought to acknowledge and confess the sins of that soul and take them in prayer to Jesus. And the souls do not like pompous funerals.

They do not like cremation, and they do not like the remains to be given or sold to science or to hospitals. Sprinkling ashes out of airplanes or throwing them into the ocean is ludicrous and does no one any good at all. It actually hurts the souls because the living are thereby much more likely to forget them rather than attending to them with prayers and loving little gestures on a regular basis. The Church only allowed cremation so that less sacrilege might occur. It again was more a political decision, and not so much a helpful or holy decision.

They do not like anything that is not prayerful or that shows them in a distorted light. Remembering them before Jesus is precisely that, putting them together again, stepping in for them and making good in front of God that which they did a little less than well.

This now reminds me of a soul that came to me once during the day. I was walking home one afternoon up in the woods and along came an extremely old woman. My first thought was, "Goodness, does she ever look old!" She wandered toward me and looked sad and somewhat lost. I greeted her and asked why she was up there on her own and that it was getting late. She answered, "No one cares for me. No one takes me in, and I have to sleep in the streets." I then thought, "Her marbles must be a little loose." I considered for a second and then offered to take her with me, knowing that if she was a nuisance she wouldn't be around for that long. "I will take you, but my place is small. It's all I have but it is a roof, and I can feed you." She cheered up instantly and said, "That is all I needed." And she was gone.

Later I learned that she, at some point in her life, had turned someone truly needy away, and therefore had to be in Purgatory until the day that another person took her in. See, in this way I made up for that sin, and all was repaired. My offering this to her was reparation for her neglect. Reparation is ALWAYS necessary and if we do not do it voluntarily, God will arrange for it.

Have the souls mentioned any other practices of Western funeral homes that they find wrong?

The safest thing to do in choosing funeral homes is to choose one where the people themselves are prayerfully active in a solid Christian Church. This will guarantee that nothing unholy will happen to the earthly remains of our loved ones.

And have they said anything about the upkeep of the grave after the funeral?

Also, and this is very important. It should be humble and lovingly kept up. It should have holy water sprinkled on it on a regular basis. It should have a blessed candle burning at all times. Both of these the Poor Souls need and love very much. Visits to the grave are seen, of course, and these visits help them and us far more than we could possibly think.

Today there are some cemeteries where for the sake of practicality the memorial plaque or stone is laid into the ground so that the lawn mowers can simply run over them with ease. This is laziness and a loveless attitude on the part of the family, and those souls will therefore need to suffer longer than if the family itself goes and cares for their resting place.

Every smallest gesture helps them and, in turn, helps us because they then are more likely to step in for us when we need protection or assistance. Even if we choose to wash the windows out of love for them, this will do so much good!

And for how long should we keep up the graves?

Here again I think it should follow that we do so for at least three generations. I say this because the Bible says that the sins of the fathers are visited upon us for three or four generations. [32] And so our prayers ought to go through the generations and not merely for those whom we personally knew. It is very good that children are led to show interest in their grandparents and great-grandparents. Things of this nature bring everyone so much good. It shows them a path and a unity. I think it is very disorienting in the modern society when families are moving so often only in the search for better money, opportunity or a bigger house. How well do we know that all people are led at some point to go back 'home'? Satan breaks up families in all directions, in the same generation as well as in between generations.

25 -- MARRIAGE, FAMILY & CHILDREN

In a marriage where the wife must suffer a lot at the hands of the husband or vice versa, is it all right for the one to leave the other?

They may, but it is certainly better that they do not. They should offer it all up. But the line one ought to draw is if physical suffering occurs because God chooses martyrs; we do not.

What in the spiritual realm might happen more between a couple married in the Church and a couple not married in the Church or a couple not married at all?

God's Blessing, the Marriage Vows, which are afterall Vows before God, the Marriage Mass and the support of all family members are all such powerful protective graces that the lack of any one or several of these will seriously weaken its needed strength and unity. In calling on God and His Church's Blessing, things certainly unfold far stronger and thus happier than without them.

Things do happen that are similar to what I see when the Poor Souls come to visit me, and among the living we would call it bilocation. Or it also happens that an angel takes on the appearance of the one spouse to bring the other a message. He or she would then see or hear, or both see and hear the other, and thereby receive protective or guiding words. This happens often and must be seen as a wonderful gift from God for a holy couple. It certainly will not happen when people live together in sin. In those cases there is far less protection from outside of this world. I would caution them very urgently to step away from that and to come back to God's protection.

It is also common that a deceased spouse would come close to accompany the still living one through the death process. What a tremendous joy this must be for both to experience! True, giving and holy love never, never dies. Yet it is only this when God has blessed the marriage and is always near to them in prayer and in their acts of selfless love.

What have the Poor Souls said about divorce?

They have said it is one of the greatest of all sins against God Himself. It hurts everyone tremendously and, of course, the innocent ones the most. It is NOTHING LESS than spiritual, emotional and mental murder committed upon God's greatest gift to us, that being our ability to participate in the creation of life and its fruit -- our children. No child of divorce will ever grow to the fullness God had planned for it. In this century, millions of times more than ever before, Satan is ripping into the families and the wombs of women, poisoning and cutting to pieces the holy threads that keep families in His plan, poisoning and cutting to pieces the babies God has given them. It is reparation for these two sins that the souls say is coming soon and will be earth shattering. And in countries such as the USA where more than

50% of marriages now break up, God will soon arrange for these matters to change quickly. He will step in for the humble, the innocent, prayerful and loving people and will punish the others for the neverending insults against love. The industries, the organizations, the attorneys, the cults, the physicians, and psychologists who lie, confuse, collude, make profits, and thereby distort the truth in order to keep this most horrid of wars going will soon experience God's wrath as it has NEVER been experienced before! God have mercy on the ones who know what they are doing! And we have the duty to inform the unknowing ones of what they're doing.

Have the Poor Souls ever told you anything about annulments in the Church?

Yes, they have told me that the Church grants far too many annulments today. Such matters must be examined far more thoroughly. I am afraid it is true to some degree that the well-connected and wellendowed have easier access to annulments and that is hardly God's wish. Of course there are cases where coercion, emotional limitations or other situations in place at the time did invalidate the marriage to begin with, but these are serious matters that must be handled very lovingly but thoroughly as well.

What else can you think of that the Poor Souls communicate to their families?

They can ask a family member to make something good that the soul itself had done badly or unfairly while here. And by following the instruction the living ones will be assisting the soul to go on its way. They can warn them to avoid this or that. They protect them, guide them, and convey love and security in various ways.

Are there things that the souls will never mention to their families?

They will not say or do anything negative or judgmental. It will always be positive, helpful, protective and thus healing.

Are families also visited by deceased relatives who are lost, who have gone to Hell, but without the family being attacked or harassed by them?

Yes, they are. But then, of course, they do not say what can be done for them because they are beyond all help and all graces. In those cases they only remind them of their own condition and of the existence of Hell.

Have the Poor Souls said anything about the women's movement?

No, not in those terms except that no women should be around the altar. In the secular world it is quite all right that they compete with men on an equal basis. Having their own careers is fine but ONLY as long as the family is not in any way ignored. Here too, both women and men commit many great sins today. If either the children or the spouse are in any way neglected, the other one will have to suffer a lot for it later. This is most definitely a serious and most divisive sin.

Have the Poor Souls ever mentioned what modern western society tends to do so often with its grandparents? Here I mean pushing them out of the home and into so-called 'Nursing Homes' where they are often, at the very least, just treated as another number and, at worst, where they are often drugged into oblivion and death.

Not specifically, but do sins of such an enormity need any clarification? These are ENORMOUS sins! How very often it is the grandparents who teach the youngest to pray, and how often are the generational differences bridged so beautifully because grandparents are there to share the wisdom they gained through many years of experience? Kicking them out of their homes is only Satan's doing.

Is it a sin for a mother not to breastfeed or hold her child?

If she is physically capable of breastfeeding and chooses not to for some self-serving reason, yes, it is. And not holding a child also stunts it emotionally later in life and is thus, of course, also a sin.

Is it better to be poor with many children or wealthy with only one or two children?

Never may we interfere with God's plan in giving us children. And He will always supply plenty for those in His plan. I know far more truly happy people among the poor than I do among the wealthy, and I know plenty of both. The wealthy are also far more burdened with the effects of their ancestors' sins. More wealthy people come to me for help in this regard than do the poor. And this is not because the poor cannot reach me. They also come.

Yet most of the world governments, as the meetings in Cairo just recently showed us, speak, however, of the serious threat of over-population. What do you respond to this?

This is selfish and misguided nonsense and again entirely orchestrated by those same banks! Of the approximately six billion on earth today, it is true that about a third are starving; but that is ONLY because of the greed of a few. There are statistics available that prove that the world could feed fifty billion or more, if the energy and food were only distributed justly. The West's greed angers God greatly, and He will do something about this very soon, I am sure. I know He will.

Who is it whose baby consumes ninety times as much as a baby does in India? And who is it who worries so much about over-population? The answers to both of these questions are the same: the West and its banks. Greed and the misguided fear of poverty make people believe, say and act out great falsehoods.

At what age is it all right for a mother to leave her child for any length of time with a non-family member?

This will depend, of course, somewhat on the exact circumstances; but, as a rule, it is a sin to do so before the age of four. The wounds incurred before that age are the most difficult to heal because they are so very far down in the subconscious.

Have the souls said anything about physical punishment upon children?

Yes, they have, and it is here that I was attacked by Germany's 'Der Spiegel' magazine a couple of years ago. They said that I supported beating children. That was a lie. The Poor Souls have said that a spanking or a slap is necessary and good when it is with a very stubborn and disobedient young child. A small slap is not harmful and will be forgotten on the conscious level very quickly, but the consequences of its stubbornness will be remembered deep down in its subconscious for a very long time. Of course this should only be done very sparingly, but if one does not do that and then waits until the child is older, it will be too late, and you will suffer at the hands of your children. An older child remembering in its subconscious that a slap came when it was only two, three or four will later on only need a particular look from the parent to act correctly. Many parents of today have already learned what fruits their overdone tolerance has produced. Physical violence in the home is a huge sin against love, but carefully placed physical discipline is a God-given necessity at appropriate ages and times.

Does the same sin committed against a child weigh more heavily than it does against an adult?

Yes, certainly, very much so. Sins against a child, if not repaired very quickly and carefully, will later on be repeated by the child as being acceptable and normal. This because the parental role model is so powerful and deeply seeded. A divorce or one act of violence, of dishonesty, of infidelity, of slander, whatever, can so easily cause a chain reaction of the same among the descendants. Being a parent is so much more serious than modern society tends to realize. People far too easily delegate these matters to so-called professionals who do not have the God-given bonds to the children as the parents do, even if the latter make a few mistakes as all humans do.

Do mentally retarded children spend any time in Purgatory?

Yes, they do; but of course it is much lighter than that of healthy children. It all depends on what the child could understand.

What are the gravest sins for children to commit, say, between the ages of six and twelve?

Disobedience and rudeness against the parents are the two worst ones.

Many parents today say that Christian parents are too authoritarian with their children. How do you respond to this remark?

No parents should be ultra-authoritarian with their children, for if they are, they will soon lose their obedience, affection and support. There are plenty of parents who are too authoritarian with their children and who are not Christians at all, so that remark is not really a valid one. Christian parents should be far more authoritative than they should be authoritarian. Any necessary strictness should come early in the children's lives. Later, the parents who should know the truths about God should teach them to the children with much love. Always being negative, with do not do this, and do not do that, is in no way being Christian. The parents should consistently emphasize the do-s, the positive, and back them up immediately with evidence they can understand. Tell them that good will come to them with those do-s. Parents should imitate God's Mercy for them and always show the same mercy and kindness to their children.

We know of the duty we that have within the family without which the society has no chance at all, but why is it that we also have the duty to help others outside our family?

The term family is only a relative one. Somewhere we are all related, no matter what scientists might on occasion try to say to the contrary. We are one family and ONLY one family.

On this subject a Poor Soul told me that someone who does not do his best for the good of all others is not worthy of life. In our search for God's justice, I think things become much clearer when we look inside the family unit as we normally define it. We are responsible and able to help our great-grandparents as we are our great-grandchildren. For the former we must pray and continue to do good deeds, and for the latter we can and must arrange a peaceful, fruitful, healthy and joyous life in faith.

What is your response to the many well-meaning Christian parents who say and act out that their children should be permitted to choose the religion that is right for them when they grow up?

Then they are simply permitting Satan in secular society to lead them away from the absolute truth about our loving God. What loving parent would let its child choose between a food that nourishes and heals and one that could slowly weaken, poison and kill them? What parent would willingly let its children go without love and warmth? Parents who say and do this have never, never prayed or even realized and nurtured their own goodness, and, in the combination of these, God Himself is being ignored and thus hurt very badly when this happens.

You have now said that there are children in Purgatory, have they also appeared to you?

Yes, children have also appeared to me. Children all the way down to the age of four are there. You know, children have a much finer conscience than do most adults. As soon as the child knows the difference between right and wrong, it carries the responsibility for it. Often it is taught that the line for this is the age of reason. This is wrong; it's really the age of conscience.

And it is very important, for instance, if a child is very ill and possibly in danger of death, and it requests a Priest to hear its confession, this request MUST be respected and followed through. I know that often it is not and that is a severe mistake on behalf of the responsible adults nearby. I know of a child of four and a half that insisted on confessing a sin. And it was very clear about the wrong it had done.

You also seem to have a special love and caring for today's children. I say this because I've heard that you teach the small children here in your village.

Yes, I have had many children around me now for a very long time; and I teach them their Catechism.

What else, if anything, have the Poor Souls said about what should and should not be in the schools?

They have mentioned that sex education should definitely not be in the schools. It is a matter that is for the parents to deal with once the child starts asking questions. It should remain under their guidance and care because children learn lasting love only from their parents. Again far too much power today is delegated away and into the hands of the secular agencies who have NO business teaching when it comes to spiritual matters of which love and sex are important parts. Secular teachers must stay away from the holiness of the family unit.

In this regard too, television does so much harm today. It portrays love as just another commodity to consume and discard. This is a huge distortion and thus a huge sin against true love, and therefore against God himself!

Have souls appeared to you, who while they were here on earth, practiced sexual deviations?

Yes, and they must suffer greatly.

What should parents do to form the consciences of their children?

Good example is the most important thing. Then by praying a lot for them and also with them. Also by blessing them often; that too is worth a lot. And then a good education and the most important one is before they go off to regular school. Jesus told us to bring His children to Him and not to block them.

You say that some children in Purgatory have visited you. Can you tell me about one or two of these cases?

An eleven-year-old girl came to me and told me she had extinguished a candle at a cemetery and had taken some of the wax with her to play with. She knew that she was not supposed to do that, and therefore she was in Purgatory for a while. I was asked to light two blessed candles and to carry whatever else was necessary for her to be delivered.

Then another much younger girl came to me because she and her twin sister had been given dolls with carts for Christmas, and their mother had told them to take great care of them. The girl who came to me soon damaged hers and, so that she would not get caught, she secretly put her damaged one in the bed in the place of her sister's healthy doll. This she had to work off in Purgatory; but, of course, I prayed and helped her on her way.

Then another case, but here there was more to learn than merely that children are also in Purgatory. There were two families living right next to each other. One was wealthy; the other one was relatively poor. One day a small girl in the wealthy family went to her mother and said that she wanted to give all her nice clothes and toys to the poorer girl next door. The mother was obviously puzzled and asked the child why she'd want to do this. Her answer was that she could always go over there to play with the other girl. To this the mother said that the other girl could always come to their home to play with her. "No, no," insisted the little girl, "I must do it, I will do it." The parents tried all they could, but nothing would change the girl's mind. Finally the parents said, "All right, go ahead and do it, but do not expect us to go out and buy all those good things again. That we will not." -- "OK, no problem" said the child and went ahead and did precisely what she said she wanted to do.

Two days later she ran out the front door without looking and was hit by a car and died. The parents in their tremendous suffering came to me to ask why this had to happen. I agreed to ask the Poor Souls about it, and soon the answer came back to me; it was this, "Their suffering in losing this girl has guaranteed that one of their boys will not be lost." So this was reparation ahead of time for something that God saw coming. God is a very loving God, for now both of these children will soon be with Him, not just one of them.

Concerning the girl who stole wax from the cemetery, I noticed that you were asked to light two blessed candles for the one that had been extinguished. Is this an example of what is meant by extra reparation?

Yes, exactly.

Earlier you said that children are still close to God and this, of course, due to their innocence. Does it then also happen that children receive special graces due to their good behavior brought on by their parents' example?

Oh yes, and very often so. I know of children who wanted to go to Mass every day and children who on their own loved listening to stories out of the Bible. These are special graces. And some might even be considered extreme at first, but the parents may never interfere with such things and must let the contact between God and their children grow as it is in God's plan for those children. I've heard of children who wanted to kneel on gravel and pray for long periods of time. The parents will have to suffer a lot if they try or succeed in stopping this. God speaks to children very clearly because their souls are, as you say, far cleaner, clearer, more innocent than ours.

Please tell me of one experience you had during your childhood that made you especially happy or that influenced you a great deal.

Certainly one of my happiest moments happened when I was fifteen. That was in 1930 or so.

One of my brothers and I were working on a farm in Bavaria. When we applied for work there the farmer had clearly promised us that we would always be able to attend Sunday Mass; but it was not long before I realized that this promise was only valid for my brother, but not for me. This was so because nearly every Sunday morning the farmer's wife became mysteriously ill and insisted that I stay at home to attend to her rather than letting me go to church with my brother. Then it was Pentecost coming around and I again wondered what the farmer's wife would do. Even late Saturday evening she was entirely healthy and so I hoped with great expectations that I would be at Holy Mass the next morning. But, at nine o'clock Sunday morning she again became sick -- with a mysterious headache or something -- and told me in no uncertain terms that I had to stay with her again because I just couldn't leave her alone when she was sick! I was broken! By one o'clock in the afternoon the headache left her and she said I could go. I ran outside and dodged around an unoccupied out-building behind which there was a bench with a peaceful view. There I cried in desperation for again having missed Holy Mass that I loved so much, and on SUCH a big day! Suddenly I was surrounded by a cloud of white doves that settled slowly all around me in the grass -- everywhere! In the grass, on my lap, all the way around me -- just everywhere!

You said a cloud, Maria. How many were there? Fifty? A hundred?

Oh! At least a hundred! Seeing such beauty I surely did not count them but they were really everywhere! And stayed for at least an hour! My tears had quickly changed to tears of joy and I was engulfed in such happiness that all else was gone. Then they left. I did tell my brother about them, but we did not tell anybody else. Over the following weeks he asked neighboring farmers whether there were any white doves or pigeons in the area and the answer was always the same -- there were none. I do not think another experience from my childhood touched me as deeply as this had. It was pure beauty!

Wow! ...and I see that this truly did touch you very deeply, but permit me to continue. Is it true that many of the accepted cases of apparitions happened to children?

Yes, it is. Children are so open to the existence of God and His Entire Kingdom. Their innocence, natural humility, dependency, sensitivity and trust allow them to experience things very differently and in a much more refined way than adults do. We must protect this cleanliness in them and allow them to be children as long as at all possible. When the world today throws them into the abusive, arrogant and over-secularized society too early, much of their beauty is destroyed and can never be retrieved. I have known many children who, for instance, have seen angels, and I do not doubt them for a minute. God gives so very much to the small among us and that is why Our Lady in Međugorje starts all her messages there with "Dear Children". She wants us to be small at heart so that God can give us more graces and gifts.

26 -- WORK AND MONEY

In this war that you have mentioned between the rich and the poor the subject of work or, more often in these times in which we live, the lack of work available is naturally a much discussed subject. Let me ask you a few simple questions about work and money. Or would you prefer to first say something about these subjects?

The greatest war today, second only to the war against the innocent babies and the family structure, is between the rich and the poor. The Freemasons are behind the movement to create a world currency and a world government, the so-called New World Order and New Age, and that world government will have all its energies aimed at destroying the Church. Even the horrid war in the Balkans at this very moment is funded by the Freemasons, and it should be no surprise at all by this time, why Our Lady chose to appear in the middle of that some ten years before anybody had an idea that it was going to explode the way it has down there.

The World Bank, the United Nations, the European Union and the International Red Cross are also synchronized with all of this and, despite all appearances, are NOT working for the benefit of the world. And behind all of this is the network of banks that are run by the Freemasons and a string of other secret societies about whom the vast majority of people know near to nothing. People's greed and fear of poverty permit them to hand Satan the funds with which he will attempt, but in the end fail, to crush our Church and thereby God. It will be at that precise moment that Our Lady with her followers will become victorious even if things do not appear so until the very last moment.

You have mentioned the greed of the West on several occasions now and you have said that God will hand out severe reparation to the West for it. Does it then follow that the centers of greed, the centers where these banks you speak of are most concentrated, will suffer more than areas where humility is more the way of life?

Yes, I think that will be the case.

Are you advising people then to leave those centers for more humble surroundings?

I advise people to come back to God and to prayer, and God wishes us to be humble so that He can help us. Then He in their prayers will advise them what to do.

Among the wealthy there is a manner of living which entails always gaining in their wealth, often referred to as the principle, by only spending the interest made from it. Then there are many people today who simply live off trading in the various currencies or from other forms of speculation. Are either of these activities or even lifestyles in God's will?

Clearly not! God wishes for the wealthy to share what they have with the poor and to do good deeds for the poor and NOT to sit on their wealth. Both these groups will have much to adjust to in the coming years and we must pray that the Holy Spirit enlighten them as fast as possible.

And were there people who already saw that the system, as it is today, is not from God, what do you suggest they do with the funds that they have accumulated if they now wish to use it according to God's will?

Do good things with it now because later it will be gone and do no one any good!

Is the idea of an Anti-Christ true?

Yes, I'm afraid it is. Some visionaries other than the ones in Medjugorje say that the Anti-Christ is already alive today. He will come as a great financial wizard, have a very powerful charisma about him and will also be considered a great healer and miracle-worker. Huge numbers of people will fall for him when, in fact, his will be the strongest manifestation of Satan ever. People must pray incessantly not to be fooled by Satan and his unlimited talent to disguise himself in any form that pleases his arrogance.

When one lends money to someone, may one then require interest from him or her upon repayment of it?

According to God, no. We should lend it out in love of brother and not in order to become richer ourselves. We may only earn money with our own work.

You tell me that an era of peace will be coming to us but only after something very big happens for the conversion of humanity. Will this era of peace also include a complete redistribution of wealth?

Yes, it will.

You say that along with this big event a complete worldwide financial collapse will also occur before we can enjoy this era of peace. How would it be easier for people to prepare for these two changes both of which, if I understand you correctly, will be enormous?

Yes, they will be enormous! People must come back to God today and give themselves to Him completely! If they do that the changes that are in store for all of us will be very much easier for them to endure.

Have you heard about the Church Organization called Opus Dei where a part of the vocation of each member is the sanctification of ordinary work? And if so, then do you know if it is good and, as you say, comes from God?

Yes, I know of it and, yes, it comes from God.

If it is a sin to demand interest from someone, is it then also a sin to buy something, usually something larger, on credit?

If one is in true need, then it would not be a sin, but the person lending the money should also see the true need with love rather than enriching himself due to it.

Does the Church today teach us about the proper and moral use of money?

Numerous Popes since the beginning of the Church have spoken about the value of work and condemned the continued use of interest. Far too little is being taught about the use of money and the present Holy Father would do the world great good to write an Encyclical about the use of it.

And one last question concerning work. Do the souls in any way help you with your own daily work?

Yes, they do; but only when it comes to work that concerns the souls themselves. When I need a particular sheet of paper, for instance, to write down an answer that they give me, all I need to do is pull one sheet out of the pile and it is the right one each and every time. So they help me help them, but that is all.

27 -- MARIAN APPARITIONS

Does Jesus' mother, Mary, really appear to people? You have mentioned
Međugorje now on several occasions. Please tell me more about it.

Oh yes, she does appear to people, and it is today in Međugorje,
Hercegovina that she appears daily to a group of young people. I've
been there already three times, but I did not have to go down there
to find out whether or not it was real. Soon after it started in June of
1981, I asked a Poor Soul if it was real, and the answer was yes.
And so are San Damiano, Kibeho, Fr. Gobbi, and other smaller cases
around the world.

You know, with Međugorje there is only one great danger, and
that is if the world were to ignore it. But there are many other cases
of messages 'from above' where the Poor Souls have told me either
'careful' or simply 'no'.

'No' is very easy to understand. Can you tell me of a case or two that are
not real? And how do you interpret 'careful'?

I will not mention names, but I know of cases here in Europe that
are entirely satanic. Right over here in Switzerland there are two cases, one in German Switzerland with a relatively small following and
the other, in French Switzerland, with a huge following throughout
the entire world. There is a very confused one in Australia, a fake in
England, one in South America and many outright evil ones in the
USA, but, then again, there are also real ones there. We must pray so
much for all those fake cases!

'Careful' can be for various reasons, but it means that some interference is happening or has happened around the person it concerns.
So one must be extra cautious. This can be the case if the person is
not cared for spiritually, or if the person chooses not to hold to a very
discerning and strong spiritual director. If there are any theological
mistakes, any mental, emotional or physical loss of freedom or an
effort to bring too much attention upon the instrument itself -- it is in
these cases one should be very careful and leave immediately. Also
the taking or the accepting of any money should warn people that

something could be way off. Another possible signal is if the 'visionary' is in any way neglecting his or her own family. There are many signals to look out for.

And please do not forget that Satan knows the truth and will use it to lure people. When we discern or are told 'careful', then it is better to ignore the entire situation than to risk being misled. Satan can fake anything he chooses to, even stigmata and healings of every sort. We must pray a lot for the many fakes in the world today and also for those who refuse spiritual leadership, refuse testing or total obedience to the Church when it comes to these matters.

If a follower of one of these fake cases comes to you, do you advise them of this fact?

The souls told me that if it was to happen that a person asks me, then I should tell them that to this or that phenomenon, the souls have said 'No!' And exactly this did happen a few months ago concerning the more widespread of these two Swiss cases.

To be candid, it's not difficult for me to imagine who you're referring to here. But tell me, why do think a person does such a thing? Or is it done unconsciously by them?

Consciously or unconsciously, due to some weakness of theirs, probably pride, Satan makes them do it. And by how this one operates it seems clearly evident that all they wish to do is cause division and to pull people away from Međugorje. My exorcist friend, who I referred to earlier, has also been able to confirm this.

I understand that you do not wish to mention names of living people who are misleading others in this manner, but would you be willing to mention a name of a deceased person about whom the souls told you 'careful'?

The Poor Souls said 'careful' when I asked about Maria Valtorta's writings. But here it could be that things happened to her writings after she had died. Again, Satan is always lurking very nearby to mess around with things, so 'careful' should not make people worry about Valtorta herself.

Has the Blessed Virgin Mary said anything through the visionaries in Međugorje about the Poor Souls?

Yes, she has spoken of Purgatory several times there. Early on the children gave two longer testimonies and a few shorter, private responses about it and then in 1986 and 1987 there was a longer message about it to the entire world and another where the necessity for Masses for the souls was briefly mentioned. (See page 225)

And do those messages confirm what you say?

Yes, they do.

You mentioned before that souls tend to congregate in prayerful or holy places. Do you know if any souls have appeared in Međugorje?

Yes, they have. Our Lady confirmed a few such visions for the visionaries there but the messages that came from them were private for the relatives concerned. But I was told about one that happened in a nearby restaurant soon after Our Lady started appearing in Međugorje.

In the next larger town where the Communists and the Police were -- both of whom, of course, at least laughed at or at worst tried to terrorize the villagers of Međugorje -- there is still today a restaurant which only the men of the town frequent. All the tables except for one were around the walls and the one in the center was always the last to be occupied. At around lunch time one day the restaurant was nearly full and some of the men were saying ugly things about both the apparitions as well as the people of Međugorje which is, afterall, only three or four miles away. Suddenly some of the men looked up when they heard a woman's voice reprimand them for saying such things about such holy matters. They saw her sitting at the normally empty table in the very center of the restaurant. She was about thirty, attractive in appearance and well-dressed. No one -- not even the waiter had seen her come in. There wasn't even a glass on her table! When the men heard her scold them, they quickly fell silent. The next time they looked up, there was no one at the table. No one had seen her enter or leave the place! This story spread all around town very, very quickly. Most certainly that was a soul sent by Our Lady to straighten things out a bit. Again, it is true that the souls show themselves more than usual around holy events.

Earlier you mentioned the warning of Garabandal. Could you tell me about Garabandal and its warning? And have you also been there?

Yes, I've gone on pilgrimage there several times. Garabandal is a mountain village in Spain where Our Lady appeared to some children in the 1960s. Out of there comes a warning that is essentially this. A moment will come when every person on earth will see the condition of his own soul and that many will die of shock when they see it. It's the same as happens to everyone during the death process, but then it will happen to all at the same time. "From whence He shall come, to judge the living and the dead." [33]

Ought we to be fearful of such warnings?

Only when we are very far from God and full of sin do we have reasons to fear them. If we try consistently to be with Him, we have nothing to fear at all. Simply said, those who pray will be safe. And also God's mercy always comes before His judgment.

A good comparison for this would be a warning on the side of the road. The fact that we see and read the sign in the road does not mean that we have already slid out of the sharp curve ahead of us that the sign is warning us about. With a childlike trust in our loving God, we are and will always be in the safest of all hands.

How else might God be warning us in these years?

He is warning us with natural as well as man-made disasters, and these include earthquakes, mass starvation and plagues, of which AIDS is not the last. No one can deny that these are happening. They are occurring with astonishing regularity, but again what the fewest of us are prepared for is a total economic collapse, and this will bring the proud and powerful literally to their knees.

Yesterday you told me that there would be a last day. Are these warnings then perhaps telling us that the last day is imminent?

No, this does not need to be the case at all. I believe God will be showing Himself clearly very, very soon because we have gotten ourselves so distant from Him. But saying that the end of the world is imminent is by my estimation, based on what the Poor Souls have told me, wrong. Remember now that the Souls have told me that things will soon be getting better again, and nothing in that implies that the final battle or any end of the world is upon us. But it will be a huge change; one can say purification. Please, we may never forget that God's mercy is also infinite.

I understand that in the early days of Fatima, the two visionary girls there asked Our Lady if they were going to go to Heaven. She answered 'yes'. Then they asked the same question on behalf of the little boy, Francesco, then only seven years old. Her answer to this was, "Only if he prays many Rosaries." Maria, how can this be true if he was only seven?

Yes, that's true. You see it is always relative to what the person was taught, even if only seven. By this answer we must presume that he was taught to pray far more than, say, children today. And I am certain if you were to research that, you would find out that this had been the case. Asking that of one of today's so secularized kids would be harsh, and Our Lady is anything but harsh. In Međugorje Our Lady asked the children in the very beginning how and how much they were praying and adjusted her requests of them to the answer they gave her. This was her motherly and gentle hand at work.

Also in Fatima, one of the girls asked Our Lady about the whereabouts of a sixteen-year-old girlfriend of hers who, I believe, had died shortly before. Our Lady answered that she was in Purgatory and would be until the end of time. How could a child of sixteen have done enough to earn that?

Oh, yes, that is easily possible. She might have been extremely stubborn or disobedient. She might have blocked very many graces, and that would have been enough to cause that.

Some people question Medugorje because the apparitions have gone on now for more than seventeen years. Do you find this to be a valid reason for concern?

No, not at all. The times are so different today than they were during Lourdes, La Salette or Fatima. These are now the times prophesied at La Salette and Fatima, but many things said there were never well publicized. Today the children in Međugorje do need this constant guidance even if only as a safeguard so that they do not fall into this world's innumerable huge temptations. Also in the messages there, Our Lady says that after these present apparitions she will not be appearing again in our times, so again this argument holds no water.

Many things about Međugorje are firsts, but how dare we challenge Jesus' permission for granting His most Holy Mother's wish to be with us in that way for a very long time. Just look at the condition of the world! We need to accept so much help if we do not wish to kill off humanity and everything else on this earth.

Have souls come to you who died in that horrible war down there in the former Yugoslav Republics? And if they have, did they say anything about their regretting not having lived Our Lady's messages while they were still alive?

Yes, three fallen Croatian soldiers have appeared to me, and one of them did confirm that Međugorje is from God. But that is all he said.

Has Our Lady in Međugorje ever mentioned that war down there in the warnings to the world that have been given to the visionaries?

The warnings are secret but the visionary Vicka was asked just that. She said no, that the war has not been mentioned as a part of the warnings. Then the person asking followed up with this, "If this indescribably horrid war is not a part of the warnings, then how big will these warnings be?" To this Vicka answered, "You have just answered your own question." And on this same subject, two other visionaries, Marija and Mirjana, also commented. Marija said, "This war is a cross for us Croatians and a warning for you" while Mirjana said that everything we need to know about them is in the Book of Revelations.

Still we must never, never worry, for all fear is only from Satan. If we try conscientiously to live with God every day, He will protect us from whatever it is that lies ahead. Praying people will be safe but those not praying will be caught off guard and be unprotected. It is that simple; and we must trust in God and His Mother with the trust of small children.

It must have been dangerous to travel to Međugorje in these last years.

Yes, Satan does everything possible to make us think this. Yet, to this very day it has never once been made inaccessible by that satanic war. If people feel called to go, they should not rely on the often confusing and dishonest press. They should not rely on insurance companies or statements made by their governments; they should rely on

Our Lady, her Angels and the Poor Souls to assist them in having a grace-filled pilgrimage.

Other than, of course, a place where daily Marian apparitions are said to occur, what is Međugorje to you and what will it become for people who go there?

The Marian apparitions ARE occurring there say the Poor Souls. They do NOT say they think they might be occurring! But to your question I predict this for those who are led to go. First of all, it is a school of prayer, and if one participates in that just a little bit, it soon turns into a school of love. There Our Lady is guiding us from a Godless and loveless world into a God-filled and therefore love-filled world like we have never before seen.

What is the Pope's opinion when it comes Međugorje?

He has often spoken in favor of it over the years, but there are many others higher up in the Church who wish to hide this fact from the faithful. Just recently he told both the Government as well as the Church leaders of Croatia that he wishes to go to Međugorje on his next visit there. He has also privately met with several of the visionaries.

Protestants complain that Catholics give too much attention to Mary. What do you say to this?

Devotion to the Blessed Virgin Mary can never go too far, as long as it stays balanced and does not turn into worship or adoration. And it was St. Louis de Montfort who said that true devotion to Our Lady includes becoming aware of and thus being active for the Poor Souls in Purgatory.

28 -- SUFFERING & REPARATION

If we were to ask of Jesus that we do our Purgatory here on earth, does He answer this request?

One should not say always, but often yes. It does happen.

I know of a case where a Priest and a woman were in the same hospital together. Both were very ill, but could still get up and spend time together. They often went outside together and got to know each other quite well. The woman, who was not old, told the Priest that she had asked exactly that of Jesus; that she could suffer enough while still here to go to Heaven straight away. To this the Priest said, "Oh, I would not dare ask that. It's just a bit too challenging." -- "No," said the woman, "if I ask that of my Jesus, I trust Him that He will grant me this wish."

A religious Sister there knew both of them and knew that the woman had often spoken those words. So, it happened that the young woman died first, and then soon thereafter the Priest did too. A short time later the Priest appeared to the Sister and told her that, had he been as trusting and devout as that woman he too would have gone straight to Heaven without any time in Purgatory.

Do entire towns or even nations get punished, or as you prefer to put it, are dealt reparation by God for the sins in their past?

> Yes, they do.

So if everyone in the West today confessed their own sins and quickly went about praying and doing extra reparation with good deeds for their relatively immediate ancestry, the reparation you say God is soon sending to us would be drastically diminished? Do I understand this correctly?

> Yes, this is true and it's that simple. Pray and confess, then pray too for your deceased family, and do some extra good deeds for them. Then God will lessen the reparation that He now has planned and which will come without people's advance knowledge.

When the souls of Priests come to you, Maria, what happens when they, of course, do not have families who can step in for them after they die?

> They have me. They have good friends, and I am one of them.

Even the ones you didn't know personally?

> Oh, of course! I will do for them whatever it is they need.

Also take on suffering?

173

Uh hm.

Are you willing to speak about this?

Jesus never gives us more than we can take.

A long time ago now a Priest came and said that if I take on three hours of suffering that it was going to save him twenty years in Purgatory. I said yes because my Priest told me I should take all that is requested of me, and I always have. Soon I was in a pain that consumed every inch of my body so entirely that I was immobile and unable to realize my where-abouts. But a joy stayed in my heart, because it remained very clear to me what this would bring for the Priest. Still, after a while, I thought this had to be three days rather than three hours. Then as suddenly as it came, it also left; and I realized that I had stayed, of course, where I had been all along. I looked at my watch, and it had been three hours and that to the very minute.

At other times it is a local pain. Once, for instance, my right arm hurt for a long time and no matter what I did or how I held it, it remained the same. This turned out to be for a soul who had mishandled someone's Will and, of course, that would entail the arm and hand with which he wrote and worked.

When we take on sufferings with God's love for us everything becomes possible; and then the very best of fruits come from them. Suffering, in other words, the cross without love is too heavy, but love without a cross does not exist.

Do they tell you then how long it will last?

No, not other than that one time. That is the worst part of it, my not knowing how long it will last; but, that time it was three hours.

Do you accept such sufferings on a regular basis or more during certain times than others?

I always accept what is brought to me but during Lent, for instance, they make their presence known to me very strongly through sufferings that I take on for them. At other times it happens whenever they request it.

Do you still take on these sufferings these days as often as in the earlier years?

No, it is less now than before because lately I have gone on lecture tours much more often than I did in the early years and my doing that also helps the souls a lot.

When you were younger, did you ever think that you were going to go around the cities of central Europe giving lectures to large halls full of people?

Never! I would have laughed loudly and been scared inside at only thinking about it. But God now gives me the strength and courage to do so and I do get to see many good fruits coming from it; and for this I am so very grateful to Him.

Have you also taken on great fears as those suffered by Jesus in the Garden of Gethsemane?

No, until now that has not happened.

The time ratio, three hours for twenty years, as you mentioned before, is it always the same or sometimes different?

Entirely different in every case. That's because there are infinitely different levels of Purgatory. A Poor Soul told me that ten years of a light Purgatory is far, far easier to take than two days of the deepest. Moreover we must not think that a soul must rise slowly through all the levels to finally walk out on the top. They can go from the deepest straight up into Heaven.

Do you think that the sufferings you take on voluntarily are similar to the sufferings in Purgatory?

Yes, they seem so to me. My body, once the sufferings have left, carries no scars or any other lasting effects from them. So that means it is entirely in the soul, and that's what makes me think they are very similar.

If we see someone with great suffering, can we step in and offer it to God for them?

Yes, but it does not count as much as when the person himself does it.

And if it is one's own suffering and one does well for a time but then loses patience, and again later offers it up in hind-sight, so to say, does this then have value?

Again yes, but not as much as doing it all the way through until it is gone.

If a person was to offer up all his future sufferings to God, knowing that he might weaken when they come about, does this have the same value as doing it while it is happening?

Yes, it would. God knows our sincerity when we offer it to Him.

So if someone suffers and does not offer it to God, the value of the suffering is lost?

In regard to that soul reaching Heaven more quickly, yes; but still that suffering occurred because most often something happened in the past and that, of course, is then repaired. With or without our help, God lets that happen. He is purely loving and knows perfectly what is best for us.

What else can you say about suffering?

Second only to life itself and the time in which to do good while we are here, suffering is the biggest gift from God there is. While suffering here, we still receive the grace to do good deeds; but once we are in Purgatory that is over forever. Suffering always heals something, and we must trust in God that it is always for our good and for His glory.

There is one enormous grace that comes with suffering that I'd like to emphasize. It is in suffering that people find each other and find each other's hearts. In suffering the other person becomes the important one and without suffering most people tend to think only of themselves first. The West has this problem to a great degree, and in the reparation that God will soon bring upon the West, people will again find each other in their suffering. That will be good and will bring the best out of people who are now only thinking about their next and bigger house or car. This too is a cleansing process. So very often what is at first considered a disaster ends up an enormous grace and gift from God.

When the suffering comes from Satan, should we behave any differently with it than when it comes from God?

All suffering comes from God insofar as He permits us also to suffer at the hands of Satan. Yet if we recognize it as coming from Satan, it is our duty to bring the person to an exorcist. Whereas, if the suffering comes from God directly, the exorcist will be able to do nothing. Some people have said, "I hope God does not love me too much!" I know a mother telling her son who was studying for the Priesthood, "Tell God He can do anything He wants with you." To this he answered, "Oh no, then He'll ask too much of me." This is not true, rest assured that God NEVER asks of us more than we can take.

Knowing that very many types of people exist and that what comes out of our psyches can never be underestimated, some might now decide to ask God for extra sufferings. For those so inclined, would you suggest such a prayer?

In general, no, not at all. People who live in the world and who have others to be responsible for should not do this for their sufferings will come about one way or the other. Prayers for extra sufferings should be left to those who lead a cloistered life, to those who are only responsible for themselves and who always have help around them. They may wish to do this but others should not. In my case I never asked for it either but I have let it happen to me for the Souls in Purgatory. And I chose not to have a family so that I could give my whole life to them. Here too my case is different from that of most other people.

Whether from the living or for the souls, is there any one subject or one sin for which you have had to suffer the most? And if there is, what is that one subject or sin?

From both among the living and the souls that subject would certainly be Communion in the hand.

Have you ever considered simply mentioning it less often?

No. It is my God-given duty to tell people about Purgatory and it is also my duty to include truthfully everything that the Poor Souls have told me about the condition of the Church. How could I possibly leave things out only in order to make my life more comfortable when the condition of the Church, as the souls have so often told me, is the worst ever since its beginning?! Then I would certainly not be a true friend of the souls!

Recently it happened that I was invited by a parish to speak and when the Priest called me he said he wanted only one subject not to be discussed. Upon my asking him what that was, he answered, "hand Communion". When I then asked the souls what I should do, they told me, "Without all the truth, there will be no lecture." And so I had to say the same thing to the Priest.

In the same way I will not authorize any book or article about me if those who publish it choose to neglect the subject of Communion in the hand.

By the appearance here in your den and by the times that your telephone has rung, it seems as though you must get a lot of mail and many, many telephone calls. Have you ever counted in any way how much mail you get or how many telephone calls come in to you each day?

No, but the other day the Post Master teased me because I received seventy-three letters on that one day. And my local Priest, Fr. Bischof, told me recently that the telephone company had told him that I get more calls than the Crisis Number in Feldkirch.

Other than the Post Master, who, Maria, is your very best friend here on earth? (laughter)

Oh, that is of course my spiritual director!

And who is your second best friend here on earth?

Anybody who is honest and says things the way they are.

Maria, as much as it saddens me, I have run out of questions to ask you. Thanks be to God and heartfelt thanks to you as well for having permitted me to pester you with so much during these two days. But before I leave, could you tell me just one more incident where the souls helped someone and did something unusual to put emphasis on their great need?

You haven't pestered me; it was a joy to hear so many thoughtful questions. I too thank God and thank you for them. And as for your request, let me think for a minute. Holy Spirit please enlighten me now. Oh, here we are.

Just recently two sisters came to me from a nearby town to ask what their deceased father needed to go to Heaven. As always, I was glad to take his name along with the years of his birth and death. Then one of the sisters said in a stern voice that if the answer I received for them had anything at all to do with money, they would not participate. I told them that this would be their business and not mine, but if they wanted an answer I would of course be happy to get one for them. Then they went home.

It was two or so weeks later that I received an answer for this name from another soul. I let the sisters know so that they would come here to pick it up. They came and I handed them the answer that was that their father needed seven Holy Masses celebrated to be delivered into Heaven. Then with it in hand they left without saying anything other than a courteous thank you. Some time went by and another woman from their town came to me on entirely different business, but it happened that she was a neighbor of those same two sisters. After we had discussed whatever it was that she needed, I simply asked her how those two sisters were doing. To this she answered, "Oh, they are doing very well now! I was with them when they discussed your letter in which you asked them why they were permitting their good father to suffer longer. They were shocked by what they read. How on earth was it possible that you knew that they had yet to arrange for their fathers' Masses?! And they then dashed over to their church to do so."

To this I said nothing, and the woman went on her way. D'you see, Nicky, I never wrote them a letter.

My God! How wonderful!

Yes! The souls are wonderful, and I beg people to start praying for them. I promise you it will not take long for the souls to jump in and help their friends in ways that will amaze them every time.

Is there anything in conclusion, Maria, which you would like to say to the world if you were given the chance to do so?

Only, as I have already mentioned earlier, the Poor Souls have told me that the Church is in the worst condition that it has ever been before in its history. But they have also told me that it will become much better and that we can look forward to peaceful times. Before that, however, a great storm will come, and it is that, about which Our Lady does not want us to worry, think or gossip.

God ALWAYS takes care of His children. This great storm will include the prophecies of La Salette which said that something that we have never seen before is coming upon us and those of Fatima, as it will also include the warning of Garabandal and the secrets held by the 'children' of Medugorje.

Finally I pass on to you that which Our Blessed Mother and the mother of Jesus advises us about this. Just pray and fast for peace on earth and bring God's immeasurable love and forgiveness to ALL of our brothers and sisters everywhere.

It seems to me that you must have a huge number of people asking you to pray for them, and if this is true what do you do for them all? You cannot pray a full Rosary or attend a Holy Mass for each one of them, so is there perhaps a particular prayer that you offer for them?

Yes, there is. The souls suggested that I pray the following for them: Glory, Praise, Gratitude and Adoration be to the Father, to the Son and to the Holy Spirit, as it was in the beginning, is now and forever shall be. Amen.

And, again Maria, what was it exactly that you yourself have learned throughout these many decades of truly extraordinary experiences?

I have learned to love God with ALL MY MIGHT!

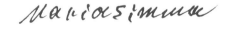

Maria Simma died on March 19, 2004

Optima philosophia meditatio mortis.
Quidquid agis prudenter agas et respice finem.

MARIA'S SUFFERINGS

The only person who was ever permitted into Maria's room during her great mystical sufferings was her dear friend and spiritual director from 1938 until † 1978, Father Alfons Matt. So it is only in his words that these can be described here, as they were in the earlier book [2] about Maria Simma in 1968:

"The suffering was relative to the sins that needed reparation."

"It was as though all her limbs were being torn apart. With great weight the soul pressed itself against her and over and over from all directions daggers were stabbed into her with great might. Another time it was as though dull iron was being pounded into her and when it met with resistance, it separated and continued into every part of her body."

"More and more souls asked for her help. The reparation for abortion and immorality consisted of terrible pains in the torso and an awful nausea."

"Then it happened as though she was lying for hours between large blocks of ice, the cold reaching the marrow of her bones. This was the reparation for apathy and religious coolness."

"Even when it was very difficult for Maria, she always accepted this freely. Often it was so severe she would not have survived it merely by natural means."

Fr. Alfons Matt

Flecken

Sonntag

Vorarlberg

AUSTRIA

(1968)

Stat Crux Dum Volvitur Orbis.

Pope John Paul II

EXHORTATIONS & WARNINGS

Dictated to Maria Simma
by the
Poor Souls

ABOUT LOVING GOD & LOVING NEIGHBOR!

Despite there being much talk and recommendation today in our Church about loving our neighbors and loving our brothers, it finds so little approval and application because one so rarely explains that true brotherly love can only grow out of love for God.

Whoever truly loves God also loves his brother out of love for God. Even if he occasionally has to reprimand sharply, it still comes out of love for God. One wishes to receive love but one seldom thinks of giving love, and for this the cornerstone must be laid in love for God. Loving others out of love for God; that brings the best fruits. Out of this too grows the strength to make big sacrifices, because in sacrificing true and blessed love shows itself. For this, a line to remember: Love without a Cross is empty; the Cross without Love is too heavy! But whoever wishes to teach love for God and love for neighbor must HIMSELF have a great love for God and for neighbor! Words soften, but examples touch the core.

Sorry to say, in our Church there are so many Priests, as is often complained about to you, who preach well on love for brother. How they emphasize that so nicely. Fine and good, if they were to place the cornerstone for it in the love for God and were themselves to go ahead and lead by good example! Where does love for God and love for neighbor remain when a Priest introduces communion with people standing and in the hands; even when so many wish to kneel when receiving Holy Communion, as it ought to be when in the presence of the Almighty God? And where does it remain when it even happens that some are passed over when they kneel to receive Holy Communion; and even when receiving their First Holy Communion, it is demanded of the children that they receive it standing and in the hand while their parents and grand-parents suffer greatly due to this?! Yes, where is all this love for God and love for neighbor? How much longer will this continue until these gentlemen realize how blinded they are, how badly they thereby fail when it comes to love for God and love for neighbor?

You yourself know by your own experiences that precisely due to receiving Holy Communion standing and in the hand much distress, discord - yes - and even quarrels within the family have been caused among the good Catholic people. Now truly think about it! Does this distress and disrespect come from God or come from Satan? Yes, receiving Holy Communion standing and in the hands is the work of Satan, and for this there is plenty of proof! Whoever fails to see this is touched by blindness.

Then comes the excuse that out of brotherly love one should go along with it. No, that which conflicts with love for God may not be done out of brotherly love! One may not go so far with brotherly love that it insults God. The Pope too is against communion in the hand and therefore requests the use of the paten when we receive Holy Communion! Where in this is obedience? Many Bishops accuse other Bishops of not following the Pope. But are those first Bishops obeying the Pope? Back then the American Bishops at first said, "We do not allow Communion in the hand because the Pope does not want it." Had the other Bishops behaved the same then there would be different fruits growing out of our Church! Why does one wish to remove the splinter from the other's eye, but doesn't even feel the log in one's own?!

Then one often hears the reasoning, "Yes, but the inner posture is important!" Precisely for this reason, away with Communion in the hand while standing because it does not lead to good inner posture. So often one hears, "As long as there was no Communion in the hand, I never had any doubts about Jesus' presence in the Holy Host; but now the doubts are surfacing everywhere!" And when theologians say, "I left the seminary because my conscience did not allow my distributing Holy Communion into the hands." While others say, "I no longer go to Holy Communion because I am handled so harshly when not wishing to receive into the hands!" Does all this lead to good inner posture? Yes, important is the inner posture and so out with Communion in the hand! You yourself know how often one hears the complaint, "I no longer feel warm in our Church!" One ought to seek the cause for this deeply and find out where things are amiss. You are entirely right when you say, "As long as Communion in the hand while standing is not forbidden in our Church, the depth of faith in our Church will not improve!" How many good Communions are no longer being received because Communion in the hand while standing is expected or lay people are distributing Communion without there being a valid reason for it! For every Communion that is, for these reasons, not being received someone will be held responsible! Only in cases of great need may the Bishop allow this and only for things to go faster is not a great need and does not suffice for this to be allowed; and, therefore, it ought not to be permitted. The Bishops ought to consider matters far more seriously to determine when there is and is not a great need.

One ought to reinstate in the seminaries a strict order, nurturing a spirit of penance and for far more prayerful sacrifice. Then there would be far more applicants and far fewer resignations, and then it would no longer be necessary to enlist lay people to assist with Holy Communion. Yes, the inner posture is important. Satan is a sly fox. Don't you see that the objection, "The inner posture is important with Communion in the hand" is the cunning of the evil enemy? That through this the most horrid of sacrileges also occur in that consecrated hosts are stolen far more frequently and sold to so-called black masses for large amounts of money? Yes, think about it seriously; how deep one has fallen, how far has one gone with this modernization within the Church. God does not let himself be modernized and neither do the Ten Commandments allow themselves to be modernized, for they stand today as they did before! Out of the schools with sex education. That is the concern of the parents and not of the teachers! Yes, back to offering prayer and back to a spirit of penance! Only in this manner can the faith improve! As long as Communion in the hand while standing is not strictly forbidden in our Catholic Church, the people will not come to a deeper faith because the reverence in front of the Holy Eucharist suffers greatly due to this. When one removes from the people the reverence in front of the Holiest of Holies, then the love for God and the love for neighbor also suffer.

COWARDICE!

Due to cowardice many today carry the blame! Many see that they are going the wrong way, but here again the cunning of the devil steps in with, "But I cannot step out of line." A Bishop said, "I have had it up to here with communion in the hand!" So why is he so cowardly as not to forbid it in his diocese where he has the right and the duty to do so? Perhaps then others would do it too. Through this much good would again be done. Yes, you still must pray and sacrifice a lot for your Bishops and Priests that they acquire this courage; that too is an act of love for God and love for neighbor! Do not complain about the Bishops and Priests who have gotten off track. That does not make them better, but through prayer and sacrifice you can save them! And one may certainly warn, remind and ask them to do this or that better. Yes, one even has the duty to do so. But this too is allowed to be done only with love and goodness and not in a brutal manner. With love and goodness you would achieve quite a lot. We ask the Bishops and Priests warmly to pray a lot to the Holy Spirit. Then they will certainly again return to the right track. May God with His immense love grant them this gift!

Yes, if everyone cared continuously to nurture the love for God and love for neighbor, how beautiful life would be here on earth! Start with small things such as a kind greeting or a sympathetic look. Especially officials and bureaucrats could achieve much good if they were to answer more lovingly, compassionately and kindly. This costs no more time, only more love and goodness and perhaps some willpower. In this way one could accomplish much good and that would be worth the bit of willpower. With this oneself becomes happier and more at peace, for the joy one gives returns into one's own heart. The sensationalists in the world do not support the world, but rather the loving souls do who attract very little attention and thereby give more love and help through their prayers. Those who patiently and for their love for God suffer in the cellars and attic rooms solve far more religious and social problems than do the most learned at their green tables.

Do not judge your neighbor, but judge yourself. That is the beginning of world peace. Were the heart free of all suspicion, all dislike, all contempt and anger, free of bad criticism; there would no longer be room on earth for lack of peace, discord, animosity and injustice! Then there would also be no war. Were love and goodness reigning everywhere in thoughts, words and especially in acts, only then would life be beautiful everywhere on earth. Were someone to begin with it today, it would bring him many blessings! Give love and goodness wherever you can, but all of it out of love for God! Only in this way can you give true and blessed love. Were everyone to start with it today, it would most quickly and safely improve and renew the world. Love, prayer and sacrifice save the world. Help with this as much as you can to save the world. And for this, pray often the following prayer that is so full of blessings:

*   *   *

LORD, FORGIVE ALL WHO HAVE EVER DONE ME INJUSTICE, WHO HAVE EVER SLANDERED ME, SO THAT I TOO CAN RECEIVE FORGIVENESS FROM YOU FOR ALL MY SINS!

LORD, GRANT ME YOUR LOVE, SO I MAY LOVE MY NEIGHBOR WITH YOUR LOVE!

LORD, MAKE ME THE GIFT OF YOUR LOVE, SO THAT I MAY LOVE ALL OTHERS WITH YOUR LOVE!

GRANT ME THE STRENGTH TO CARRY ALL SUFFERING PATIENTLY OUT OF LOVE FOR YOU, BECAUSE I KNOW I CAN SAVE MANY SOULS BY DOING SO; AND THEN I ALSO FEEL THE SUFFERING LESS SEVERELY!

FOR THIS GRACE I PRAY TO YOU, OH JESUS, AND THE SAME FOR ALL SOULS SUFFERING PHYSICALLY OR MENTALLY, SO THAT IN THIS WAY MORE SOULS CAN BE SAVED. ESPECIALLY FOR THE SOULS OF PRIESTS, SO THAT SOON THERE WILL BE ONE SHEPHERD AND ONE FLOCK.

* * *

Pray that the Priests again give more honor to the Mother of God:

* * *

O MARY, YOU MOTHER OF THE HEAVENS AND OF THE EARTH, YOU MOTHER OF PRIESTS, SEND THE HOLY SPIRIT TO PRIESTS SO THAT THEY RECOGNIZE YOU AS OUR MOTHER, OUR COREDEMPTRIX, OUR STRONGEST HELPER IN THE PRIESTHOOD.

* * *

Mary must again be brought into daily life, and then with Mary you will again be able to lead misled men back to God. Through Mary to Jesus, that is the surest way to God! Then so many Priests will once again learn the humble kneeling before God, when receiving Holy Communion and at the Holy Mass. It is proper to kneel during the Confiteor, during Intercessory prayer, during the Sanctus and especially during the Consecration, then during the Agnus Dei and also during the Priest's blessing.

Yes, then many hearts will again be happy and feel warm in Church! Through prayer and sacrifice you will achieve what is necessary to save one's own soul, necessary to save the souls of Priests and also those of many others. Pray with trust to the Holy Spirit the entire Pentecostal Prayer:

*   *   *

COME, O SPIRIT OF HOLINESS FROM HEAVEN'S GLORY, SEND YOUR STREAM OF LIGHT; COME YOU FATHER OF THE POOR.

COME, LIGHT OF HEARTS, AND REST WITH THE SEVENFOLD GIFTS, CONSOLER IN LONELINESS, REFRESHMENT FULL OF LOVELINESS.

COME, O FRIEND OF SOULS, INTO TIREDNESS SEND REST, INTO THE HEAT BREATH COOLNESS, CONSOLE HIM WHO CRIES WITHOUT CONSOLATION.

O, YOU LIGHT OF BLISS, MAKE READY OUR HEARTS FOR YOU; PRESS INTO OUR SOULS.

WITHOUT YOUR LIVING PAIN, NOTHING IN MAN CAN WITHSTAND, NOTHING GOOD CAN BE IN HIM.

WASH CLEAN WHAT IS SOILED, HEAL WHAT IS WOUNDED, QUENCH WHAT STANDS DRIED OUT, SOFTEN WHAT IS HARD, MELT WHAT IS FROZEN, STEER WHAT GOES ASTRAY.

HOLY SPIRIT, WE BEG YOU, GIVE WITH MUCH GRACE TO ALL OF US THE POWER OF YOUR SEVEN GIFTS, GIVE MERITS IN THIS TIME AND PURE BLISS AFTER A FULFILLED JOURNEY. AMEN.

*   *   *

Another timely prayer to the Holy Spirit:

*   *   *

ENLIGHTEN US, O HOLY SPIRIT, AND GRANT US THE GRACE THAT, EVEN IN THE VERY LAST MOMENT, THE TERRIBLE JUDGMENT WHICH IS PLANNED FOR SINFUL HUMANITY MAY BE TURNED AWAY.

LORD, MAKE ME AN INSTRUMENT OF YOUR PEACE!

WHERE HATE IS SOWN, LET ME SOW LOVE;
WHERE THERE IS INJURY, LET ME SOW PARDON;
WHERE THERE IS CONFLICT, LET ME SOW HEALING;
WHERE THERE IS DOUBT, LET ME SOW FAITH;
WHERE THERE IS DARKNESS, LET ME BRING LIGHT;
WHERE THERE IS SADNESS, LET ME BRING JOY.

LORD, LET ME STRIVE NOT TO BE CONSOLED, AS TO CONSOLE;
NOT TO BE UNDERSTOOD, AS TO UNDERSTAND;
NOT TO BE LOVED, AS TO LOVE.

FOR IT IS IN GIVING THAT WE RECEIVE;
IT IS IN PARDONING THAT WE ARE PARDONED;
IT IS IN DYING THAT WE ARE BORN TO ETERNAL LIFE.

* * *

ADVICE ABOUT OUR GREAT HELPERS, THE MIGHTY ANGELS!

In these times it is very necessary to again honor the Guardian Angels more and to trustfully nurture contact with your Guardian Angel. Evil spirits have pushed their way into the Church. You alone will not be able to deal with these evil powers, and you need the Angels' protection now more than ever before! The more trustingly you call upon the Angels, the more power they have to protect you! And because in 70 to 80% of all accidents, evil is in the works, do call upon the Guardian Angels of the drivers before going anywhere, also the Guardian Angels of the passengers that they protect you from all mishaps, also the Guardian Angels of the other drivers whom you will encounter. Was this to be done, less than half as many accidents would occur. And sorry to say even some Priests today deny the existence of Angels. So many children in religion class hear nothing anymore about their Guardian Angels. Here their parents should show more care that the children pray daily to their Guardian Angels and that more should be said to them about their Angels' duties. Seek good books about the Angels. Only in eternity will you recognize how much gratitude you owe them for things you never thanked them for and how much more they could have helped you had you not blocked their way to speak to you. Before big events and days in court, pray to the Holy Spirit and to your Guardian Angel that they help you to handle things correctly!

Pray this way:

* * *

HOLY SPIRIT, GIVE ME THE STRENGTH TO ANSWER THINGS COURAGE-OUSLY WITH THE TRUTH WITHOUT WOUNDING LOVE!

HOLY SPIRIT, MY GUARDIAN ANGEL AND ST. MICHAEL THE ARCHANGEL, DRIVE AWAY THE EVIL POWERS AMONG US.

HOLY SPIRIT, YOU SPIRIT OF TRUTH, GIVE ALL THOSE PRESENT COURAGE AND STRENGTH FOR THE TRUTH, MAY LIES AND DECEPTIONS BE TURNED ASIDE BY THE POWER OF THE ANGELS. AMEN.

* * *

Yes, believe and trust far more in the Holy Angels!

ABOUT GOOD USE OF TIME!

Only once in eternity will you recognize what you did with your time during your life, with all the years, days and hours; and what you could have done with them. There too you will recognize what chances you missed during life to make everything good; and once there in eternity, it will be too late. What would people not do to start a new life if they knew what eternity was! And here are some more lines to remember:

Long is not eternal, but eternal is long.
This is a true yet serious thought.
Pick roses while they bloom for tomorrow is not today.
Let no hour slip by, for this time is fleeting.
We build many firm houses and are in them only as guests.
But for where we will be eternally, we build very little.

God gives you time so that you can progress with your souls. Man wanders through life but once, and not a second time as is taught by many today. This is wrong! God gives us only one time to live here on earth! It is Satan's trickery to think that you've been on earth before or that one comes to earth again in another body. These are falsehoods!

What great things could one make out of time? What treasures could one win or lose? Costly and short is time, it does not come again. Fulfillment of God's will must be the password for your entire lives! Why does man dive into time-bound things? Because he thinks so little about eternity. Seek in everything to fulfill God's will. Do not get disturbed if you make mistakes over and over. What is important is always to get up again and to start anew. To err is human, getting up again is blessed, and to stay in sin is satanic. Recognize in humility that you are sinful, but no one need despair if he falls over and over because Christ died on the Cross for us so that we can get up repeatedly. Most of our falls are due to weaknesses, superficialities, carelessness, but seldom malice. So do not get disturbed about your own faults, and much less, about those of others. Do not judge others! Those who do so again and again are those who should work on themselves the most. A good word can heal, a nasty word can kill; so never judge others. Let no day go by without a good word or a good deed! One should carry the other's burden. Only in this way is the law of Christ fulfilled. If only everyone was eager never to judge another -- to sow peace where conflict exists -- and only to pass on the good about another but never a mistake. Take care only to help the other in this manner, but never to injure him; then there would never again be a war. Was this the case, not half as many people would be in Purgatory and Hell would be empty. Do good for others as long as you have time for it. A time will come when you can do no more and will only reap what you have sown. Do not judge others but only yourself. That is the beginning of peace on earth. A good Christian has a firm decision in him only to fulfill God's will. He is kind and gentle to his brother. He always turns back to God in humility and simplicity. He gets used to tolerating the mistakes of others and his own. You must work yourself forward from mediocrity to holiness. Many wish to be good Christians; but to strain for holiness, that seems too much for them! And still God's Church needs truly holy and not merely somewhat holy men! The tide of ruin is stronger than the mediocre, so how should it be conquered by mediocrity?!

It is so important to be loyal in small matters, because it strengthens humility and leads to great things. In small things the great truly show themselves. The strict fulfillment of small duties takes no less power than do heroic acts. Small things add a lot more to the total sum of man's good than do the large ones. He who is loyal in small matters is also loyal in great matters. He who is disloyal in small matters is also disloyal in the great.

ABOUT GRACES TOWARD HOLINESS!

Treasure far more the graces to become holy! It was the goal of all of God's holy functions. This grace brings to you God's friendship and heightens it. It makes you similar to God. It gives love between same and same. Being a child of God makes you related to Him. It gives you a share of Christ's dignity as Son and makes you connected with God! It lends a participation in the Godly nature. As God's child you live God's holy and wonderful life. The grace to become holy is afterall God's living stream of life which floods from Him and through you to all others. You are part of God's nature, of his mystery-filled nature. God's eye through which you look is your faith! God's hand with which you reach is your hope. God's heart out of which you live is your love. In these three lie something of God's sacred sight, of God's providence, of God's bottomless love! And thus they are also Godly virtues! The grace of God, which brought such greatness to others, will also be granted to you, if only you do not lose trust in it. Think about it often and pray that you can always learn to understand better what immense treasure we carry in our souls with the graces to become holy.

ABOUT SPEAKING AT THE RIGHT TIME!

The expression exists: Speaking is silver, silence is gold. Yes, but speaking can also become gold! Today good Christians are silent too often. How much good can come about and how much evil be avoided with good words. It would not have gone so far with the decline in faith in our Church, if one had stepped in more strongly against this unending modernization in our Church! Yes, man's fear today is great. How heavily will it have to be answered to when one sees clearly that this or that leads to the abyss and one stays silent even though one could speak and knows what should be said, but stays silent in order not to be pushed back. What responsibility! Pray especially for the

Priests and Bishops who out of human fear cause so much damage in the Church. Many see the abyss but do not turn away in order not to be pushed aside. Sorry to say, so many Priests and Bishops walk the path to the abyss and pull so many others with them -- but not for much longer, for God will soon arrange powerfully for order if people do not turn back themselves beforehand.

ABOUT REVERENCE BEFORE GOD!

Have more reverence for God! Kneel humbly; do not stand proudly in front of God! To stand before God is something everyone can do; but to bend the knees humbly, that is infinitely bigger and not everyone can do it! Yes, it even happens that Priests forbid the good faithful to kneel. To this one need no longer obey. Because of this Catholics have already left the Church and many no longer go to Holy Mass or to Holy Communion! What a responsibility! Yes, the spirit of sacrifice must once again become alive. And the Priestly habit on the street also belongs to reverence for God. Already many Priests could have served where they were needed, but because they were not dressed as Priests, they could not be found. Go back to your Priestly and religious habits, and then people will again have more reverence for Priests.

ABOUT THE INFINITE VALUE OF A SINGLE MASS!

Why aren't the words "Sacrifice of the Mass" used today instead of "Eucharistic Celebration" or merely "Feast of the Mass"? Christ offered Himself on the Cross to the extreme, offered Himself bloody; and the Holy Sacrifice of the Mass is after all the renewal of Christ's offering on the Cross. It is the greatest sacrifice! The Sacrifice of the Holy Mass is treasured so little because it has lost its sacrificial character. Through the offering of the Mass, you bring God the worthiest sacrifice so that you can offer Him your entire needs and dealings! Through nothing does one become so happy as through giving all of oneself united with Christ's sacrifice on the Cross.

Through Christ the Cross has become a sign of strength of character, for love and loyalty -- love and loyalty until death. The Cross is the sign of inner strength and the carrying of the Cross are steps on the path to inner strength. There are Priests who only rarely offer Holy Mass on weekdays, and so many hunger for it so badly! Is this worthy of a Priest? Often the complaint of believers "I no longer know if this Holy Mass is still valid the way this or that man offers it" is legitimate; but, please, still go to Holy Mass and ask our Loving Lord with all trust that He correct all that is invalid at the Holy Mass. He will do it too. Only with Priests where you know for sure that they no longer complete the Consecration ought you to stop participating. If you no longer have the opportunity to go to a good Mass, then take yourself spiritually into a Holy Mass that is still offered legitimately. Have with you a good Missal and pray the Mass where you are with all the Priests who at that moment are offering Holy Mass. Always when you are unable to attend a Mass you should in this way participate spiritually! But it is wrong to say that the present form of Holy Mass is not valid. If you only knew how much one single Holy Mass was worth, then even during workdays the churches would be at least half full!

The good books explaining the Sacrifice of the Mass by Fr. Martin von Cochem have been made unavailable. They have been purged! This is persecution of the Holy Mass from within the Church! But today again a good book is available, and it is Celebrate Mass With The Heart by the Franciscan Priest, Fr. Slavko Barbarić, OFM. [34] And why do so few attend weekday Holy Mass? Because people are no longer conscious of its infinite value. Too little is explained, both in schools and in sermons. A person will make great sacrifices for earthly things that soon disappear; but eternal values are cherished far too little because one knows so little about them! Yes, even some Religious Orders have stepped away from weekday Mass! Many religious go on vacation without attending weekday Mass even though they have the opportunity. Christ offers Himself for us at every Mass but so few are present to whom He can give these graces! A huge treasure is offered to you at Holy Mass: Jesus' Wounds, His Life and His Death, His Precious Blood! Treasures may not lie dormant; you must reach out for them and work with them! You must take the treasure of the Precious Blood and continuously bring it to the Father through Holy Mass as reparation for your sins, as the cost of the conversion and salvation of souls and as a request for rich graces for the needs of the Church and of all men. Yes, if you knew the worth of one single Mass, you would offer everything to receive this grace. Every new step in the life of grace is a miracle of Godly love and signifies a transformation for your soul!

At every Consecration your past life is lifted to a higher level of graces and then you live these higher graces. Take your sufferings and your prayers, your worries and your work; take everything into the sacrifice of the Holy Mass. At your death all the Holy Masses that you attended in sincerity during your lives will be your greatest intercessors. Even with the strictness of God's justice and even if your sins are ever so numerous and heavy as a mountain, next to God's justice stands His Infinite Mercy in the Sacrifice of Holy Mass. The many who think they have no time to go to Holy Mass during the week should try it and see if they cannot get along with their work as though they had never been to Holy Mass! As long as no duty is neglected, for duty comes first

That which the Gospel does not promise, you may not promise either; and that is a life without a Cross! The Gospel without the Cross belongs to Heaven, suffering without the Gospel belongs to Hell, and the Gospel with suffering belongs here on earth. With the Cross of suffering, we help the Lord save souls. Were you to know the value of one single mass, you would give everything to save just one soul. For your soul the Son of God became man and died on the Cross, and for it, he founded the Church. If you were able to see the beauty of a soul covered with graces, you too would be willing to die for a single soul. St. Francis of Assisi said, "Take everything from me, O Lord; just let me save souls." St. Gemma Galgani said, "I asked Jesus to give me Crosses so that I can through suffering win souls for him!" Study the lives of the Saints. From their teachings you can gain wisdom to see the value of a single soul. Yes, the Saints belong in the lives of all people, in the houses of God's people. They have disappeared from so many churches! The Saints are great models, they were people like you; they were your pathfinders and for this reason they belong inside all of God's houses and not outside of them. If you walk in their steps you can also achieve what they did. But before all else, honor the Blessed Mother again in your lives. Today she is pushed away by so many Priests and even her virginity is often questioned. A Priest who turns away the Virgin Mary is no longer Catholic! And for this reason so many have left the Priesthood. We greet Mary in the Litany, "You, Mother most worthy of Love!" Yes, Mother, not sister! "See here your Mother", is what Jesus said! Through Mary to Jesus, that is the surest way to God. It is a great bequest that Jesus gave us! This applies to every person! This should bring joy and consolation to everyone in all of life's situations. The word "Mother" refreshes every broken courage. It is a word of security. Yes, she is the Mother most worthy of Love! Think now about the kindness she showed in her relationship with God and with all men. She was also loving and worthy of love during her daily works. Always polite. Politeness is a virtue and shows love for neighbor in its loveliest and finest form. But she was also the humblest of God's servants. Yes, all leaders of the Church, all Priests and Bishops must again become humble to win back the trust of the faithful. Humble recognition of guilt receives forgiveness, grace and mercy. Love and practice humility. The humbler a man is before God, the more God can make of him. God placed His Graces in loving motherly hands. Mary, Mother of all Graces! What a loving, consoling thought. All graces that flow to us after Christ's death for salvation went through the hands of Mary! Her loving gentle hands touched all graces that were ever received by men. With what reverence you must handle and stay loyal to these graces. Mary is mediatrix of all graces! What responsibility this fact carries! How much it should sadden us if ever a grace, which has come through her hands, is not received by us and must go back into Mary's hands. This is often the case today. With special reverence you ought to think about every grace toward holiness that came to you with your Holy Baptism and all others in this new supernatural life which also came to you through Mary. Through this Mary became our real Mother! She bore us for God as God's children, which we are. From this convincing position, Mary deserves, after God, our greatest honor, our deepest love and our highest trust! She is for us the praying power who always listens to us and never turns anyone away.

ABOUT ADORATION OF THE HEART OF JESUS!

Jesus says, "Learn from me, I am humble and gentle of heart!" Yes, adoration of the Heart of Jesus has also gone way down in the Catholic Church! Today the Church ignores the Heart of Jesus Fridays, the source of so many graces, in many towns! God's Heart scorned by his creations! The Heart of Salvation forgotten by those it saved! The Heart of Jesus must be in the artery of the life of the Church. It is the living spring out of which never-ceasing truth and graces flow. It enlivens and strengthens you towards Eternal Life. Through this Heart our Church is everything that she is. We stand here as children of the Catholic Church in the immediate and living proximity of the Divine Heart. We live from Him and eke out a living through his good deeds. Sink into the Heart of Jesus, let yourself be refreshed by the Heart of Jesus and let us live through the Heart of Jesus. The Divine Heart is the Sacrificial Cup, the gift of sacrifice; in it is his Precious Blood! Heart and Blood reveal and make clear at the same time His Sacrificial Love and His Sacrificial Way of Being. And this He offers again and again in the Holy Mass. We honor the Heart of Jesus best when we acquire His Being. To love the Father over everything, to be entirely open to His Will! To love men to the extreme and to be good to them! MAY THE HEART OF JESUS LIVE IN PEOPLE AGAIN!! This is what we should always pray! It is a call of deepest love, a prayer of rare content! In Jesus' Heart lives the entire Holy Trinity, the Almighty Father, the beauty and wisdom of the Eternal Son, the surrendered Love and Kingdom of the Holy Spirit. In it lives the entire Love of the Savior! In it pulses the entire fullness of the shed Precious Blood. In it are hidden all the deep secrets and all the effectiveness of the Holy Eucharist and of all the other Sacraments. Out of it flow all the rich, large and small graces that are granted to any creature. Yes, this Heart with all its infinite, wonderful riches should live and reign in men's hearts, in yours and all other human hearts. A true devotee of the Blessed Mother and of the most Sacred Heart of Jesus overcomes all hardships. Practice to stay quiet when something unloving comes upon you, not to complain, but rather to be happy with it because you are suffering with the Heart of Jesus. THAT would be true devotion to the Heart of Jesus.

ABOUT MISSION WORK!

A person who is not ready to help the health of his neighbor's soul is not worthy of life! In some way every Catholic is called to this. It is a duty of your faith! Faith pushes through its inner strength and its last goal to spread the Glorification of God through the entire world, and it's the faithful duty of honor to tend to this spreading. It is a duty of love for God and for neighbor! So many souls could be saved if Catholics would participate in Mission work with heart and hand. A duty of obedience! Go and teach all races! A duty of gratitude for the great fortune of believing the true faith. Whoever is penetrated by this fortune feels eager with strength to help others to become so lucky. How grateful the souls in Heaven will be toward you for having helped bring them this grace through words, writings, prayers and sacrifice; and especially by example, through love and goodness in word and deed! And all this out of pure gratitude to God! Patient suffering for God saves many souls.

ABOUT EUCHARISTIC LOVE!

Care more for Eucharistic Love that today, through the modernization of the Church, suffers so greatly. Repay the Eucharistic Lord's Love with Eucharistic returned Love! For this, we pray:

199

*   *   *

YOUR EUCHARISTIC LOVE, O JESUS, I WISH TO REPAY AS MUCH AS I CAN! FOR THIS REASON I WISH, WHEN POSSIBLE, TO BE PRESENT THOUGHTFULLY AT HOLY MASS EVERY DAY AND AS OFTEN AS I CAN TO TAKE YOU INTO MY HEART AND AS LONG AS DUTY ALLOWS TO VISIT YOU! OFTEN I WISH TO REST WITH YOU IN THOUGHT, TO GREET YOU IN ALL TABERNACLES OF THE WORLD, ESPECIALLY WHERE YOU ARE MOST NEGLECTED! SPIRITUALLY I WISH TO VISIT YOU IN EVERY CHURCH IN THAT YOU GAVE ME GRACES THROUGH YOUR EUCHARISTIC LOVE! ALSO WHERE CRIMES OCCUR AGAINST YOUR ALTARS OR YOUR MOST HOLY SACRAMENT! ALSO WHERE YOU ONCE LIKED TO REST, BUT WHERE YOU WERE PUSHED AWAY OFTEN BY A PRIEST WHO DID NOT PERMIT THIS. ALSO IN POOREST LITTLE MISSION CHAPELS AND HUTS, DO I WISH TO VISIT YOU WHERE PERHAPS NOT EVEN THE SMALLEST LIGHT STILL FLICKERS. I ALSO ALWAYS WISH TO ASK THE HOLY ANGELS THAT THEY INCLUDE IN THEIR DEVOTION ALL THE TINIEST CRUMBS THAT FALL FROM YOUR EUCHARISTIC TABLE OR WHICH FIND THEMSELVES IN THE CORPORAL OR THE TABERNACLE. AMEN.

Turn this or similar prayers into real deeds; and thereby you will receive very many graces.

YOUR TASK!

Think about it! God gave you, for your entire lifetime, a particular task! He expects this task from you and only from you! Only you can achieve this. No one else can replace you! If this task is not truly completed, then it stays undone into eternity. You are responsible for all advice you give to all who come to you for help. Therefore, pray a lot to the Holy Spirit that you advise them all well and bring them nearer to God! Let love and goodness prevail with all. Ask God's blessings for everyone who enters and leaves through your doors. This is your task. Let nothing discourage you. With God's help you will overcome all difficulties, for saving souls needs sacrifices. But every person also has a task given to him by God! Namely that he works on his soul and on his abilities as much as he can! That these always multiply and improve in order to honor God more. That he improves his soul and those of others, and that he always helps his neighbor toward eternal bliss. In every gift that God gives him, there lies a task, a demand, and a responsibility. Thank God for this, your task and see to it that you always support it. You do not know how much longer you have to accomplish it. May everyone fulfill his task with strength. God's love touches you with every good thought and wish that travels through your soul, in every joyful decision in your will to do good, in every pure joy which refreshes you, in every quiet push to love which touches your heart, in every suffering that comes over you, in every good word you hear spoken, in every good example that draws you to imitate, in every praise that comes to you deserved; also in every scolding, in every humiliation which returns to you, in every test of patience which reaches you, in every lack of love which you must carry. Therefore you should never get excited because in everything God's love touches you! All this you should see as gentle, loving graces that God in His great Love sends you, which you must notice and use, or for which you, at least, should be grateful. Everything serves you for the best, if you truly love God!

You should write down and spread these instructions and teachings. Many will glean much good from them and be grateful to God forever! And were you only to multiply for one soul the graces for holiness, then your work will have been worthwhile. Therefore work as long as you can still work."

* * * * * * * * * * *

I received these exhortations from the Poor Souls by dictation. I believe they are very important and to be taken seriously. May the good Lord grant His Blessing that they serve everyone who reads and takes them to heart and may they lead them toward eternal bliss.

Maria Simma

"... will rise to a disciplinary curative time of punishment."

FR. BISCHOF'S TESTIMONY

Maria Simma, born here in Sonntag, spent most of her eighty-seven years in our Parish. Her modest home is very close to the church. To live near to the church is very important to her and this becomes evident in her attending Mass every day. She treasures the Holy Mass above all else. Her religious life is defined by prayer, sacrifice, reparation and through her courageous testimony for maintaining and spreading of the true Catholic faith in unity with the Pope. She has a great devotion to the Blessed Virgin Mary and often makes pilgrimages to Marian Shrines. Her lifestyle is simple and humble.

People with a true Christian faith and a deep piety can be the best examples for others who then, with their help, can be kept on the right path. In this manner Maria was always and is still today in her advanced years sought out by many for advice, orientation in religious life and assistance in all kinds of situations. Despite her living in tiny Sonntag in small Vorarlberg and without attracting attention upon herself, she is known well beyond Europe. From the farthest parts of the globe people have come to visit her. So uncountable are the letters she receives containing an enormous variety of intentions and problems that her ability to answer them all promptly has been taxed far beyond her capabilities. In the truest sense of the word Maria Simma also practices a telephone apostolate of spiritual direction. There too she spends much time attending to the many seeking her advice at all hours. She speaks and guides them with the fundamentals of God and of prayer, and therein always helping and consoling those who call. God distributes His grace wherever and however He wishes.

Fr. Fridolin Bischof
Parish Priest of Sonntag
Vorarlberg, Austria
since 1976

"... will rise to a disciplinary curative time of punishment."

THE AUTHOR'S TESTIMONY

During the year 1990 the author prayed the St. Bridget Prayers that are to be recited for one year. In September of that year he first heard about Maria Simma and her astonishing apostolate. On December 30, 1990, the 'Information Operator' in Vienna, Austria gave him Maria's telephone number. On December 31, 1990, he called Maria for the first time and in two draining minutes told her of his recent history, to which she responded, "Kommen Sie sofort!" (Come immediately!) On January 1, 1991, he arrived in front of her church at precisely 3:00 p.m. after one of the most frustrating and exhausting drives of his life.

Although the distance entailed no more than 200 miles with at least half of this being on German and Austrian Highways, he needed the assistance of four Automobile Club Emergency Vehicles, fought two severe blizzards and lost a chain that had disintegrated with a resounding bang. Half way around the world during the very same hours his wife, while driving a very familiar stretch of road, came upon some black ice, lost control and went tumbling into a ditch while in the process demolishing her vintage Volvo sedan. She escaped without as much as a scratch.

Back in Sonntag the author entered the church just as Adoration of the Blessed Sacrament began. Having a good idea already what Maria looked like from photographs in the older book about her and believing she would be there, he slipped in and looked at each of the fifteen or so women present. She was not one of them on that day. The women, while being led by the Priest, prayed the Rosary and sang enthusiastically in between the prayers. The Priest knelt facing the monstrance with his back toward his parishioners. After the first decade he spoke and his very first words were, "Knock and it will be opened." The author smiled, left the church and pushed his way up Maria's steep drive on foot, fighting as he went the second serious blizzard of this most memorable day. So it was a bit after 3:00 p.m. that he rang Maria's doorbell and she called him up to see her for the first of what proved to be many visits. After hearing his story in a much more than purely outlined form, she took the author to her front door and pointed toward another village about four miles southwest and across the valley from Sonntag. Over there next to the church, she explained, he would be able to find the only man she knew who could help him. He drove away with much newly found hope in his heart and quickly found his way to him.

It was four months later that he returned to Maria as translator and driver for a friend whose associates had already made a short audio cassette for the French speaking world and who therefore initially thought it was her assignment to write a more in-depth book about Maria. This was why the author arrived with a recorder in hand to start, although at first unwittingly, upon the lengthy and obstacle-strewn path toward his finally putting this book together.

The day after that initial interview with Maria and just before leaving the Grosseswalser Valley, her friend across the valley gave the author and his companion a twelve-inch statue of the Madonna of Fatima. This was puzzling them because neither they nor anybody at their destination needed more Marian images than they already had. During the long drive that followed the author and his friend who, of course, was also very interested and active for the Poor Souls decided to pray a Rosary for them and occasionally discussed the possibility of writing this book. It was during this Rosary that two interesting things happened.

Driving along, he asked out loud, "What should we do with this Madonna lying behind me on the back seat?" Within a few seconds he heard, "Give it to the first woman standing on the right side of the road." It was not his passenger who had spoken because she had, with a friendly shrug, quickly also expressed her own ignorance, yet it had still been a soft clear voice to his right. It was not internal and was not the result of a normal process of thought inside his mind. It was a quick and clear answer. As he heard this he was already driving a long, gentle, right curve with small trees blocking the view beyond, say, fifty or sixty yards. Five to ten seconds after hearing this answer; there she was, an old peasant woman standing on the right shoulder of the road. Saying nothing at first to his passenger, he slowed down a little and stared at the woman thinking the somewhat curious thought of whether she was alive or a Poor Soul. Hardly logical if it was she who had the need for their Madonna! Only then did he mention to his friend what he had heard, and she called out, "Turn around! Turn around!" Having quickly done so, they drove up to the old woman and rolled down the window. She was eighty or more and had only two teeth in her wrinkled mouth. She spoke a dialect too strong for either of them to understand, but reached for and embraced the Madonna while starting to cry and smile simultaneously. She held it tight in her arms as a small child would hold a large doll. As they waved good-by, she bubbled, "Thanks to God, thanks to God, thanks to God." He again turned the car around and through the rearview mirror saw her hobble toward her house still clutching the Madonna in the same way.

They continued their drive and their fifteen decades of the Rosary for the Souls in Purgatory. A short while later they again discussed the possibility of a book based on the long interview with Maria. He then asked out loud, "What should the title be, especially so that people today will really want to reach for it? I do not want it to sound like, God forgive me, just another religious book." His passenger said nothing at first but suddenly jumped and called out, "I've got it. I've got it!" -- "You've got what?!" -- "The title, the title! You just asked for it, and here it is." -- "So what is it? Tell me!" -- "Get us out of here!!" -- "Why? What's wrong?!" he asked, stepping on the throttle while quickly checking in all directions. "No, no! That's the title for the book, silly!"

It certainly was!

It too had come to her from the outside and for this reason the author felt obliged to put quotes around these so deeply appropriate words.

Only after much thought, many discussions and understandable hesitations, not the least of which was that he had never written anything of any consequence before, he went on to ask God for confirmation whether it was really he who was meant to write a book about Maria Simma.

And how, might the reader be asking him or herself, does the author claim to have gone about doing that?! He went about it in three ways, always remaining as careful and thorough as at all possible. By this point, as should already be clear, no matter where he went he was always active among praying people. So first he himself prayed about it a great deal. Furthermore he sought out among those surrounding him a half dozen or so truly loving, wise and observant people who knew both him and his story well and who had a far more experienced and thus matured prayer life than his. Gently but firmly all responses and signs he was given in these ways over several months seemed to point consistently toward the affirmative.

Although exceedingly rare and needing experienced and well discerned handling, there is among praying people a truly rare and, for the most part, carefully hidden group of individuals who, like Maria Simma, are gifted in extraordinary ways. Among these are what is referred to as inner-locutionaries, who are permitted to hear loving, gentle and always protective guidance from above. Then finally when it happened that he also received two strong nudges in the same direction from entirely separate inner-locutionaries, in these cases to the Virgin Mary, he set about in trust doing the clearest and most thorough job he possibly could.

Maria gave him the book written with her in 1968 by Fr. Alfons Matt, three German audio-tapes of some of her talks and the Poor Souls' Exhortations. Then between the summer of 1991 and the spring of 1996, he returned to visit Maria some thirty or more times. Nearly each time he had more questions or sought clarification on already discussed matters.

It is with Maria's permission that he remained with a conversational format, and therefore, what you have now read is a composition of the long initial interview made in the spring of 1991, their many meetings as well as those other sources. Please be trusting and understanding toward their mutual decision to publish it in this format for no other seemed to fit the situation quite as well. For this they both offer you their heart-felt thanks.

It was already by late November 1993, that only small details in this book were left to be polished out. To take particular care that everything contained in it was the truth; the author did three things. First he asked reputable and praying theologians to comb through it as critically as they could. None to date have expressed any objections. Then he took the book to one of the already mentioned inner-locutionaries who is also an exorcist who physically feels anything deceptive, false or evil when he prays over it. Having done so over "Get Us Out Of Here!!", he expressed that everything in it was clean and true. And finally to be extra certain of again the same, Maria Simma was permitted to ask a soul in Purgatory if the souls there were in agreement with everything contained herein. The soul's answer was, "We object to nothing." Then besides this, and entirely un-solicited by either the author or Maria Simma, the soul continued with, "All the attacks against Nicky and his family over these years happened because of his book." In December 1994 and January

1995 this two-tracked procedure of proofing was repeated. Both responses were again positive. When Maria again asked a visiting soul whether everything in this book was still all right and the truth. The soul's answer was, "Yes, everything in it is the truth."

What were these attacks as referred to by the souls in late 1993, the reader may ask; or how did they show themselves? Here he responds with only a basic outline of his many years of pain, chaos, and loss.

He witnessed inside his own house demonic activity so hateful, so angry, so surreal and so frightening that it managed to paralyze his legs, freeze his voice box, instantly block his memory of what he had heard, and in a few seconds turned his shirt sopping wet on what was already a cool and damp February evening. He has suffered to the very core of his soul an absence from his family whom he loves beyond all imaginable parameters and for whom he would instantly permit himself to be martyred if so requested by God. A divorce and its accompanying court judgment were creatively concocted against him under so-called "emergency conditions", and the latter entailed some 120% of the total that his entire family was ever worth. All this was done in his absence, and more specifically yet, while he was in Medjugorje. He lost his internationally recognized gallery of antique woven art. He lost his house, his show dogs and art inherited from his good and gentle father, whom he has recently helped to deliver into Heaven. He was deemed mentally ill, although four Psychiatrists testified in writing that there was not a single shred of evidence to uphold such a charge. He was unjustly imprisoned twice by the State, both times only to be exonerated entirely, because all charges leveled against him soon proved to be completely fictitious. He was also held briefly in an Institute for the Criminally Insane from where he was released quickly when its chief Doctor admitted openly to not knowing the reason why he had been brought there under force to begin with. This latter enterprise proved to be an attempt to kill him, while attempting to hide the action under a jacket of Officialdom. He has also had rocks thrown at him by a complete stranger. And still, throughout all the above, his unwavering and completely blind loyalty toward his family has remained solidly in tact.

The author has several reasons to share the above so publicly.

The first is to hopefully further awaken non-believers to the fundamental truths that Maria speaks while through his willingness to mention, albeit understandably in brief, his own story, his experiences reciprocally confirm what she says.

The second is to admit again clearly that it was nothing other than his own familial crisis that led him to want to meet Maria, correctly sensing that her friends, both the living and the deceased, would surely assist both him and his family. This they have done and to a degree that is very far beyond even his healthy and always hopeful imagination at the time.

The third is to ask all readers who may have major or minor distress in their immediate presence or at a distance to persevere, to never lose hope, to hand everything to Our Lady, knowing, whether they believe in God or not, everything will then again be as it should -- in peace.

The fourth is to express two very important and absolute truths; truths so solid that they can be called spiritual laws, which are as follows:

-- God responds to His children as much as they trust in Him, and it is relative to this trust that He can then work miracles through them.

-- To any spiritual attack of any sort and of any size, from the tiniest to the most immense, there will not only be a resolution, but in addition a reward, a Godgiven grace which without exception will be LARGER than the attack itself.

With these two truths you can guide your entire life.

The fifth is to kindly solicit from those so inclined a short prayer:

> May, through the intercession of our Holy Mother Mary,
> through the Archangels Saints Michael, Gabriel, and Raphael,
> the Good Lord humble the hearts of the proud,
> strengthen the hearts of the fearful,
> console the hearts of the suffering,
> free the hearts of the bound,
> enlighten the hearts of the deceived
> and heal the hearts of the hateful.
> Amen.

The Poor Souls in Purgatory are begging us to help them and will return the favors in ways that will astound us every time. Over the years, since first having met Maria and having himself started praying a lot for the souls, the author can personally testify to several other occasions when he experienced the souls and numerous times when they guided and assisted him in situations that are not mentioned in this text. This because here too he wanted the testimony to come from someone with many decades more experience than he has. Just one such encounter occurred during the first ten days of January 1994 when a few minutes before breakfast an older female voice said the following to him:

"You do not yet understand how big this book will be."

Having herein been advised by Maria Simma that the Poor Souls may only speak with Our Lady's permission and, at the same time, due to their enlightenment that they are only able to speak the truth as it is shown to them at that one moment, every one of us will therefore be able to watch the above statement unfold. Thereby we ourselves can test whether what Maria says about the souls as well as what the souls have told her and the author will turn out to be the truth.

And obviously, if this does turn out to be the case, it will then indirectly be Our Lady who is asking us and our families to take this book very seriously and to help the Poor, Holy or Chosen Souls in all the ways already discussed in these pages. Please also to do this by asking all your friends, as well as enemies, to read this book for the good of their families, and in this manner for the good of the entire world.

Were there, after all this, still some doubters to be found as to whether Heaven itself finds praying for our deceased brothers and sisters good, necessary and healing and these perhaps among self or otherwise proclaimed Biblical scholars, the author kindly points them to Matthew 16:18-19. And while they meditate on those words spoken by Jesus Himself, may this little book bring all the rest of us who have already come to trust in Maria Simma much closer to the reality of God and His Mother who love us beyond any and all measurement.

Only in being with Jesus through Mary with our hearts will a true peace and joy come to this troubled, broken, and thus so volatile world.

Nicky Eltz

The time to seek God is during life.
The time to find God is at death.

The time to own God is eternity.

St. Francis Sales

EPILOGUE

Maria Simma's visionary experiences are a valuable contribution to apparitionology and so the succeeding discussion will be of greater interest to ardent students of apparitional experiences than to readers who have, through far simpler ways, already discovered the love of God.

The technological revolution has nearly erased the impression of the Creator, the 'factory mark' from us; and our generation is on the verge of losing the sense of a Beyond, the mysticism. The alienation of this century from the traditional religious faith also stems partly from the confusion created by the scientific promotion of the evolutionary theories and the recent erroneous view that human beings are nothing but highly complex neural computing machines. Both of these views attempt to make the belief in life after death outmoded and irrelevant. There is, on the other hand, growing evidence in the field of parasciences to discard the mechanistic views of the mind and to suspend the skepticism in different forms of personal survival after the physical destruction of the body. Above all else, Marian apparitions, and particularly the recent scientifically investigated ones, offer compelling evidence to believe not only in different forms of discarnate survival but also in the validity of Holy Sacraments and the historical existence of Jesus Christ, the fruit of God's love for all human beings and in a special way for females. The Divine incarnation through Mary accelerated the spiritual evolution of human society, but it is the apparitions of Our Blessed Virgin throughout the centuries -- a manifestation of the Holy Spirit -- that have been maintaining the rhythm of this higher dimensional evolution that also embraces the Holy or Poor Souls awaiting beatific vision.

What happens after the dissolution of the physical body is a basic curiosity of every intelligent human being. Medical scientists also have stepped into the crucial issue of discarnate survival that earlier belonged only to the philosopher, theologian or para-psychologist. In medical practice this topic has special bearing in counseling the grieving families, helping suicidal patients and the current debate over euthanasia. Ideally, research into life after death should have beneficial effects for both the living and the deceased and Maria Simma's experiences serve both these purposes -- when she requests the living to pray for the Poor Souls while they offer us a proof for discarnate survival and assist us in uncountable ways.

"Get Us Out Of Here!!" is based on Maria Simma's apparitional experiences over several decades and these are unusual and quite unique in the history of apparitions. They are an encounter with the Poor Souls awaiting liberation from the trapped state of passive contemplation to a free active contemplation with the Creator. These discarnate personalities have a spiritual purpose for visiting Maria both for their own relief of suffering and for those in the terrestrial sphere. Nicky Eltz had to prepare this book aiming at a spiritual goal and at the same time satisfy the scientific criteria of a paranormal investigation. His aim is not at all to offer intellectual entertainment for the readers but rather a spiritual stimulus and this he has admirably succeeded to achieve.

Even though new techniques of monitoring and visualizing brain activity have great diagnostic value, they have also unfortunately reinforced the materialistic views of the mind. In taking into account some of the new information obtained through psychical research, the brain can be compared to a musical instrument with an invisible musician. Many scientists are now able to believe that we exist in a physical space as well as in a personal mental space or higher dimensional space, a concept that can also accommodate or help us appreciate spiritual space. Our minds may be existing in higher dimensional spaces yet the mind is still shrouded in mystery. The views of the mind that are dominated by scientific materialism are under challenge by experiences such as Maria's, those of the visionaries of Međugorje as well as other Marian visionaries and are to be discounted as sophistry.

The lack of a scientific model of a non-physical realm is a block for many scientists towards accepting the reality of a celestial visitation. As there are alternate universes, there are higher dimensional spaces. The "objects" in these subatomic spaces are invisible to us because the electrons have a higher rate of vibration to those in the physical world. They are invisible to us as the leaves of a working fan are invisible but we know the leaves exist.

Soul and spirit are terms used interchangeably but they represent two interrelated realities and one is the vehicle of the other. Maria Simma has noticed this difference. Human beings have a template of the physical body and one of these terms refers to it. Animals also have a template of their physical body, but no soul.

Maria's unusual experiences with the Poor Souls prove that the deceased can give guidance to the living. A person standing on the top of a hill has more visibility than the ones in the valley. In a similar way, discarnate personalities have advantages over the living and can predict the consequences of human actions but without infallibility. Neither discarnate personalities nor even angelic spirits can predict our future with infallibility. Many of the accomplished predictions reported have strong alternative para-psychological explanations. Any fulfilled prediction of a geophysical event made well in advance with precise temporal details of its occurrence is to be considered as a true case of precognition, and to this I would like to add that such information only the Creator possesses. The visible signs promised at Garabandal and Međugorje are to be considered as examples of such a prediction because a geophysical event could be involved there at a future date when the permanent sign is left. Moreover, the Marian visionaries of both these apparitional sites have the temporal details well in advance of when these confirmatory signs will come into reality. An obedient servant of the Almighty can be instrumental in giving such a message under the inspiration of the Holy Spirit yet such incidences are extremely rare. There are not many predictions given through the visionaries even though Marian apparitions have occurred right from the early days of Christianity. The Međugorje visionaries are entrusted with ten special messages or prophecies even though several thousand apparitions have occurred at Međugorje.

Mother Mary has reaffirmed the existence of negative spirits more than fifty times at Međugorje and Simma's experiences add to this heavenly confirmation. Negative entities succeed in making our lives less normal, misleading us to swim away from the shore and are therein destructive. Even though awareness of wild animals generates anxiety and discomfort in a person who travels in the forest, that knowledge will force him to take precautions from the attack of wild animals. A person who is unaware or denies the presence of wild animals in the forest may be relaxed for a while but can become prey to them during his journey through the forest. Such is the case regarding the knowledge of negative entities for us human beings struggling on this earthly planet. They influence us through the machineries of civilization. Behind the veil of this visible world there is a spiritual struggle involving all human beings and we can get drained out if we are not well equipped to cope with it.

The negative entities have been "hiding behind the psychiatric terms of delusion, hallucination and psycho-dynamic jargons" but have been more active than ever before. Spiritual influence means that human behavior also has got a para-psycho-dynamic. We should not be unduly concerned about the process of their influence on us but only accept the remedial measures prescribed by the Mother of Mercy. As there are 'tempters', there are also 'helpers' -- the angels. A belief in the existence of evil spirits without a parallel belief in good spirits and the Holy Spirit can be unhealthy. Virtuous spirits out-number evil ones for there are more angels than stars in the sky. Our Lady is urging us for a global liberation from the captivity of Satan and his soldiers through prayer and fasting.

Maria has reaffirmed the spiritual causation of illnesses. The telesomatic concept is gaining ground in scientific circles. According to this concept, a physical illness can be equivalent to a resisted telepathic message. This concept can also be extended to even some of the physical mishaps. In simple physical terms, the telesomatic concept is analogous to throwing a light object at a preoccupied person who does not listen to verbal messages in order to invite his attention more urgently. When the Poor Souls fail to communicate with the living, they occasionally use physical methods but without being spiritually destructive. They are doing so either for the benefit of the living or for themselves and it is this that can result in illnesses. Psychosomatic and telesomatic conditions are easily misdiagnosed and here I would also like to caution the reader not to ignore the natural causes of illnesses. It is understandable if a physician is heavy on the physical side of illnesses, but at the same time recognizing both of the above conditions. It is in this line of research that Dr. McAll's so courageous works are of great value. None of the medical concepts fully unravel the mystery of physical and psychological sufferings. The Lord's denial to the curious disciples of ancestral sins while healing the fellow born blind and his subsequent clarification, "He is blind because God's power might be seen at work in Him" alone is the final explanation. St. Paul also questioned the fruitfulness of tracing ancestral shortcomings in his instructive letter to Timothy. The telesomatic concept might some of the time include only the 'ancestral call' and not the after-effect of their terrestrial misdeeds. Dr. McAll's concept of the revengeful wandering souls explains some of the untold human sufferings. It is also a highly useful concept in this transitional period from the scientific denial of the existence of negative entities into a better and frightful understanding of the evil ways of the unknown spirit world while the HEALING THE FAMILY TREE MINISTRY has made many families more insightful in the paranormal sense.

Međugorje and Maria's views on depression ought to be given due importance by the medical profession. Depressive illness has become time-consuming and financial burden for the health systems. This illness is only a "common cold of the mind" and can be a state of the maturation process but is potentially dangerous when the patient has death wishes. Psychoanalysts have been trying to bring out past traumatic memories to find the cause of depression. Memories repeated get multiplied and become more emphatic and Our Lady has, afterall, warned us about the tyranny of memories. Biochemists are trying to find a chemical cause of this illness and have been successful in presenting a few useful theories; but they are only straws in the wind. In pure medical terms, depression is explained as a complex neurotransmitter disease. Biological psychiatrists may be able to prove a few cases originating solely due to biochemical changes but the alternate view is that such changes are responsible for only unmasking a long existed depression. The chemical defense mechanisms in the brain may be weakening for everyone as a part of aging process. Categorization of depressive illness and various other psychiatric disorders is still a moot point. Depressive illness may be the result of the sum of negative life experiences along with the unresolved anger and guilt, constantly confronting with the brain chemistry, thereby producing biological symptoms. In other words, depression starts from childhood and if not neutralized, progresses throughout life. It is also explained that depression is the aftermath of a cognitive revolution following a coup in the mind. Thus, it has a biological aspect as well as a cognitive aspect.

The Queen of Peace has isolated the "agent blue" (depression virus) along with the prophylactic measures when she warned that negative entities are the causative agents of depression. These depressed patients are only the wounded soldiers of a spiritual battle and deserve more respect and understanding. A depressed patient may be closer to God as he is in a state of suffering. In this vein, the Međugorje visionary Mirjana was asked by a pilgrim whether he had become ill because he had been a "bad Christian". Mirjana's response was that it was the opposite of what the pilgrim thought and that in actuality he had become ill because he was a good Christian. Depressive illness may be even a final spiritual defense mechanism against further spiritual attack on the community and the people who had a physical exhaustion chose or happened to be in the forefront of this battle for the rest of the community. My experience in psychiatry in two cultures has shown to me that many of the depressed patients are trapped apparently in a human network of manipulation. These sociological influences are intertwined with the psychological and the spiritual factors to cause depression. If these spiritual views are accepted, it becomes obvious that depression has a collective human responsibility and, in these days of world union through mere technology, a global blame as well. Depression is a psycho-bio-socio-spiritual condition and the biological aspects of this universal phenomenon should not be underestimated. Let us hope that the future research will shed more light into specific biochemical aspects of depressive illness. The Souls through Simma attribute merely sixty percent of depression to spiritual causes and so the biologically oriented medical scientists have enough room to accommodate the chemical theories.

The Poor Souls visiting Maria are chosen by the Mother of Mercy. Their visitations have a special purpose and are not to be confused with non-intentional appearances reported in paranormal literature. Spontaneous apparitions are still a matter of controversy as there are, apart from the survival hypothesis, several complex para-psychological explanations for this phenomenon. Collective apparitions cannot be explained away with the telepathic hypothesis of apparitions and are objective and paranormal. Non-intentional apparitions are taciturn and rarely speak. For some unknown reasons, their capacity for verbal communication is limited whereas the Poor Souls visiting Maria are capable of to-and-fro verbal communication. This, I believe, is a distinguishing feature between the spontaneous appearances and the purposeful apparitions of the Poor Souls. Simma's unique experiences will take off the general fear of celestial visitors. A belief in purposeful apparitions as those described in this book can be a stepping stone to break off the skepticism of religious apparitions and help unwilling people to accommodate the concept of Marian apparitions in their scientific thinking. Apparitional studies seemed forever to have been clouded with folklore, but this book has made them a respectable research topic and will help establish them on a normal scientific basis.

The following are the six theories of apparitions popular today in the scientific literature of parapsychology.

A) PHANTASMOGENIC CENTER Theory -- This Theory promotes the view that the 'appearer' generates an image of himself in the mind of the percipient who, in turn, sees a phantom. The discarnate personality is present at the apparitional site, but the seer does not perceive the soul of the dead individual.

B) ETHERIC BODY Theory -- This one claims that the astral body of the 'appearer' present at the physical site is seen, through the normal senses, as an apparition.

C) ESP-PK Theory -- Here the 'appearer' is present at the physical sight. The extra sensory perception powers of the seer together with psycho-kinetic powers of the 'appearer' result in the actual sighting of the apparition. Here there are both paranormal perception and perception through the normal sensory channels of the percipient at work. I consider this theory of great use in explaining true apparitional occurrence.

D) RETROCOGNITION Theory -- This theory suggests that certain apparitions prove only persistence and localization of something that carries small, superficial and probably obsessive traces of the experiences by a deceased human personality. In other words, an apparition is the result of the percipient's ESP of past events.

E) CLAIRVOYANCE Theory -- The protagonists of this theory believe that the apparition is solely created by the percipient, utilizing it's own clairvoyant impression of the 'appearer'.

F) TELEPATHY Theory -- According to this theory, the apparition occurs only in the mind of the percipient. Tyrrell preferred to consider that apparitional cases are analyzed as products of mid-level elements of the personality, but collective apparitions cannot be explained away with the telepathic hypothesis. Well authenticated cases of collective apparitions have been reported, and they also support the very existence of individual apparitional experiences. Moreover, many of the Marian apparitional experiences are collective ones.

In parapsychology, a "drop-in communicator" is one who is completely unknown to the medium and sitters at the time of the communication, and they have great theoretical importance in the post-mortem survival research. Simma's celestial visitors are apparently similar to the "drop-in communicators" of mediumship. It is the unfamiliarity of these visitors that make these apparitional experiences more authentic. Here the one who appears is different on each occasion and therefore totally unfamiliar to the percipient, yet unlike the mediums, Simma does not initiate the spiritualistic communication, but only remains receptive to them in a very casual and natural way without going into altered states of consciousness. Here I have to reaffirm that she is not acting as a medium. The experience and the agents can be fake in actively initiated mediumship communication. The Church cautions against humanly initiated spiritualistic communications, but Simma's experiences do not fall into this category at all. Simma sees the apparitional figure in the objective space without going into intensified state of attention, and therefore self-hypnosis is a very weak counter-argument. The unfamiliarity, the changing identity and the multiplicity of the apparitional figures on its own, defend her celestial experiences from an alternate explanation based on auto-hypnosis.

The searching behaviour of Maria's celestial visitors and the furnishing of requested information concerning others after a latent period is not observed in any form of pseudoor true hallucinatory experiences. It is true that pseudo-hallucinations are most frequently visual but they are characteristically comprised of complex scenes or fragments of action that are repetitive and stereotyped and that often reproduce the scenes of a real past event of emotional significance for the individual. Simma's experiences are totally different from the afore-mentioned statements concerning pseudo-hallucinations.

There is a popular misconception that parapsychology, the modern term for psychic studies, is a substitute for religion. Parapsychology is mind-centred and religion is God-centred. Spiritualism or spirits (the French term for the same) involves doctrines and practices based on the belief of survival after personal physical extinction and communication between the living and the deceased, usually through mediumship, but without the Creator. While both parapsychology and spiritualism are without God, the former is strongly opposed to the latter. It must be pointed out that mediums go into a trance state while they attempt to contact with the discarnate realm. Simma does not go into an altered state of consciousness and so her apparitional experiences should not be confused with the mediumistic trance state. It is also alleged that interest in the paranormal phenomenon without the mystical qualities can distract people from the true spiritual and mystical goals of religion. In these respects "Get Us Out of Here!!" is a valuable contribution.

During the last three decades a number of books and articles have been published about the survival of human personality after the dissolution of the physical body. Unfortunately many are the result of armchair research and run the risk of being fictional and could also lead to the creation of an intellectual Disneyland. The scientific promises of life after death have nearly without exception been ultra-optimistic without clear supporting evidence. So it is quite welcoming to have a contribution like that of Maria Simma who has no material motives but only a spiritual one that she is willing to share with the whole human society.

Parapsychology has the advantage of exposing the magical belief systems from true mysticism. On the other hand, it is also running the risk of opening once again the floodgates of superstitions. Proof oriented research in parapsychology is harmless and can be useful, but process oriented research in parasciences can lead to unveiling of many new and hitherto unknown destructive forces.

Any human assessment about the future is conditional. "In Portugal, the dogmas of the faith will always be preserved." These words of the Holy Virgin spoken to the Fatima visionaries in 1917 also mean that faith will be fragile or even lost in many parts of the world in the years to come. So it is logical to think that the above views of an impending crisis in faith, which might be initiated by pathological scientific developments, have a probable relevance to the Fatima revelation. At Međugorje, Our Lady has cautioned against dwelling on future mishaps and so I am prudently reserving elaboration of this topic. "Get Us Out of Here!!", written in the background of Marian apparitions, will be of immense value to the present and future generations who are going to be bombarded with pseudo-scientific literature about the life after death and the spirit world; and will persuade them to find refuge in the mantle of the Mother of the Savior. It will be one of the functions of Theistic Metapsychiatry, founded on Marian apparitions, to monitor the developments in para-sciences.

During analysis of the paranormal phenomenon, there are gaps and interrelated facts that are complimentary but the gaps get filled as the research progresses. If the gaps are given undue importance, facts can be overlooked and the conclusion can be delayed. There is only thin margin between scientific analysis and scientific dissection, which is particularly true of a delicate topic like the apparitional experience. In these days, before opening the door, everybody looks through the peep-hole and verifies the identity of the visitor. Likewise, Maria had monitored her unique personal experiences for herself in a strict manner, both objectively and subjectively, before she began to welcome the celestial visitors. One should not forget that the messages of the Poor Souls are more important than the process of their visitation.

These apparitional occurrences have taken place in the Austrian cultural ambiance. The views that culture interprets the apparition and the apparitions are adapted to the culture are probably valid in the early stages of an apparitional occurrence. The truth may also be that a favorable culture mediates a paranormal event to take place more easily. The visionary experiences of this senior citizen of Austria have, however, outgrown the cultural components and barriers. Simma has not kept a diary recording her experiences with the Holy Souls, as she herself never had the intention of presenting them to the world community. So, naturally, the answers to the questions of the author have been mixed with her own inner psychological wisdom and while being an honest instrument in conveying the messages of the Poor Souls, Maria, of course, can make mistakes like all the rest of us mortals. Many of the investigations in parapsychology conclude conditionally based on the reliability of the percipients and the informants. The percipient and the informant of the paranormal cum mystical occurrences described in "Get Us Out Of Here!!" are reliable and why should we hesitate to trust these celestial visitors along with Maria Simma? In January of 1995, when I met her in her mountainside home, she impressed me as being a gold mine of spiritual wisdom. Her encounters with the Holy Souls are, I believe, complementary to the Marian apparitions of recent times. Even though the biblical belief is that we will know for certain whether we and others are saved only after the final judgment, Our Lady herself has given information about the spiritual state of certain deceased people in her apparitions at Fatima as well as Međugorje. These support and justify Simma's information about the whereabouts of a certain number of discarnate souls in the spiritual realm.

The Poor Souls' confirmation through Maria Simma about the spiritual aspect involved in the conflicting life events of the author well before as well as during his task of preparing this book is itself illustrative of the completion of the "paranormal triangle". All of us must negotiate hurdles while struggling to reach our allotted positive goals. Yet the truer, cleaner, deeper and thus more healing these positive goals become, the more the "tempters" try to harass their architects. Because this book is so strongly counter-balancing the direction that this century's most influential thinkers have taken, the "tempters" tried a truly astonishing variety of ways to damage the author, his loved ones and his work. The author's dedication of "Get Us Out of Here!!" is, I believe, most appropriate for the "tempters" will go a very long way to keep today's respected scientists, most of whom still remain untouched by God's majestic love for them, away from the truth of a loving Creator. Still the Poor Souls and the "helpers", themselves also guided by the Queen of Peace, the Mother of Mercy and the Queen of Angels, were watching the race and prompting him from, as mentioned earlier, on top of their hills and the "tempters" continued causing painful schisms among the good ones who in truth were meant to assist him. Therefore the Author's Testimony is an extremely clear and thus valuable reflection of the para-psycho-dynamics of our everyday life.

Dr. J. Paul Pandarakalam
Department of Psychiatry
Billinge Hospital
Wigan, England

Author's note:

Dr. James Paul Pandarakalam is the Founder of Theistic Metapsychiatry, Interim President of the Theistic Metapsychiatrist's Peace Association and an Associate of the American Society of Scientific Exploration. He is the author of a parapsychological study of Međugorje, LIKE A HEAVENLY BREEZE.

A short reading list on the revelations of Fatima, Portugal:

FATIMA IN LUCIA'S OWN WORDS
Compiled by Fr. Kondor, SVD
by the Postulation Center,
Fatima, Portugal
(English distributor: Augustine
Publishing, Devon, England)

FATIMA, THE GREAT SIGN
by Francis Johnson
AMI Press
Washington, NJ 07882 (1980)

TWO HOURS WITH SISTER LUCIA
by Carlos Evaristo
St. Anne's Oratory
P-2496 Fatima Codex
PORTUGAL (1994)

THE WHOLE TRUTH OF FATIMA
by Frère Michel de la Sainte Trinité
Immaculate Heart Publications
P.O.Box 1028
Buffalo, NY 14205 (1984)

MEĐUGORJE TESTIMONIES & MESSAGES CONCERNING PURGATORY

In July 1982 and January 1983 Međugorje visionaries gave the following two testimonies about Purgatory:

"There are many souls in Purgatory. There are also people who have been consecrated to God - some Priests, some religious. Pray for their intentions, at least the Creed, seven Our Father-s, seven Hail Mary-s and seven Glory Be-s. There are a large number of souls who have been in Purgatory for a long time because no-one prays for them."

... and ...

"In Purgatory there are different levels; the lowest is close to Hell and the highest gradually draws near to Heaven. It is not on All Soul's Day but on Christmas that the greatest number of souls leaves Purgatory. There are in Purgatory souls who pray ardently to God, but for whom no relative or friend prays on earth. God makes them benefit from the prayers of other people. It happens that God permits them to manifest themselves in different ways close to their relatives on earth in order to remind them of the existence of Purgatory and to solicit their prayers to come close to God, who is just but good. The majority of people go to Purgatory; many go to Hell and a small number go directly to Heaven."

Then on November 6, 1986 Our Lady gave the following message to the world through Marija Pavlović-Lunetti:

"Dear Children,
Today I wish to call you to pray daily for the souls in Purgatory. For every soul prayer and grace are necessary to reach God and the love of God. By doing this, dear children, you obtain new intercessors who will help you in life to realize that all earthly things are not important for you; that only Heaven is that for which it is necessary to strive. Therefore, dear children, pray without ceasing that you may be able to help yourselves and the others to whom your prayers will bring joy. Thank you for having responded to my call."

And in January 1987 Mirjana (Dragićević) Soldo received an extraordinary and very long message that among other things also included:

"Take time to come to God at Church. Come into the house of your Father! Take time to come together and with the family request graces from God. Do not forget your deceased. Bring them joy with the Holy Mass."

The above testimonies and messages about Purgatory have been printed with the permission of the Međugorje Parish Office. Any other testimonies or 'messages' concerning Purgatory other than these, that may appear in other books, might or might not have been given privately through the visionaries. Despite those other testimonies' potential credibility, no 'messages' concerning Purgatory other than the above were meant for world-wide publication.

FURTHER READING IN SUPPORT OF MEĐUGORJE (PARTIAL LIST)

ALBRIGHT, Judith M.; OUR LADY OF MEDJUGORJE, Riehle Foundation, Milford, Ohio, USA, 1988.

ASHTON, Joan; MOTHER OF ALL NATIONS, Harper & Row, San Francisco, USA, 1989 and THE PEOPLE'S MADONNA, Harper Collins, Great Britain, 1991.

BARBARIC, Fr. Slavko, GIVE ME YOUR WOUNDED HEART and CELEBRATE MASS WITH YOUR HEART and PRAY WITH THE HEART and FASTING, Franciscan University Press, 1988 and THE WAY OF THE CROSS and FOLLOW ME WITH YOUR HEART and ADORE MY SON WITH YOUR HEART and IN THE SCHOOL OF LOVE, Faith Publishing Co., Milford, OH, USA and MOTHER, LEAD US TO PEACE!! and BE SIMILAR TO MY HEART and PEARLS OF THE WOUNDED HEART and FAST WITH THE HEART, Parish Office Medjugorje, 1989-2001.

BATY, Edward; MEDJUGORJE 1981--1995, United Kingdom, 1995. BEDARD, Robert, MEDJUGORJE: PROPHECY FOR OUR TIME?, Catho-

lic Renewal Centre Publication, Ottawa, Canada

BUBALO, Fr. Jakov; RUPCIC, Fr. Ljudevit; KRALJEVIC, Fr. Svetozar, KOSICKI, Georg W.; MIRAVALLE, Mark; KRMPOTIC, Vesna; NINE YEARS WITH OUR LADY AND HER CHURCH BETWEEN TWO MOUNTAINS, Medjugorje Publishing Group; Medjugorje, 1990.

BUBALO, Fr. Janko; A THOUSAND ENCOUNTERS WITH THE BLESSED VIRGIN MARY IN MEDJUGORJE, Friends of Medjugorje, Chicago, Illinois, USA, 1996.

CARROLL, Richard L.; A PRIEST LOOKS AT MEDJUGORJE, Vantage

Press, New York, 1989.

CARTER, Rev. Edward; THE SPIRITUALITY OF FATIMA AND MEDJUGORJE, Faith Publishing Co., POB 237, Milford, OH, USA (1994)

CAVAR, Stipe, THE FIRST MONTHS OF THE APPARITIONS IN MEDJUGORJE, Medjugorje, 2000.

CONNELL, Janice T.; QUEEN OF THE COSMOS, Paraclete Press, Orleans, 1990 and THE VISIONS OF THE CHILDREN, St. Martin's Press, 175 Fifth Ave., NYC, NY, USA, 1992.

CRAIG, Mary; SPARK FROM HEAVEN, Ave Maria Press, Notre Dame, IN, USA, 1988.

DeMERS, John, INVITED TO LIGHT, A SEARCH FOR THE GOOD NEWS IN MEDJUGORJE, Trinakria Press, 1990.

DONOFRIO, Beverly, LOOKING FOR MARY or THE BLESSED MOTHER AND ME, Penguin Compass, NYC, NY, 2000.

DUGANDZIC, Marija, MEDJUGORJE IN THE CHURCH, Information Center MIR Medjugorje, 2002.

GIRARD, Fr. Guy; GIRARD, Fr. Armand; BUBALO, Fr. Janko; MARY, QUEEN OF PEACE STAY WITH US, Editions Paulines, Maison St. Pascal, Canada, 1988.

GRANT, Robert; NEW WINE, NEW WINE SKINS, Grant Books, Worcestershire, England, 1988.

GRILLO, Girolamo; OUR LADY WEEPS, Ave Maria Press, Toronto, Canada, 1998.

HANCOCK, A.; BE A LIGHT: MIRACLES AT MEDJUGORJE, Donning Co., Norfolk, Virginia, USA, 1988.

HELD, Aloys Gerald; WHAT THEY SAY ABOUT MEDJUGORJE, Andrew B. Thul, 1992.

HON, Joan; A TRIP TO MEDJUGORJE, Hope Publishers, Ltd, Marina House, Singapore, 1989.

HUMMER, Franz; MEDJUGORJE, Franciscan University Press, Steubenville, OH, USA.

KLANAC, Darija; AT THE SOURCES OF MEDJUGORJE AND OBJECTIONS, Ziral, Mostar, Bosnia & Herzegovina, 1999.

KORDIC, Ivan; THE APPARITIONS OF MEDJUGORJE, A Critical Consideration, 1985.

KRALJEVIC, Fr. Svetozar; PILGRIMAGE -- REFLECTIONS OF A MED-JUGORJE PRIEST, Paraclete Press, Orleans, MA, USA, 1991 and A PIL-GRIM WITH OUR LADY, Cork Medugorje Centre, Cork, Ireland and THE APPARITIONS OF OUR LADY AT MEDJUGORJE, Information Center Mir, Medjugorje, 1999.

LAURENTIN, Fr. René & JOYEUX, Dr. Henri, SCIENTIFIC & MEDICAL STUDIES ON THE APPARITIONS AT MEDJUGORJE, Veritas Publica-tions, Dublin, Ireland, 1987.

LAURENTIN, Fr. René and LEJEUNE, Dr. René; MESSAGES AND TEACH-INGS OF MARY AT MEDJUGORJE, CHRONOLOGICAL CORPUS OF THE MESSAGES, Riehle Foundation, Milford, Ohio, USA, 1988.

LAURENTIN, Fr. René; LATEST NEWS OF MEDJUGORJE, JUNE 1987 and THE APPARITIONS AT MEDJUGORJE PROLONGED, A MERCI-FUL DELAY FOR A WORLD IN DANGER? and SEVEN YEARS OF AP-PARITIONS, LATEST NEWS FROM MEDJUGORJE, NR. 7 TIME FOR HARVEST? and THE CHURCH AND APPARITIONS, THEIR STATUS AND FUNCTION, CRITERIA AND RECEPTION and REPORT ON AP-PARITIONS and EIGHT YEARS, RECONCILIATION, ANALYSIS, THE FUTURE, NR. 8, and THE APPARITIONS OF THE BLESSED VIRGIN MARY TODAY, Veritas Publications, 7-8 Lower Abbey Street, Dublin, Ire-land, 1990 and MEDJUGORJE -- HOSTILITY ABOUNDS, GRACE SU-PERABOUNDS"- TESTAMENT, Ave Maria Press, Toronto, Canada, 1998, most published by Riehle Foundation, Milford, Ohio, USA.

Maillard, Sr. Emmanuel; MEDJUGORJE, THE WAR DAY BY DAY, Florida Center for Peace, POB 431306, Miami, FL, USA, 1993.

Maillard, Sr. Emmanuel & Nolan, Denis; MEDJUGORJE -- WHAT DOES THE CHURCH SAY?, Queenship, Santa Barbara, USA, 1998.

Maillard, Sr. Emmanuel; MEDJUGORJE, THE 90s, THE TRIUMPH OF THE HEART, Queenship Publishing, Santa Barbara, CA, USA, 1997.

MANUEL, David; MEDJUGORJE UNDER SIEGE, Paraclete Press, Or-leans, MA, USA, 1992.

MARIN, Jacov; QUEEN OF PEACE IN MEDJUGORJE, APPARITIONS, EVENTS, MESSAGES, Riehle Foundation, Milford, Ohio, USA, 1989.

McGINNITY, Fr. Gerard; PRAYING THE ROSARY WITH THE QUEEN OF PEACE, Ronan Press Ltd, Lurgan, Ireland, 1985.

MILICEVIC, Ivo; RADILOVIC, Julio; & ZELENIKA, Goran; MEDJU-GORJE OUR LADY AND THE CHILDREN, Mirago, Zagreb, Croatia, 1990.

MIRAVALLE, Mark; THE MESSAGE OF MEDJUGORJE, THE MARIAN MESSAGE TO THE MODERN WORLD, United Press of America Inc., Lanham, MD, USA, 1986 and HEART OF THE MESSAGE OF MEDJUGORJE, 1988, and MEDJUGORJE AND THE FAMILY, Franciscan University Press, Franciscan Way, Steubenville, OH, USA, 1993, and MARY, COREDEMP-TRIX, MEDIATRIX, ADVOCATE, Queenship Publishing, Santa Barbara, CA, USA, 1993.

NUIC, Fr. Viktor; HERZEGOVINIAN AFFAIR, K. Kresimir, Zagreb, Croatia, 1998.

O'CARROLL, Fr. Michael; MEDJUGORJE: FACTS, DOCUMENTS, THE-OLOGY and IS MEDJUGORJE APPROVED?, Veritas Publications, Dublin, Ireland, 1986 & 91.

O'CONNOR, John, MEDJUGORJE, THE STORY AND THE MESSAGE, Medugorje Herald, Galway, Ireland, 1989 and MEDJUGORJE, WHERE THE COCK CROWS AND THE BIRDS SING, Marian Promotions, Galway, Ireland, 1986.

OREC, Fr. Leonard; HORVATIC, Dubravko; RUPCIC, Fr. Ljudevit; BAR-BARIC, Fr. Slavko; LAURENTIN, Fr. René; KUSTIC, Fr. Zivko; FRANIC, Archbishop Frane; BUBALO, Fr. Jakov; KRALJEVIC, Fr. Svetozar; KOSICKI, Fr. Georg W.; MIRAVALLE, Mark; KRMPOTIC, Vesna, MEDJU-GORJE TODAY, Medjugorje Publishing Group, Sonnenhaus Verlag J. Rastic, Trochtelfingen, Germany

OSTOJIC, Fr. Zoran; QUEEN OF PEACE, CROATIAN -- ENGLISH PRAYER BOOK, Croatian Franciscan Publications, Chicago, ILL, USA.

PANDARAKALAM, Dr. James Paul; LIKE A HEAVENLY BREEZE, Panda-rak Paul Bros. Publications, Kerala, India, 1997.

PARSONS, Heather; A LIGHT BETWEEN THE HILLS and MARIA, AND THE MOTHER OF GOD, Robert Andrew Press, Ireland, 1994-97, and THE ANTIDOTE, Paraclete Press, Orleans, MA, USA, 1997.

PELLETIER, Joseph A.; THE QUEEN OF PEACE VISITS MEDJUGORJE, Assumption Publication, Worcester, MA, USA, 1985.

PERVAN, Fr. Tomislav; QUEEN OF PEACE, ECHO OF THE ETERNAL WORLD, Franciscan University Press, USA, 1990.

PLUNKETT, Dudley; QUEEN OF PROPHETS, THE SPIRITUAL MESSAGE OF MEDJUGORJE; Darton, Longman and Todd, London, England, 1990.

Riehle Foundation; MEDJUGORJE, A PLACE OF PRAYER and MEDJUGORJE AND MEDITATION, WITNESSES, TEACHINGS, Milford, Ohio, USA, 1992.

RODGERS, Peter; CROATIAN -- ENGLISH PRAYER BOOK, Medjugorje Centre, London and MEDJUGORJE HANDBOOK, A PILGRIM'S GUIDE, The Medjugorje Centre, London, England, 1986-88.

Rooney, Sr. Lucy & Faricy, Fr. Robert SJ, MARY QUEEN OF PEACE, Soc. of St. Paul, 2187 Victory Blvd., Staten Island, NY, USA, 1984 and MEDJUGORJE UNFOLDS IN PEACE AND WAR, Morehouse Publishing Co., POB 1321, Harrisburg, PA, USA, 1993 and MEDJUGORJE UP CLOSE, MARY SPEAKS TO THE WORLD and MEDJUGORJE JOURNAL Franciscan Herald Press, 1434 West 151th Street, Chicago, IL, USA 1986 & 88.

RUPCIC, Fr. Ljudevit; THE TRUTH ABOUT MEDJUGORJE, Ljubuski -- Humac, Yugoslavia, 1990.

SCHMITZER, Iana; OUR BLESSED MOTHER'S MESSAGES TO THE WORLD, Bernard Ellis, Bletchingley, Surrey, England, 1990.

SEGO, Kresimir; TIME OF GRACE, Ziral, Mostar, Bosnia & Herzegovina,"1996.

SEWARD, Desmond; THE DANCING SUN, Harper Collins Publishers, 77-85 Fulham Palace Road, Hammersmith, London, England, 1994.

SHAMON, Rev. Albert J. M.; OUR LADY TEACHES ABOUT PRAYER, Riehle Foundation, Milford, Ohio, USA, 1989.

ST. JAMES' Press, WORDS FROM HEAVEN, POB 380244, Birmingham, AL, USA, 1990.

STARKEY, Mary Kay, COME AND SEE ... MEDJUGORJE, A PRACTICAL GUIDE BOOK FOR PILGRIMS, Phoenix, Arizona, USA, 1990.

STELZER-DUGANDZIC, Marija; OUR LADY SPEAKS AS A MOTHER, Information Center MIR Medjugorje, Bosnia & Herzegovina, 2001.

SULLIVAN, Randall; GRACE PERIOD, NYC, NY, USA (in press).

TOYE, Charles R.; MEDJUGORJE AND THE TRIUMPH OF THE IM-MACULATE HEART and MIRACLE OF THE SUN AT MEDJUGORJE and PRAYER OF THE HEART FROM OUR LADY OF MEDJUGORJE and „IN THE END MY IMMACULATE HEART WILL TRIUMPH", A CRITICAL REVIEW, Send Your Spirit Publishing, Reading, MA, USA, 1987-94.

TOTTÜ, George; MEDJUGORJE, OUR LADY'S PARISH, Medjugorje In-formation Service, East Sussex, England, 1985 and MARY, MOTHER OF GOD, MOTHER OF MAN, FATIMA, MEDJUGORJE AND 1981, Private Publication, 1985, and MEDJUGORJE, SCHOOL OF PRAYER, Pika Print Ltd., Enfield, Middlesex, England, 1988, and LIVING THE GOSPEL WITH OUR LADY, Manchester Medugorje Centre, Manchester, England, 1991, and THE MEDJUGORJE MESSAGE ABOUT MARIAN HOLINESS OF LIFE, Longon, England, 1994 and THE MEDJUGORJE MESSAGE AND POPE JOHN PAUL II, Scanplus Ltd., London, England, 1995.

VINCENT, R.; „PLEASE COME BACK TO ME AND MY SON", Milford House, Milford, Co. Armagh, N. Ireland, 1992.

WALLACE, Mary Joan; MEDJUGORJE, ITS BACKGROUND AND MES-SAGES, Follow Me Communications, Huntington Beach, CA, USA, 1989.

WATTERS, John; A MESSAGE OF PEACE, MIR, TESTIMONY, Pika Print Ltd., Enfield, Middlesex, England, 1992.

WEIBLE, Wayne; LETTERS FROM MEDJUGORJE and MEDJUGORJE, THE MESSAGE and MEDJUGORJE, THE MISSION and MEDJUGORJE, THE FINAL HARVEST, Paraclete Press, Orleans, MA, USA, 1989-96.

YEUNG, Andrew Jerome; THE WAY TO MEDJUGORJE, YUGOSLAVIA, Ave Maria Centre for Peace, Toronto, Canada, 1998.

ZIMBAR-SCHWARTZ, S. L.; ENCOUNTERING MARY: FROM LA SALETTE TO MEDJUGORJE, Princeton University Press, Princeton NJ, USA, 1991.

FOR READING SLANDEROUS OF MEDJUGORJE

AUBOYNEAU, Cyrille; THE TRUTH ABOUT MEDJUGORJE -- THE KEY TO PEACE?, F.X. de Guibert, 27 Rue de L'Abbe Gregoire, F-75006 Paris, France, 1993.

BAX, Mart; MEDJUGORJE: RELIGION, POLITICS, AND VIOLENCE IN RURAL BOSNIA, VU Boekhandel/Uitgeverij, Amsterdam, Netherlands. 1995.

JONES, E.M.; MEDJUGORJE, THE UNTOLD STORY, Fidelity Magazine, Part 1 (Sept 1988) Part 2, October 1988; MEDJUGORJE GOES UP IN FLAMES, February 1991, Notre Dame, IN, USA.

SIVRIC, Fr. Ivo; THE HIDDEN FACE OF MEDJUGORJE, Psilog Inc., Saint Francois-du-lac, Quebec, Canada.

ZANIC, Msgr. Paul, Bishop of Mostar, THE TRUTH ABOUT MEDJUGOR-JE, Fidelity Magazine, May 1990 (Among a plethora of other writings by the Bishop.)

PERIC, (Collected by) Ratko Peric, Bishop of Mostar, MIRROR OF JUS-TICE, Mostar, Bosnia & Herzegovina, 2002.

IN RESPONSE TO SOME OF THE ABOVE

BARTULICA, MD, Nicholas; MEDJUGORJE: ARE THE SEERS TELLING THE TRUTH? A Psychiatrist's Viewpoint, Croatian Franciscan Press, Chicago, IL USA, 1991.

FRANIC, Msgr. Frane, Archbishop of Split; A RESPONSE TO BISHOP ZANIC'S DOCUMENT, Riehle Foundation, Milford, OH, USA, 1990.

HEBERT, Fr. Albert; MEDJUGORJE: AN AFFIRMATION AND DEFENSE, POB 309, Paulina, LA, USA, 1990.

NOLAN, Denis; MEDJUGORJE: A TIME FOR TRUTH, A TIME FOR ACTION, Queenship Publishing Co., POB 42028, Santa Barbara, CA , USA, 1993.

RUPCIC, Fr. Dr. Ljudevit; THE TRUTH ABOUT MEDJUGORJE, (A response to the pamphlet „Medjugorje" by Msgr. Pavao Zanic, Bishop of Mostar), Parish Office, Medjugorje, Croatian Protectorate of Herceg-Bosna, 1990.

RUPCIC, Fr. Dr. Ljudevit; THE GREAT FALSIFICATION: THE HIDDEN FACE OF MEDJUGORJE by FR. IVO SIVRIC, Parish Office, Medjugorje, Croatian Protectorate of Herceg-Bosna, 1991.

FURTHER READING ON PURGATORY

DIE SEHERIN AUS DEM RUHRGEBIET: Ursula Hibbeln
(THE VISIONARY FROM THE RUHR AREA: Ursula Hibbeln)
by Robert Ernst
Christiana Press
CH-8260 Stein-am-Rhein
Switzerland (1988)
(In German only, but an exceptional book. According to Maria Simma: "the best". Ought to be published in English)

HEALING YOUR FAMILY TREE
by Fr. John Hampsch, CMF
Performance Press
P.O. Box 7307
Everett, WA 98201-0307 (1986)
(Valuable yet in an awkward self-answered Q/A format; also somewhat overloaded with Psychology.)

MEINE GESPRÄCHE MIT ARMEN SEELEN
(My Conversations with Poor Souls)
by Eugenie von der Leyen
Christiana Press,
CH-8260 Stein-am-Rhein
Switzerland (1979)
(In German only, and not for the faint-hearted. A breath-taking and somewhat shocking testimony, and ought to be published in English.)

FEGEFEUER,LEIDEN,FREUDENUNDFREUNDEDERARMENSEELEN
(Purgatory, Sufferings, Joys and Friends of the Poor Souls)
by Ferdinand Holböck
Christiana Press,
CH-8260 Stein-am-Rhein
Switzerland (1992)

(In German only. Wonderful witnesses throughout Church history by Saints as well as many others. Very informative, and also ought to be published in English.)

HEALING THE FAMILY TREE
by Dr. Kenneth McAll
Queenship Publishing Co.
P.O. Box 42028
Santa Barbara, CA 93140 (reprinted 1996)

HEALING THE HAUNTED
by Dr. Kenneth McAll
Bignell Wood
Brook Lyndhurst
Hampshire   SO43 7JA
England (1989)

GUIDE TO HEALING THE FAMILY TREE
by Dr. Kenneth McAll
(same as above or)
The Handsel Press, Ltd
The Stables,
Carberry EH21 8PY
Scotland (1994)
(The first two are an adventure, written in short episodes describing specific healings instigated by Dr. McAll. The latter is a medical compendium describing the many specific illnesses that have so far responded to prayer.)

CHARITY FOR THE SUFFERING SOULS
An Explanation of the Catholic Doctrine of Purgatory
by Rev. John A. Nageleisen
TAN Books & Publishers, Inc
Rockford, IL 61105 (reprinted 1977)
(Exactly that. With Imprimatur.)

HOW TO AVOID PURGATORY
by Fr. Paul O'Sullivan, O.P.

TAN Books & Publishers, Inc.
Rockford, IL 61105 (reprinted 1992)
(Small pamphlet, worth reading.)

THE HOLY SOULS, "Viva Padre Pio"
Padre Pio of Pietrelcina Editions (1990)
Nat'l Ctr of Padre Pio, Inc.
Rd#1 Box 134 (Old Rt 100)
Barto, PA 19504
(Bl. Padre Pio is one-of-a-kind.)

ESCHATOLOGY -- DEATH AND ETERNAL LIFE
by Joseph Cardinal Ratzinger
Friedrich Pustet
Regensburg (1990)
(Serious teaching.)

AN UNPUBLISHED MANUSCRIPT ON PURGATORY
by Reparation Soc. of the Immaculate Heart of Mary, Inc
100 E. 20th St.
Baltimore, MD 21218-6091 (1968)
(Very beautiful!)

PURGATORY, EXPLAINED BY THE LIVES AND LEGENDS OF THE
SAINTS
by Fr. F.X. Schouppe, SJ
TAN Books & Publishers, Inc.
Rockford, IL 61105 (1923, reprinted 1968)
(Good yet long with slow heavy reading, only for the in-depth permanent student.)

MEINE ERLEBNISSE mit ARMEN SEELEN
(My Experiences with Poor Souls),
by Maria Simma and Fr. Alfons Matt,
Christiana Press,
CH-8260 Stein-am-Rhein,
Switzerland (1968)

(Simple and very good. Only about a third of it is not already in this book. English is out of print.)

... and ...

New Cathecism of The Roman Catholic Church, (1993)
(Two paragraphs on Purgatory!)

Whatever you would wish at your dying hour
to have done in health,
that do now while you may.

St. Angela Merici

PRAYERS FOR THE POOR SOULS

A short effective prayer:

O Mary, Mother of God, flood all of humanity with the graces of your burning love, now and at the hour of our death! Amen.

Prayer which will deliver many souls from Purgatory:

Eternal Father, I offer You the most precious blood of your Divine Son, Jesus, in union with the Masses said throughout the world today, for all the holy souls in Purgatory, for sinners everywhere, for sinners in the universal church, those in my home and within my own family.

Prayer for our deceased parents:

Lord God, you commanded us to honor our parents. Kindly have mercy toward the souls of my father and mother; forgive them their sins and allow me to see them again in the joy of Eternal Light! Through Christ our Lord. Amen.

Prayer for a particular soul:

Almighty Eternal God, in your fatherly goodness, be kind to the soul of your servant .... Cleanse him (her) whom you have called from this world of all his faults, take him into the Realm of Light and Peace and into the Community of your Saints and give him his share of Eternal Delight in your Kingdom. For this we pray through Jesus, Our Lord. Amen.

God, You Creator and Savior of all the faithful, forgive all the sins of all your servants' souls! Let them receive forgiveness through our pious prayer, for which they have always been yearning. Amen.

Prayer from the Mass for the deceased:

O Lord, You always love to distribute Mercy and Graces. For this reason I never cease asking of You to think of the souls of your servants whom You have taken from this world. Do not leave them under the power of the enemy and do not ever forget them. Order Your Holy Angels to take and lead them to their heavenly home. They hoped for You, they believed in You. So do not let them endure the punishments of Purgatory, but let them have the Eternal Joys. Through Christ, Our Lord. Amen.

Prayer for the most neglected souls:

Jesus, for the sake of the agony that you endured during Your fear of death in the Garden of Gethsemane, at the Scourging and Crowning, on the way to Mt. Calvary, at your Crucifixion and at your Death, have Mercy on the souls in Purgatory and especially on those who are completely forgotten! Deliver them from their bitter pains, call them to You and embrace them in Your arms in Heaven!

Our Father... Hail Mary...

Lord, grant them eternal peace. Amen.

This prayer is of great help to the Poor Souls:

O Lord, Jesus Christ, through the Sacred Blood that You shed during Your fear of death in the Garden of Gethsemane, please deliver the souls of your faithful from the sufferings of the fires of Purgatory, in particular those who are most neglected, and lead them to their place in your Splendor to glorify and praise You in Eternity.

Our Father... Hail Mary...

O Lord, Jesus Christ, through the Sacred Blood that you shed during your merciless flogging, please deliver all the souls of the faithful, in particular those who are closest to their liberation, and lead them to seeing You so that they may glorify and praise You in Eternity.

Our Father... Hail Mary...

O Lord, Jesus Christ, through the Sacred Blood that you shed during Your painful Crowning, please deliver all souls of the Christian faithful from the dungeon of Purgatory, in particular those who would have to suffer there very much longer, and lead them into the Blessed Community of the Chosen, so that they may glorify and praise You in Eternity.

Our Father... Hail Mary...

O Lord, Jesus Christ, through the Sacred Blood that You shed during Your gruesome Crucifixion, please deliver all the souls of the departed, in particular those of my father, my mother, my brothers and sisters, my relatives, my benefactors, and lead them to Eternal Joys, so that they may glorify and praise You in Eternity.

Our Father... Hail Mary...

O Lord, Jesus Christ, through the Sacred Blood that poured from Your Blessed Side, please deliver all Poor Souls from Purgatory, in particular those who during their lives especially served Your Blessed Virgin Mother, and lead them to Your Eternal Glory so that they may glorify and praise You in Eternity.

Our Father... Hail Mary... Amen.

Rosary for the Poor Souls in Purgatory:

On the large beads we pray:

O Poor Souls draw the fire of God's Love into my soul, to reveal Jesus crucified in me here on earth rather than hereafter in Purgatory.

On the small beads:

Crucified Lord Jesus, have mercy on the souls in Purgatory. At the end three times:

Glory Be to the Father...

Prayer of Sacrifice for the Poor Souls:

Almighty, Eternal God! Because it is Your Will that we pray for the Poor Souls, I offer You, through Mary's most unblemished hands, all the Masses that are celebrated today, for Your highest Honor and for the redemption of the souls in Purgatory. Humbly I beg of you, erase their guilt through the overly rich merits of Your most Beloved Son and have Mercy on them. For the restitution of the praise, the love, the honor, the thanks and the merits that these souls neglected to show and to gather, I offer You all the Praise, the Love, the Honor, the Thanks and the Troubles of Your Son through which He Honored You while here in the world.

In reparation for all neglects and tepidity, which these souls committed, I offer You the Glowing Zeal with which Your Son did all His Works here on earth and which are now renewed and brought to You in all Holy Masses.

In reparation for all mistakes and all that was left undone by these souls, I offer You all Virtues which Your Son practiced in Totality and which He now still practices and completes in all Holy Masses.

For the cleansing of all stains of sin that these souls still show, I offer You the Sacred Blood which Your Son shed while here on earth and which He now continues to offer to You in all Holy Masses.

As discharge from all punishments and torments, which these souls endure, I offer You the bitter Passion and Death of Your most Beloved Son, which He now renews and continues in all Holy Masses.

For their rescue from the burning dungeon, I offer You the infinite merits which Your Son earned on earth and which He now still exercises and distributes in all Holy Masses.

Finally, in order to do enough to fulfill Your strict Justice, I offer You all virtues and merits which the entire Life, Suffering and Death of Your most Beloved Son, His Holiest Mother, all Saints and Chosen Ones who together suffered more than the dear Poor Souls left undone. Amen.

Sevenfold Prayer for the Poor Souls:

1) Lord, Almighty God, through the Sacred Blood which Your Divine Son shed in the Garden of Gethsemane, I ask You to free the souls in Purgatory, in particular those who are most neglected! Lead them into Your Glory so that they praise and glorify You in Eternity. Amen

Our Father... Hail Mary... Lord, grant them Eternal Peace.

2) Lord, Almighty God, through the Sacred Blood which Your Divine Son shed during the cruel Scourging, I ask You to free the souls in Purgatory, in particular those who stand the closest to the entrance to Your Delight. Let them begin to praise and glorify You now in Eternity. Amen.

Our Father... Hail Mary... Lord, grant them Eternal Peace.

3) Lord, Almighty God, through the Sacred Blood which Your Divine Son shed at the painful Crowning of thorns, I ask You to free the souls in Purgatory, in particular those in most need of our intercession! Do not let them wait any longer to praise and glorify You in Eternity. Amen.

Our Father... Hail Mary... Lord, grant them Eternal Peace.

4) Lord, Almighty God, through the Sacred Blood which Your Divine Son shed in the streets of Jerusalem as He carried the Cross on His Holy Shoulder, I ask You to free the souls in Purgatory, in particular the one who in Your Eyes has the greatest merits so that he can, from the high and glorious throne that awaits him, praise and glorify You in Eternity. Amen.

Our Father... Hail Mary... Lord, grant them Eternal Peace.

5) Lord, Almighty God, through the Sacred Flesh and Blood of Your Divine Son, Jesus Christ, which He Himself on the evening before His Death offered to His Beloved Apostles as food and drink, which He thereby left behind as continuous Offering and life-giving Sustenance for the faithful of the entire Church, I ask You to free the souls in Purgatory, in particular the one who honored this Secret of His Infinite Love the most, so that he with Your Divine Son and the Holy Spirit may, through this Holy Sacrament, praise and glorify You in Eternity. Amen.

Our Father... Hail Mary... Lord, grant them Eternal Peace.

6) Lord, Almighty Father, through the Sacred Blood that Your Divine Son shed from His Hands and Feet while on the beam of the Cross, I ask of You to free the souls in Purgatory, in particular the one for whom I must pray the most. Do not let that one stay there any longer due to my fault so that he may praise and glorify You in Eternity. Amen.

Our Father... Hail Mary... Lord, grant them Eternal Peace.

7) Lord, Almighty God, through the Sacred Blood and Water which flowed from the Side of Your Divine Son in front of the eyes of His Holy Mother and to Her greatest anguish, I ask You to free the souls in Purgatory, in particular the one who honored the highest Mother of Heaven the most intimately! Let him soon enter Your Glory in order to Praise and Glorify You with Mary in Eternity. Amen.

Our Father... Hail Mary... Lord, grant them Eternal Peace.

A fruitful prayer for the Poor Souls as given to St. Matilda: (Mechtildis)

OUR FATHER WHO ART IN HEAVEN: We most humbly beseech you - good, merciful and eternal Father - forgive the Poor Souls who You Yourself have taken as Your children, who did not love You and who pushed You away from them and neglected to give You sufficient honor. As reparation and penance I offer You all the love and good deeds of Your most beloved Son, Jesus Christ Our Lord.

HALLOWED BE THY NAME: I most humbly beseech you - good, merciful and eternal Father - forgive the Poor Souls who did not give glory to Your name, who often spoke unworthily or thoughtlessly. As reparation and penance I offer You all the sermons with which Your most beloved Son, Our Lord Jesus Christ, honored Your name while here on earth.

THY KINGDOM COME: We beseech You most humbly - good eternal and merciful Father - forgive the Poor Souls who did not attend to Your Kingdom with a burning love and a yearning wish but who often enriched themselves with earthly goods. As reparation and penance I offer You the great offering that Your most beloved Son, Our Lord Jesus Christ, made so that all can be taken into Your kingdom.

THY WILL BE DONE, ON EARTH AS IT IS IN HEAVEN: We beseech You most humbly - good, eternal and merciful Father - forgive the Poor Souls who did not serve Your will but often followed their own will and who thereby did not do Your will. As reparation and penance we offer You the Holy and Divine heart of Your Son, Our Lord Jesus Christ, and its total will service.

GIVE US THIS DAY OUR DAILY BREAD AND FORGIVE US OUR TRES-PASSES AS WE FORGIVE THOSE WHO TRESPASS AGAINST US: We beseech You most humbly - good, eternal and merciful Father - forgive the Poor Souls who offered no resistance to big temptations but who fell to the urgings of evil and into ruin. As reparation and penance we offer You the obedience, the tiring work, all the bitter sufferings and the death of Your most beloved Son, Jesus Christ Our Lord.

AND DELIVER US FROM EVIL: We most humbly beseech You - good, eternal and merciful Father - forgive the Poor Souls and lead them as well as our souls, through the merits of Your most beloved Son, Our Lord Jesus Christ, into the kingdom of Your Holiness, which You Yourself are. Amen.

Rosary for the Poor Souls in Purgatory

Here we pray the Sorrowful Mysteries. Before each decade, we pray what concerns the particular mystery, and instead of ending the decades with Glory Be..., we pray: Lord, grant them Eternal Rest and let Perpetual Light shine upon them!

1) Lord, Jesus Christ, through Your bloody sweat of fear that You shed on the Mount of Olives, we ask You to have Mercy on the Poor Souls in Purgatory! Deliver them from their fear and pain and console them with the Cup of Heavenly Comfort!

2) Lord Jesus Christ, through Your painful Scourging which You tolerated so patiently for us sinners, we ask You to have Mercy on the Poor Souls in Purgatory! Retract from them the pain of Your Anger and give them Eternal Relief.

3) Lord Jesus Christ, through Your painful Crowning which You suffered so patiently for us sinners, we ask You to have Mercy on the Poor Souls in Purgatory and give them the crown of Eternal Delight!

4) Lord Jesus Christ, through Your painful Carrying of the Cross, which You suffered so patiently for us sinners, we ask You to have Mercy on the Poor Souls in Purgatory! Remove from them the heavy burden of suffering and lead them into Eternal Peace!

5) Lord Jesus Christ, through Your painful Crucifixion, which You suffered so patiently for us sinners, we ask You have Mercy on the Poor Souls in Purgatory! Turn Your Holy Face toward them and let them today be in Paradise with You!

After the fifth decade we pray:

Lord Jesus Christ, through your five Holy Wounds and through all of Your Sacred Blood that You shed, we ask You to have Mercy on the Poor Souls in Purgatory, and in particular for our parents, relatives, spiritual guides, and benefactors! Heal their painful wounds and let them enjoy and participate fully in Your Salvation. Amen.

Prayer for Specific Souls in Purgatory:

O Jesus, You suffered and died that all mankind might be saved and brought to eternal happiness. Hear our pleas for further mercy on the souls of:

My dear parents and grandparents,   Jesus,   have   Mercy!
My brothers and sisters and other near relatives, etc...
My Godparents and sponsors of Confirmation,
My spiritual and temporal benefactors,
My friends and neighbors,
All for whom love or duty calls me to pray,
Those who have suffered disadvantages or harm through me,
Those who are especially beloved by You,
Those whose release is near at hand,
Those who desire most to be united with You,
Those who endure the greatest sufferings,
Those who are least remembered,
Those whose release is most remote,
Those who are most deserving on account of their services to the Church,
The rich, who now are the most destitute,
The mighty, who now are powerless,
The once spiritually blind, who now see their folly,
The frivolous, who spent their time in idleness,
The poor who did not seek the treasures of heaven,
The tepid, who devoted little time to prayer,
The indolent, who neglected to perform good works,
Those of little faith, who neglected the frequent reception of the Sacraments,
The habitual sinners, who owe their salvation to a miracle of grace,
Parents who failed to watch over their children,
Superiors who were not solicitous for the salvation of those entrusted to them,
Those who strove for worldly riches and pleasures,
The worldly-minded, who failed to use their wealth and talents in the service of God,
Those who witnessed the death of others, but would not think of their own,
Those who did not provide for the life hereafter,
Those whose sentence is severe because of the great things entrusted to them,
The Popes, Kings and rulers,
The Bishops and their counselors,

My teachers and spiritual advisers,
The Priests and religious of the Catholic Church,
The defenders of the holy faith,
Those who died on the battlefield,
Those who fought for their country,
Those who were buried in the sea,
Those who died of apoplexy,
Those who died of heart attacks,
Those who suffered and died of cancer or AIDS,
Those who died suddenly in accidents,
Those who died without the last rites of the Church,
Those who shall die within the next twenty-four hours,

My own poor soul when I shall have to appear before Your judgment seat,

Eternal rest grant unto them, O Lord, and let perpetual light shine upon them forever more with Your Saints because You are gracious.

P. The Lord be with you.
S. And with Your spirit.

May the prayer of Your suppliant people, we beseech You,
O Lord, benefit the souls of Your departed servants and handmaids. That You both deliver them from all their sins and make them partakers of Your Redemption. Amen.

Rosary for Divine Mercy:

Begin with:

Our Father... Hail Mary... I believe in God...

On the large beads:

Eternal Father, I offer You the Body and Blood, Soul and Divinity of Your dearly Beloved Son, Our Lord Jesus Christ, in atonement for our sins and those of the whole world.

On the small beads:

For the sake of His most sorrowful Passion, have Mercy on us and on the whole world.

In conclusion pray the following three times:

Holy God, Holy Almighty One, Holy and Immortal One, have Mercy on us and on the whole world.

Litany for the Poor Souls:

Lord, have Mercy on the deceased!
Christ, have Mercy on them!
Lord, have Mercy on them!
Christ, graciously hear us!
Christ, listen to us!
God the Father in Heaven, have Mercy on them!
God the Son, Savior of the world, have Mercy on them!
God the Holy Spirit, have Mercy on them!
Holy Trinity in One God, have Mercy on them!
Holy Mary,   *pray for them!*
Holy bearer of God,   etc....
Holy Virgin of Virgins,
Mother of God,
Mother of Mercy,
Gate of Heaven,
You Consoler of the downtrodden,
All Holy Angels and Archangels,
Saint Michael,
All holy patriarchs and prophets,
Saint John the Baptist,
Saint Joseph,
All holy apostles and evangelists,
All holy disciples of the Lord,
All holy innocent children,
All holy martyrs,
All holy bishops and faithful,
All holy teachers of the Church,
All holy priests and deacons,

All holy monks and hermits,
All holy virgins and widows,
All saints of God, pray for them!
Be gracious toward them; spare them, O Lord!
Be gracious toward them;   *deliver them, O Lord!*
From everything painful,   etc....
From all Your anger,
From the strictness of Your Justice,
From the gnawing worm of their conscience,
From their deepest sadness,
From the harsh captivity,
From the tearing fire,
From the painful yearning,
From all punishments,
Through Your wonderful Incarnation,   *deliver them, O Lord!*
Through Your Holy Nativity,   etc....
Through Your Holy Name,
Through Your Baptism and Your Fasting,
Through Your deepest Humility,
Through Your complete Obedience,
Through Your deepest Poverty,
Through Your Patience and Tenderness,
Through Your immeasurable Love,
Through Your bitter Suffering,
Through Your bloody Sweat of Fear,
Through Your Captivity,
Through Your painful Flogging,
Through Your disgraceful Crowning,
Through Your scolding Ridicule,
Through Your unjust Judgment,
Through Your grueling Carrying of the Cross,
Through Your horrible Crucifixion,
Through Your agonizing Abandonment,
Through Your Holy sacrificial Death,
Through Your five Holy Wounds,

248

Through Your pierced Heart,
Through Your Glorious Resurrection,
Through Your wonderful Ascension,
Through the arrival of the Holy Spirit,
Through the Merits and Intercession of Your Holy Mother,
Through the Merits and Intercession of all Your Saints,
We poor sinners we implore You, *hear us, O Lord!*
That You might protect the suffering souls in Purgatory, etc...
That You might rescue them from their pains and agony,
That You might share with them all the good works of Christianity,
That You might always hear all of our prayers for them,
That You might through St. Michael the Archangel and the Holy Angels lead them to Eternal Light,
That You might delight them soon with seeing Your face,
That You might grant our deceased parents, siblings, friends and benefactors Eternal Delight,
That You might deliver those souls where we share the guilt for their punishment on the other side,
That You might have special Mercy on all souls who no longer have anyone on earth to think of them,
That You might grant all souls of deceased Christians Eternal Peace,
That You may pour merciful Love toward the Poor Souls into the souls of all living Christians, hear us, O Lord!

Son of God, King of Eternal Delight.
Lamb of God, You wash away the sins of the world, protect them, O Lord!
Lamb of God, You wash away the sins of the world, listen to them, O Lord!
Lamb of God, You wash away the sins of the world, have mercy on them, O Lord!
Let us pray!
O God, Lord over life and death, show Your infinite Mercy to those servants who believed and hoped in You.
Grant them all reprieve of their guilt and punishment and deliver their souls from the sufferings on the other side.
For this we pray through the intercession of the Blessed Virgin Mary and through Christ Our Lord. Amen.

Novena of Graces for the Poor Souls in Purgatory:

First Day:

The reason that so many Souls suffer in Purgatory is the sins they committed in this life. This is the source of their suffering.

O Jesus, my Lord and Savior, I too have often deserved Hell. What a torture the thought to be lost forever! O my God, have patience with me, I love You for You are infinite goodness. I regret with all my heart for having hurt and insulted You, and I promise to improve myself. Grant me, O God, Your Graces; have Mercy on me and have Mercy also on the Poor Souls who suffer in Purgatory.

Oh Mary, Mother of God, agent of all Graces, Mother of Eternal Peace, come to the assistance of the Poor Souls with Your powerful intercession! Through Your mighty intercession may Christ, Your much loved Son, our Lord and God, permit them to partake in His Delight and Glory. Amen.

Our Father... Hail Mary...
O Lord, grant them Eternal Rest,
and may Perpetual Light shine upon them.
Lord, let them rest in Peace. Amen.

Second Day:

The Poor Souls suffer under the thought of the lost time on earth during which they could have earned merits to reach the Kingdom in Heaven. This loss they can no longer make up, because with the end of this life ends also the time to earn merits for Heaven.

Almighty, Eternal God, what have I earned during my earthly life to deserve Eternal Life? My senses and thoughts were for the greatest part directed toward timely matters. I thank You that You still give me more time to repair the evil and to earn merits for Eternity. I regret with all my heart for having fallen away from You, O God of Goodness. Stand by me so that from now on nothing will ever again be more important than my loving and serving only You. Have Mercy on me and also have Mercy on the Souls who suffer in Purgatory.

O Mary, Mother of God, full of grace, come and help the Poor Souls with Your mighty intercession! Through Your mighty inter-cession may Christ,

Your much beloved Son, our Lord and God, permit them to partake in His Delight and Glory. Amen.

Our Father... Hail Mary...
O Lord, grant them Eternal Rest
and may Perpetual Light shine upon them.
Lord, let them rest in peace. Amen.

Third day:

The great agony of the Poor Souls is the dreadful appearance of their sins for which they must now suffer in the place of cleansing. In this world one is not enough aware of the ugliness of sins, but will be most clearly in the other world!

Eternal Father, Holy God, Holy Almighty God, Holy Immortal God, I love You more than anything, for you are infinite Goodness and I regret with all my heart for having hurt You. I intend with all seriousness never again to fall away from You. Grant me again, O God, Your Grace! Have Mercy on me and have Mercy on the souls who suffer in the place of cleansing!

O Mary, Mother of God, full of grace, come and help the Poor Souls with Your mighty intercession! Through Your mighty inter-cession may Christ, Your much beloved Son, our Lord and God, permit them to partake in His Delight and Glory. Amen.

Our Father... Hail Mary...
O Lord, grant them Eternal Rest
and may Perpetual Light shine upon them.
Lord, let them rest in peace. Amen.

Fourth Day:

Already now it should hurt us to have insulted God, Eternal Love, so often. The Souls in Purgatory, however, recognize how infinitely good God is in a much clearer way and therefore love Him with all their strength. Because of this, they suffer an indescribable pain for having hurt the great God, a pain much greater than any other pain.

Almighty, Eternal God, I love You above all else because You are infinite goodness and I regret with all my heart for having hurt You. I intend with all seriousness never again to sin. Let me be persistent from now on. Have Mercy on me and have Mercy on the souls who suffer in Purgatory!

O Mary, Mother of God, full of grace, come and help the Poor Souls with Your mighty intercession! Through your mighty intercession may Christ, Your much beloved Son, our Lord and God, permit them to partake in His Delight and Glory. Amen.

Our Father... Hail Mary...
O Lord, grant them Eternal Rest
and may Perpetual Light shine upon them.
Lord, let them rest in peace. Amen.

Fifth Day:

The Souls in Purgatory suffer not knowing when their agony will come to an end. They are, however, certain that they will be delivered some day. Yet alone the uncertainty of the length of their penance is a great pain to them.

I love You over everything, O Infinitely Good God, and I regret with all my heart for having hurt You. I intend with all seriousness, O God, to bring You joy. Let me rest, O God, in Your Peace! Eternal Father, Holy God, Holy and Strong God, Holy and Immortal God, and have Mercy on me and have Mercy on the Poor Souls who suffer in Purgatory.

Oh Mary, conceived without sin, pray for us who escape to you for protection! Holy Mary, unblemished Virgin and Mother of God, come and help us and the Poor Souls in Purgatory with your mighty intercession! Amen.

Our Father... Hail Mary...
O Lord, grant them Eternal Rest
and may Perpetual Light shine upon them.
Lord, let them rest in peace. Amen.

Sixth Day:

A great consolation for the Poor Souls are thoughts about the bitter Passion of Jesus Christ and of the Blessed Sacrament at the Altar because they feel themselves saved through His bitter Passion and because they received so many graces through Communion and still do. But just as great is the immeasurable pain knowing how thoughtless they had been during their lives about these two greatest proofs of Jesus Christ's Love for them.

My Lord and my God, you died on the Cross for me. You gave Yourself to me so often during Holy Communion and I so often took You for granted with ingratitude. I intend with all seriousness, You Great and Holy God, not to hurt You again. Grant me, O Savior, Your Mercy and Love! O God, my highest Gift, have Mercy on me and have Mercy on the souls who suffer in the place of Oh Mary, Mother of God, Mother of all men, come to help the Poor Souls with your mighty Intercession!

Our Father... Hail Mary...
O Lord, grant them Eternal Rest
and may Perpetual Light shine upon them.
Lord, let them rest in peace. Amen.

Seventh Day:

The incredible pain that the Poor Souls suffer, and which is entirely dependent upon our help, increases when they consider the kind deeds of God. They had Christian parents, grew up with faith, nothing was lacking when it came to God's graces. All this emphasizes even more their ingratitude during life.

Almighty God, Eternal God, I too was an ungrateful creature. You waited for me with great patience, forgave my sins so often; and I, after so many promises, hurt you again and again. O my God, Father in Heaven, have Mercy on me! I regret having hurt You and promise to offer You reparation. Have Mercy on me and have Mercy also on the Poor Souls. Remove from them all guilt and all punishment. Deliver them soon and let them be intercessors for me and all my intentions!

O Mary, our Protectress and Helper, come and help the Poor Souls with your mighty intercession!

Our Father... Hail Mary...
O Lord, grant them Eternal Rest
and let Perpetual Light shine upon them.
Lord, let them rest in peace. Amen.

Eighth Day:

The Poor Souls, who are unable to help themselves, suffer from the fact that so many people on earth do not know what they do. They live their lives without ever thinking of God, of Eternity and thereby about the purpose of their lives and to prepare already now to meet their Creator at the hour of their death.

Almighty, Eternal God, protect me from a lazy and apathetic heart. Let me recognize now the true values in life, to count my days and to always come closer to You until I can see, adore and praise You in your Eternal Kingdom.

Oh Mary, conceived without sin, pray for us who seek protection from You. Holy Mary, Mother of God, agent of all graces, come to us and to all the Poor Souls with your mighty intercession!

Our Father... Hail Mary...
O Lord, grant them Eternal Rest
and let Perpetual Light shine upon them.
Lord, let them rest in peace. Amen.

Ninth Day:

The sufferings of the Poor Souls are enormous - their own failures, the lengthy cleansing. Yet even so, the greatest suffering is to be separated from God and to be denied seeing Him.

Almighty, Eternal God, how could I have collected so many years of distance from Your graces? Forgive me, my Lord and my God! Do not permit me to ever again lose Your Graces! I also beg You for Graces and Mercy for the Poor Souls! Lighten their sufferings, shorten their time of banishment and let them see Your Delight soon!

Holy Mary, Mother of God, pray for us poor sinners and especially at the hour of our death. Amen.

Oh Mary, Virgin conceived without sin and Mother of God, agent of all graces, Queen of all Saints, victorious in all of God's battles, come help us and the Poor Souls with Your mighty intercession.

Our Father... Hail Mary...
O Lord, grant them Eternal Rest
and let Perpetual Light shine upon them.
Lord, let them rest in peace. Amen.

An old and very beautiful Russian prayer:

As the tree loses its leaves, so does our life lead toward its end every year.
The festival of youth becomes empty.
The light of joys is extinguished.
The lonely age comes closer. Friends are dying. Relatives leave.
Where are you the lucky and joyful ones?
Quiet are the graves, but the souls are in Your hands.
One feels the loving looks that come out from the other world.
Lord, shining sun, warm and brighten the homes of the dead.
Lord, may the bitter times of separation disappear.
Give us a joyful reunion in Heaven.
Lord, help us all to become one with You!
Lord, give to those who have gone to sleep the childlike cleanliness and youthful bliss,
And may their eternal life become an Easter Feast! Amen.

A long and important Prayer for the Poor Souls by Arnold Guillet:

Most Holy Trinity, almighty eternal God, once You permitted the holy Curé of Ars to see the beauty of a human soul. It was an explosion of beauty and light that exceeded all human capability to understand, and John Maria Vianney would have died on the spot had You not kept him alive.

How is it possible that the human soul is so beautiful? Simply because every soul is a thought of Yours, a reflection of Your beauty, and because You created it after Your picture and image, no one the same as another, everyone with unmistakable features and merits.

How quickly a person, weakened by original sin, loses his innocence, how he permits himself to be pulled back and forth between good and bad, between God and the devil and how often he ends in contradiction and entanglement and heavy guilt. But still You repeatedly stretch Your forgiving hand to us after the fall -- when we may again get up and experience Your forgiveness. But also after You have forgiven us we are not spared the rust of sin and the payment for all our guilt. According to Paul's words we are cleansed "as though through fire", and according to the words of Your Son there is no return from the place of cleansing until "every penny is paid". The Souls in Purgatory know of Your eternal perfection, they know that You hate sin, they know that You live in the inaccessible light and no soul would dare, even if it could, to

255

step in front of You when still the smallest mark of sin was on it. The yearning for You burns them like fire and they themselves burn to be purified in the fire of Your love, the way iron is purified in fire.

Father in Heaven, Your Son, Jesus, permitted us to call You Abba, dear Father. You love Your children and You sent Your Son here so that He save us. Father, have mercy on the Poor Souls in Purgatory. For them we offer You through the painful and Immaculate Heart of Mary the Precious Blood of Your Son, Jesus. We beg You, through the merits of Your Son, shorten their time of cleansing, dry their tears, as it is written in Holy Scripture, press them soon to Your heart and hold them in Your lap forever.

Jesus, Son of the Father, You became man through the Blessed Virgin Mary, You became our brother and went there to prepare for us a place in Heaven. Have mercy on the souls in Purgatory, wash them with Your blood, expiate their failings through Your merits and recognize their names before Your Father, before all Angels and Saints in Heaven.

Holy Spirit, You who exudes from the Father and the Son, You are the third person of the Divinity. The Father created us, the Son delivered us and You, Holy Spirit -- You made us holy. For this reason Purgatory was more than anything Your making, Your burning Spirit of Divine Love. You cleanse them because You love them. You cleanse them because You wish to make them beautiful, the way God conceived them. Holy Spirit, for the honor of God's will, make of them "a new creation" (Gal 6:15), hasten the work of Your hallowing and completion, for every soul that may enter into the bliss of Heaven in the shine of newly found innocence the Angels and Saints are joyful.

Holiest Trinity, God Father, Son and Holy Spirit, we the fighting Church on earth, we beg You for the suffering Church in Purgatory, for our brothers and sisters in the place of cleansing. Hear our prayers, that they may intervene for us with You. Amen.

"... will rise to a disciplinary curative time of punishment."

PRAYERS TO THE ANGELS

Prayers to St. Michael the Archangel:

Saint Michael, the Archangel, defend us in battle; be our protection against the wickedness and snares of the devil. May God rebuke him, we humbly pray; and do thou, O Prince of the Heavenly Host, by the power of God, thrust into Hell Satan and the other evil spirits who prowl about the world seeking the ruin of souls. Amen.

Prince of the heavenly hosts, conqueror of the infernal dragon, you received from God the strength and power to destroy through humility the pride of the powers of darkness. We implore you help us to true humility of heart, to unshakable fidelity, to fulfill the Will of God and to fortitude in sufferings and trials. Help us to stand before the judgment seat of God. Amen.

To St. Gabriel the Archangel:

You Angel of humanity, you trusting messenger of God, open our ears also for the quiet warnings and calls of the most loving Heart of Jesus! Always be in front of our eyes, we beg you, that we understand the word of God correctly, that we follow, obey and fulfill that which God wants of us! And assist us in staying awake for when the Lord comes to get us so that He does not find us asleep!

To St. Raphael the Archangel:

You arrow of love and doctor of God's love, wound our hearts, we beseech you, with burning love and do not let the wound heal so that we stay on the path of love every day and so that we overcome everything with it!

To our Guardian Angel:

You caring protector given to me by God for my weakness. Holy Guardian Angel, my guide and consoler, my teacher and advisor, I thank you for your loyalty and love and beg you to always stay at my side and always remain my friend and helper. When I sleep, stay with me; when I am awake guide my steps; when I am sad, console me; when I am weak, save me from dangers; when I doubt, advise me; from sin, protect me. Dear angel, push me to do good; keep me in a state of grace; keep me from a fearful death; in the darkness of this world light my way; in my ignorance, teach me; of all attacks, warn me; from the evil one, protect me; pray for my intentions; in the hour of death, accompany my soul upward to bring me to my heavenly place so that I can be with you in blissful Adoration of the Almighty and all good Father in Heaven. Amen.

A Call to the Angels to help the Souls in Purgatory:

Jesus, Our Lord, You spent the night before Your Passion on the Mount of Olives, in the Garden of Gethsemane. In front of Your eyes You saw all the sins of the world -- a burden which crushed You and which pressed blood out through Your pores. The Apostles slept and did not have the strength to keep watch with you during this hardest of hours. Only Your heavenly Father was moved and sent an Angel in order to console and strengthen You during Your mortal anguish.

Lord, see our brothers and sisters in Purgatory. They suffer more than a human can while here on earth and You wish us to be merciful toward their anguish and distress. You give us the chance to do something for them, to keep watch with them, to pray for them, to make an offering on their behalf; but most of all, we can bring them the Holy Mass. Yes, we may even send our Guardian Angel so that he may in the Power of Your Blood console and strengthen them. How merciful God was with His Son on the Mount of Olives, and in this way he wishes us also to be merciful toward the suffering Church in Purgatory.

Jesus, remember Your loneliness on the Mount of Olives. Remember how much good it did for You when the Angel of Your Heavenly Father strengthened and supported You. Teach us to be as merciful and as supportive as Your Father, and fill the Poor Souls with the same consolation, which You received on the Mount of Olives.

Mary, Queen of Angels, have mercy toward your suffering children in Purgatory. Send them your angels to help them.

Saint Michael the Archangel, Saint Gabriel the Archangel, Saint Raphael the Archangel, you nine choirs of Holy Angels, you Seraphim and Cherubim, you Thrones and Dominations, Princes and Powers, you Archangels and

Angels, we pray, in the name of God and in the name of your Queen, our heavenly Mother Mary, go quickly and help our brothers and sisters in Purgatory. They suffer great anguish, they thirst for the Eternal God more than the stag thirsts for a spring's water. Strengthen them and lead them further on the path to heavenly Fatherland. Amen.

Petition to the Holy Angels:

Almighty and Eternal God the Trinity, before we beseech Your servants, the holy angels, and call upon them for help, we fall on our knees and adore You, Father, Son, and Holy Spirit. We honor and praise You for all eternity, and may all angels and men, whom You created, adore, love and serve You, O Holy, Almighty and Immortal God! Mary, Queen of Peace and Queen the Angels, you also graciously accept the supplications we address to your servants. We beg you, our Mother, our Mediatrix of all graces and all-powerful Intercessor, bring all our petitions to the throne of the Most High that we may find grace, salvation and help! Amen.

You great and powerful holy angels, you have been given to us by God for our protection and help.

We beseech you in the name of God the Trinity,   *come help us!*
We beseech you in the name of the Precious Blood of
Our Lord Jesus Christ,   etc...
We beseech you in the all-powerful name of Jesus,
We beseech you by all the wounds of Our Lord Jesus Christ,
We beseech you by all the sufferings of Our Lord Jesus Christ,
We beseech you by the heart of Our Lord Jesus Christ,
We beseech you by the holy word of God,
We beseech you in the name of God's love for us, the wretched,
We beseech you in the name of God's faithfulness to us, the wretched,
We beseech you in the name of God's mercy towards us, the wretched,
We beseech you in the name of Mary, the Mother of God and our Mother,
We beseech you in the name of Mary, Queen of Heaven and earth,
We beseech you in the name of Mary, Our Queen of Peace,
We beseech you by your own beatitude,
We beseech you by your own fidelity,
We beseech you by your warfare for the kingdom of God,

We beseech you; cover us with your shield,
We beseech you; protect us with your sword,
We beseech you; guide us with your light,
We beseech you; save us under the protective mantle of Mary,
We beseech you; hide us inside the heart of Mary,
We beseech you; keep us in the hands of Mary,
We beseech you; lead our way to the gate of life, the open heart of Our Lord,
We beseech you; guide us safely to the heavenly Father's house,
All you nine choirs of holy angels,
You, our special companions who have been given to us by God,

COME HELP US, WE BESEECH YOU!

The Precious Blood of Our Lord and King calls out to you for help from within us, the wretched, *come help us, we beseech you!*

The heart of Our Lord and King calls out to you for help from within us, the wretched, *come help us, we beseech you!*

The Immaculate Heart of Mary, Most Pure, your Queen, calls out to you for help from within us, the wretched. *come help us, we beseech you!*

Amen.

Help Us, Great and Holy Brothers, Fellow-Servants Before God:

Protect us from ourselves, from our own cowardice and tepidity, from our self-seeking and avarice, from our envy and mistrust, from our craving for satiation, comfort and recognition, free us from the bonds of sin and attachment to worldly things, take from our eyes the blindfold we ourselves have put over them so that we need not see the misery around us, but can complacently think about and pity ourselves. Set the road of holy restlessness for God in our hearts so that we do not cease to seek God with longing, contrition, and love!

Seek in us the Precious Blood of Our Lord which was shed for our sake. Seek in us the poor, faded, ruined image of God, after which God once formed us in love! Help us to know and adore God, to love and serve Him! Help us in the battle with the powers of darkness that insidiously stalk and oppress us! Help us so that none of us may be lost, but that rejoicing, we may one day be united in eternal happiness. Amen.

Daily prayer to the Angels:

(It would be good to recite this in the morning and then to call upon the angels often during the day. Can also be prayed as a Novena.)

St. Michael, assist us with our angels, help us and pray for us!
St. Raphael, assist us with our angels, help us and pray for us!
St. Gabriel, assist us with our angels, help us and pray for us!

Many wish to be good Christians; but to strain for holiness, that seems too much for them! And still God's Church needs truly holy and not merely somewhat holy men! The tide of ruin is stronger than the mediocre, so how should it be conquered by mediocrity?!

The Souls in Purgatory to
Maria Simma

ST. BRIDGET PRAYERS FOR 12 YEARS

These prayers, as given by the Lord to St. Bridget of Sweden, are to be prayed for 12 years. He promised to all who pray them the five graces already listed by Maria Simma on page 39 of this book. Was the person praying these to die before the twelve years are over, the Lord will accept them as having been prayed in their entirety. If a day or a few days are missed due to a valid reason, they can be made up for later.

This devotion was pronounced good and recommended by both the 'Sacro Collegio de propaganda fide', as well as by Pope Clement XII. And Pope Innocent X confirmed this revelation as being from the Lord.

1) The soul who prays them suffers no Purgatory.

2) The soul who prays them will be accepted among the Martyrs as though he had spilled his blood for his faith.

3) The soul who prays them can chose three others whom Jesus will then keep in a state of grace sufficient to become holy.

4) No-one in the four successive generations of the soul who prays them will be lost.

5) The soul who prays them will be made conscious of his death one month in advance.

*   *   *

O Jesus, now I wish to pray the Lord's Prayer seven times in unity with the love with which You sanctified this prayer in Your heart. Take it from my lips into Your Divine heart. Improve and complete it so much that it brings as much honor and joy to the Trinity as You granted it on earth with this prayer. May these pour upon Your Holy Humanity in Glorification to Your Painful Wounds and the Precious Blood that You spilled from them.

1) THE CIRCUMCISION
Our Father ... Hail Mary...

Eternal Father, through Mary's unblemished hands and the Divine Heart of Jesus, I offer You the first wounds, the first pains and the first Bloodshed as atonement for my and all of humanity's sins of youth, as protection against the first mortal sin, especially among my relatives.

2) THE SUFFERING on the Mount of Olives
Our Father ... Hail Mary...

Eternal Father, through Mary's unblemished hands and the Divine Heart of Jesus, I offer You the terrifying suffering of Jesus' Heart on the Mount of Olives and every drop of His Bloody Sweat as atonement for my and all of humanity's sins of the heart, as protection against such sins and for the spreading of Divine and brotherly Love.

3) THE FLOGGING
Our Father ... Hail Mary...

Eternal Father, through Mary's unblemished hands and the Divine Heart of Jesus, I offer You the many thousands of Wounds, the gruesome Pains and the Precious Blood of the Flogging as atonement for my and all of humanity's sins of the Flesh, as protection against such sins and the preservation of innocence, especially among my relatives.

4) THE CROWNING of THORNS
Our Father ... Hail Mary...

Eternal Father, through Mary's unblemished hands and the Divine Heart of Jesus, I offer You the wounds, the pains and the precious Blood of Jesus' Holy head from the Crowning with Thorns as atonement for my and all of humanity's sins of the Spirit, as Protection against such sins and for the spreading of Christ's Kingdom here on earth.

5) CARRYING the CROSS
Our Father ... Hail Mary...

Eternal Father, through Mary's unblemished hands and the Divine Heart of Jesus, I offer You the Sufferings on the way of the Cross, especially His Holy Wound on His shoulder and its precious Blood as atonement for my and all of humanity's rebellion against the Cross, every grumbling against Your Holy Arrangements and all other sins of the tongue, as protection against such sins and for true love of the Cross.

6) CRUCIFIXION of JESUS
   Our Father ... Hail Mary...

Eternal Father, through Mary's unblemished hands and the Divine Heart of Jesus, I offer You Your Son on the Cross, His Nailing and Raising, His Wounds on the Hands and Feet and the three streams of His precious Blood that poured forth from these for us, His extreme tortures of the Body and Soul, His precious death and its non-bleeding Renewal in all Holy Masses on earth as atonement for all wounds against vows and regulations within the Orders, as reparation for my and all of the world's sins, for the sick and the dying, for all holy priests and laymen, for the Holy Father's intentions toward the restoration of Christian families, for the strengthening of Faith, for our country and unity among all nations in Christ and His Church, as well as for the Diaspora.

7) THE PIERCING of JESUS' SIDE
   Our Father ... Hail Mary ...

Eternal Father, accept as worthy, for the needs of the Holy Church and as atonement for the sins of all of Mankind, the precious Blood and Water which poured forth from the wound of Jesus' Divine Heart. Be gracious and merciful toward us. Blood of Christ, the last precious content of His Holy Heart, wash me of all my and other's guilt of sin! Water from the Side of Christ; wash me clean of all punishments for sin and extinguish the flames of Purgatory for me and for all the Poor Souls. Amen.

MARY'S SEVEN SORROWS
AS GIVEN TO ST. BRIDGET

Whoever thinks about the Passion of Christ must also think about His mother. The mother of God gave to St. Bridget the revelation that whoever prays seven Hail Marys daily while meditating upon her tears and sorrows and then spreads this devotion will be promised the following graces:

1) Peace within the family.

2) Enlightenment into God's mysteries.

3) Fulfillment of all their wishes -- as long as these within God's will and are useful for their souls' health.

4) And eternal joy in Jesus and Mary.

* * *

1st Sorrow: Simeon's revelation. Hail Mary......

2nd Sorrow: Flight into Egypt. Hail Mary......

3rd Sorrow: Losing 12 year-old Jesus in the Temple of Jerusalem.
Hail Mary......

4th Sorrow: Meeting on the Way of the Cross. Hail Mary......

5th Sorrow: Crucifixion, Death, Lancing
and Removal from the Cross on Calvary. Hail Mary......

6th Sorrow: The dead Body of Christ in the arms of His mother.
Hail Mary......

7th Sorrow: The Burial of Jesus; Mary's tears and loneliness.
Hail Mary......

NOTES

Chapter 3:

(1)　See　　MEINE GESPRÄCHE mit ARMEN SEELEN
　　　　　　(My Conversations with Poor Souls),
　　　　　　by Eugenie von der Leyen, Christiana Press
　　　　　　CH-8260 Stein-am-Rhein, Switzerland (1979)

Chapter 4:

(2)　See　　MEINE ERLEBNISSE mit ARMEN SEELEN
　　　　　　(My Experiences with Poor Souls),
　　　　　　by Maria Simma and Fr. Alfons Matt,
　　　　　　Christiana Press
　　　　　　CH-8260 Stein-am-Rhein,
　　　　　　Switzerland (1968)

On the subject of Maria's mental health the author hereby quotes the publisher of this previous book (German Edition):

"We were permitted to make photocopies for our archives of a six-page psychological report prepared by Dr. Ewald Böhm of Innsbruck as requested by a Professor of Theology in Innsbruck. It is important to recognize within this report that when it comes to Maria Simma, a hysterical or pathological condition is completely out of the question." Then, a bit further on, he continues with: "The publisher is also ready to make available to any serious critics further testimonies and documentations that are in our possession."

(3)　Concerning cases of private revelation such as Maria Simma's the Second Vatican Council said the following:

One English version:

"...Such graces, whether of great enlightenment or of modest and general acceptance, must be accepted with great thanks and consolation because they are especially well suited and useful to the needs of the Church. However, one should not take these too lightly. Nor may one presumptuously expect fruits from their apostolic truth and their ordered use stands with those who have the leadership within the Church and to whose attention they have been brought; not to extinguish its Spirit, but to test everything and to keep what is good."

(Decree concerning the lay apostolate, "APOSTOLICAM ACTUOSITA-TEM") One French version of the very same text:

"... De la réception de ces charismes mĉme les plus simples, résultent pour chacun des croyants le droit et le devoir d'exercer ces dons dans l'Eglise et dans le monde, pour le bien des hommes et l'édification de l'Eglise, dans la liberté du Saint Esprit qui "souffle où il veut" (Jean 3,8), de mĉme qu'en communion aec ses frère dans le Christ et très particulièrement avec ses pasteurs. C'est à eux qu'il appartient de porter un jugement sur l'authenticité et le bon usage de ces dons, non pas pour éteindre l'Esprit, mais pour éprouver tout et retenir ce qui est bon (cf. 1 Thes. 5,12.19.21) (4)."

(Décret sur l'apostolat des laïcs "APOSTOLICAM ACTUOSITATEM")

The above discrepancy in translation from the original Latin is merely one very good example of what human hands have done to the Holy Spirit of Vatican II and its documents.

(4) See   HEALING THE FAMILY TREE
              by Dr. Kenneth McAll
              Queenship Publishing Co.
              P.O. Box 42028
              Santa Barbara, CA 93140 (American edition, 1996)

    and   HEALING THE HAUNTED
              by Dr. Kenneth McAll
              Bignell Wood, Brook Lyndhurst
              Hampshire SO43 7JA England (1989)

    and   GUIDE TO HEALING THE FAMILY TREE
              by Dr. Kenneth McAll
              (same as above, or)
              The Handsel Press, Ltd
              The Stables,
              Carberry EH21 8PY
              Scotland (1994)

(5)   In the summer of 1993 a soul gave Maria Simma an answer concerning Robert F. Kennedy. It was, "He is delivered."

(6)   Since February 2002, when a fire badly damaged her house again, Maria Simma has moved into a Home for the Elderly, for she was no longer able to live alone. She therefore is no longer able to receive names of the deceased as before. Instead she requests that the readers of this book keep praying for the Souls in Purgatory and never to underestimate your prayers. The author kindly requests that the readers pray also for Maria, for she has been such a heroic intercessor for the Poor Souls.

7)   See   DEATH KNOWS NO SECRETS
              by Nicky Eltz
              available in Međugorje or on Internet under www.white-lily.info

Chapter 5:

(8)   See   Jeremiah 1:5
              (All Biblical References are per New American Bible.)

(9)   For the St. Bridget's Prayers to be prayed for a year:
      See   PIETA PRAYER BOOKLET and order from:
              Lillian M. Faulhaber
              Miraculous Lady of the Roses
              1186 Burlington Drive
              Hickory Corners, MI 49060

Chapter 7:

(10) See   ST. MICHAEL AND THE ANGELS
              Compiled from Approved Sources
              TAN Books & Publishers, Inc.
              Rockford, IL 61105 (1983)

Chapter 8:
(11) See   THERESE NEUMANN, MYSTIC & STIGMATIST 1898-1962
              by Adalbert Albert Vogl
              TAN Books & Publishers, Inc.
              Rockford, IL 61105 (1987)

(12) See   Documents of Vatican II
      also   MEMORIALE DOMINI by Pope Paul VI

The Pope's Letter (DOMINICAE CENAE) to
All Bishops & Priests
Instruction of Oct 18-22, 1968 and May 29, 1969
(see Acta Apostolic Sedis 61, 1969)

This includes the following:

"In view of the state of the Church as a whole today, this manner of distributing Holy Communion (on the tongue) therefore should be observed, not only because it rests upon the tradition of many centuries but especially because it is a sign of reverence by the faithful toward the Eucharist. The practice of placing Holy Communion on the tongue of the communicants in no way detracts from their personal dignity. This traditional manner of administering Holy Communion gives more effective assurance that the Holy Communion will be given to the faithful with due reverence, decorum and dignity."

And this then is also followed by the votes of all the world's Bishops which were overwhelmingly against Communion in the hand.

also   THE MYSTERY & THE CULT OF THE HOLY EUCHARIST
The Pope's Letter (DOMINICAE CENAE) given to
All Bishops & Priests
Given at the Vatican February 24, 1980
Polyglotte Vaticane
Also to be found in OSSERVATORE ROMANO

This includes the following:

"How eloquently the rite of the anointing of Priests' hands in our Latin ordination tells that a special grace and power of the Holy Spirit is necessary precisely for Priests' hands! To touch the Holy Eucharist and to distribute them with their own hands is a privilege of the ordained."

also   THE INSTRUCTION INESTIMABLE GIFT
(INAESTIMABILE DONUM) ON SOME NORMS CONCERNING THE CULT OF THE EUCHARISTIC MYSTERY The Holy Cong. for the Sacraments & Divine Worship (Holy Thursday) April 3, 1980

This includes the following:

"The Holy Eucharist is the gift of the Lord, which should be distributed to lay-men THROUGH THE INTERMEDIATION OF CATHOLIC PRIESTS who are ordained especially for this work. Laymen are neither permitted to take the Sacred Host by themselves nor the Consecrated Chalice."

Chapter 9:

(13) For further reading about the Freemasons in America see:

CHRISTIANITY AND THE SECRET OF
THE MASONIC LODGE
by John Ankerberg & John Weldon
Ankerberg Evangelistic Assoc.
P.O. Box 8977
Chattanooga, TN 37411 (1989)

BEHIND THE LODGE DOOR
by Paul A. Fisher
TAN Books & Publishers, Inc.
P.O. Box 424
Rockford IL 61105 (1993)

THEIR GOD IS THE DEVIL -
PAPAL ENCYCLICALS & FREEMASONRY
by Paul A. Fisher
American Research Foundation
P.O. Box 5687

Baltimore, MD 21210 (1990)
NEW WORLD ORDER
By William Still
Huntington House Publishing
P.O. Box 53788
Lafayette, LA 70505 (1990)

(14) The man to whom Maria refers here is Fr. Jerzy Popieluszko; Priest and Spiritual Director to many in Poland's Solidarity Movement of the early '80s. He was murdered on October 19, 1984 and found having been beaten, tied up with wire, with plastic bags pulled over his head, drowned and weighted down with rocks.

See   THE WAY OF MY CROSS,
              MASSES AT WARSAW BY FATHER JERZY POPIELUSZKO
              translated by Fr. Michael J. Wrenn
              Regnery Books
              950 North Shore Dr.
              Lake Bluff, IL 60044 (1986)

Chapter 10:

(15) See Matthew 12:31-32; and then a bit further on, in Matthew 25:46, it says, "Those who've done good will rise to everlasting life and those who've done evil will rise to damnation" as it does also in John 5:29. However, when going back to the Greek and Aramaic, we discover that this translation is not correct and that what Jesus really said was, "disciplinary curative time of punishment." These words exactly fit Maria's definition of Purgatory.

(16) See   THE HOLY SOULS, "Viva Padre Pio"
              Padre Pio of Pietrelcina Editions, 1990
              Nat'l Ctr of Padre Pio, Inc.
              Rd#1 Box 134 (Old Rt 100)
              Barto, PA 19504

     also   "SEND ME YOUR GUARDIAN ANGEL"
              by Fr. Alessio Parente OFM Cap
              -- same --

(17) See 2 Maccabees 12:43

(18) The following can be quoted from a Masonic plan in the year 1925: "How can one rob the faithful of their belief in the true presence? ... First one must bring people everywhere to recieve communion while standing, then one must place the Host in their hands. Prepared in this fashion, they will come to see the Eucharist as a mere symbol of a general brotherly meal and will thereby fall away."

Going back further still, well into the 19th Century, we may here also quote Stanislas de Guaita. He was a fallen away Priest, a kabbalist, a satanist and a model for all Freemasons.

"When we have succeeded in having Catholics receive Communion in the hand, then we will have met our goal."

Then the following was published first by Marquis de la Franquerie in 1819 and then also in the following:

DER STILLE KRIEG GEGEN THRON UND ALTAR (oder)
DAS NEGATIVE DER FREIMAUREREI, NACH
DOKUMENTE
(THE SILENT WAR AGAINST THRONE AND ALTAR (or)
THE NEGATIVE OF FREEMASONRY, ACCORDING TO
DOCUMENTS)
by G.M. Pachtler
2nd Edition, 1876

On page 83 Pachtler writes that these secret instructions occurred in 1819. He also gives it's entire title as being:

ISTRUZIONE PERMANENTE, CODICE E QUIDA PRAT-
ICA DEI PREPOSTI ALL'ALTA MASSONERIA

And it's original text was in CIVILTA CATTOL. 4TH EDITION, 1875, page 598.

"The thought is the liberation of Italy, from which on a particular day the liberation of the entire world, the Brotherly Republic and the Unity of mankind, must radiate... Our goal is afterall much more than that of Voltaire and the French Revolution: therefore the entire destruction of Catholicism and the idea of Christianity itself...

The Pope, whoever he may be, will never come to the secret Brotherhood, therefore the secret associations must undertake the first steps toward the Papacy and the Church with the intention of putting both in chains. Our assignment is not one of a day, of a month or of a year. It may take many years or perhaps a century. We do not afterall intend to win the Pope over to us, to make of him a neophyte of our principles or an apostle of our ideas. That would be a laughable dream. And even when the circumstances turned out that it were to happen that a Cardinal or a Prelate was to come to us with all his heart or as a trick on the consecrated ones of our secrets, still we could not wish to elevate him onto Peter's Throne. Yes, such a selection would be our ruin. For just as he would have come to apostasy out of pure ambition, in the same manner his wish for power would also have him offer us up. What we seek and what we must strive for is, as the Jews wait for their Messiah, is a Pope according to our needs... And so in order to make a Pope according to our hearts, we must raise a generation out of which a man will rise who will be worthy of our rule. One must leave the old or mature men entirely aside. Instead aim straight at he youth and perhaps even at children... Once your good reputations have become well founded in the Colleges, High Schools, Universities and Seminaries, and once you have the trust of the professors and the youth; make sure that especially the candidates for the Priesthood seek your company... After a number of years this young clergy will, due to the power of circumstances, occupy all Offices. It will reign, manage, judge, form the sovereign's (Pope's) advice and be obligated to pick the next Pope... Throw out your nets like Simon Barjona in the inner Sacristies, the Seminaries and Convents, not at the bottom of the sea. And if you do not rush things, we promise you a catch as wonderful as that of St. Peter. The fisherman has turned into man-catcher, and you will even catch friends at the foot of the Apostolic Throne. In this way you will have a revolution in your nets of the Crown and Cape at whose tip the Cross and the large papal flag will be carried; a revolution which will need only a little help in order to spread the fire in all four directions of the world..."

(19) See Documents of Vatican II where this statement is confirmed -- yet confirmed only as long as the reader makes absolutely certain that the version he is reading is the true translation. There are vast differences and sometimes even omissions of whole sentences between translations of those documents. And here, as a very appropriate example, see alone how the document referring to the attention that the Church wishes to give to the charisms of the laity differ between the French and the English shown here in the above Note (3).

See   THE PAPAL DECREE CONCERNING HAND COMMUNION
Sacred Congregation of the Holy Liturgy
Benno, Cardinal Gut, Prefekt
May 29, 1969

also   LITURGICAL SHIPWRECK
by Michael Davies
TAN Books & Publishers
P.O.Box 424
Rockford, IL 61105 (1994)

Chapter 11:

(20) See   Apostolic Constitution: 'Universi Dominici gregis'
                     Spring 1996

Chapter 12:

(21) See   Leviticus 26:40; Daniel 9:20; Baruch 3:1-8 and Numbers 14:19

(22) See   John 19:26-27

(23) See   PREPARATION FOR TOTAL CONSECRATION
                     According to ST. LOUIS de MONTFORT
                     Montfort Publications
                     Bay Shore, L.I. New York 11706-8993 (1992)

Chapter 17:

(24) See   Luke 12:48

Chapter 18:

(25) See   AN UNPUBLISHED MANUSCRIPT ON PURGATORY
                     by The Reparation Soc. of the
                     Immaculate Heart of Mary, Inc
                     100 E. 20th St.
                     Baltimore, MD 21218-6091 (1968)

Chapter 19:

(26) See   Matthew 19:14

Chapter 20:

(27) The following is a partial list of occult practices popular in the United States and much of the West:

Astrology	Ouija Board Game
Dungeons & Dragons Game	Palm reading
Channeling	Santeria
Enneagrams Fortune-telling	Seances
Freemasonry	Tea leaf reading
I Ching	Tarot cards
Numerology	Wicca

276

(28) According to the British organization, CHILDWATCH, four thousand children are sacrificed annually in Great Britain alone. This organization is proceeding with many Law suits in order to solve these murders. Children are tortured in unbelievable ways before they are killed. A fourteen year-old girl was impregnated eight times and each time forced to have an abortion. The embryos were first frozen and then later consumed at 'black masses' as 'Last Suppers'.

(29) See   IN GOD'S NAME
by David A. Yallop
Jonathan Cape Ltd
30 Bedford Square
London WC18 3EL (1984)

(Good journalism but poorly discerned concerning Pope John Paul II.)

Chapter 21:

(30) See   THE DOGMA of HELL
by Fr. F.X. Schouppe, SJ
TAN Books & Publishers
P.O. Box 424
Rockford, IL 61105 (1989)

Chapter 22:

(31) See   Matthew 8:5-13

Chapter 24:

(32) See   Exodus 20:5, 34:7

Chapter 27:

(33) In the last ten days of November 1992 the following occurred in Međugorje. This has been quoted from an open letter sent from the village by Sr. Emmanuel which also appears in her book MEĐUGORJE, THE WAR DAY BY DAY.

"A group of pilgrims here had a staggering experience which happens normally only at the moment of death. In an instant their entire lives unfolded in front of their eyes as if in a movie. They were able to see with precision and clarity each occasion in their lives where they had said 'yes' to God and where they had said 'no'. Their consciences were taken over by such a light as in a broadcasting of the Holy Spirit, with shadows of their sin and brightness of their love given. They felt a profound regret. All received at the very same moment a great healing, both physical as well as spiritual. In this manner a drug addict was completely delivered from the drug. They all had no more than the desire from that time on to put God and His Love at the center of their lives."

Exhortations and Warnings:

(34) See   CELEBRATE MASS WITH THE HEART
                by Fr. Slavko Barbarić, OFM
                Faith Publishing Co.
                P.O.Box 237
                Milford, OH 45150 (1994)

Some, and most especially some among the German speaking readers, will know that the 'Exhortations and Warnings' in this book were originally dictated by the souls to Maria and published in 1978. The first sentence of this paragraph seemed appropriate only for the older German reading public. This is because Fr. Martin von Cochem was German and died in 1712, and because it was obvious that his books would not easily be made available to the American public, the author asked Maria whether the souls would perhaps also mention another book about the Holy Mass which the American readers would have no trouble in finding. He took this request to Maria in mid January 1994 and asked her whether she would be willing to ask this of a soul. Despite there not having been any answers forthcoming for the living in some two months prior to this, she agreed. That very night a soul came and, having given some answers for the deceased, remained in Maria's presence thereby giving her, as already explained in the text, the signal that she was permitted to ask further questions of it. Upon her question concerning a good and available book about the Holy Mass, the soul expressed that the author was permitted to mention Fr. Slavko's recently written book.

Were anybody so distrusting as to suspect collusion between the author and Fr. Slavko, please drop this notion quickly for, as the reader can easily see, Fr. Slavko gave his preface to the author on July 1, 1993 and it was a full five and a half months later that the soul mentioned to Maria that their teaching may include naming his book. Fr. Slavko never found out that the Poor Souls clearly liked what he had written and had even been allowed to say so. If there is any collusion to be found anywhere, it is between Mary, the Mother of God, and Fr. Slavko, whereas Maria Simma and this author have merely played the role of messengers in once again exposing the truth of the very closely knit cooperation between the former two.

ACKNOWLEDGMENT

The author extends his heartfelt and eternal love and gratitude to the following who in numerous ways, knowingly or unknowingly, participated in the creation of this book.

To Maria Simma who so heroically has given her entire life back to God. To Karl H. who was present from the very first day that the author met Maria, and who has been actively and prayerfully supportive of him and of this book ever since. To Fr. Walther Bertel for being Maria's very special friend.

To all the past and present Franciscan Priests and Sisters of Međugorje, and in a very special ways to Fr. Slavko, Sestre Maria, Fr. Ivan, Sestre Milena.

To all the visionaries, inner-locutionaries and other prayerful lay people residing in or near Međugorje, both Croatian as well as others, who supported the author on his path in faith and thus, peripherally, in the writing of this book.

To Drs. Kenneth & Frances McAll for their deep and prayerful support of this book and its author, and for their unwavering wish to assist all those around them at all times.

To Sr. Emmanuel of the Community of the Béatitudes for her assistance in composing questions to ask Maria; and to her and her lambs at the time -- Bernard, Cécile and Maurice -- for supplying the author with spiritual, mental, physical, and often humorous tender loving care and support throughout months of war, both spiritual and military. Also to those others who in any way assisted over the years in supplying questions which the author then passed on to Maria, and then came to use in this book.

To Dr. J. Paul Pandarakalam for being a plenipotentiary ambassador between the soldiers of Marian mysticism and those of the scientific medical community and who, due to his efforts, should from now on, with God's grace, come much closer to one another in their mutual search for truth and health.

To many pilgrims of Međugorje who, due to their responding to Our Lady's call in very special ways, have become life-long friends of the author; and may they rest in God's Peace, Light and Joy, Cuni Soldo and Thomas Tempel.

To friends and relatives too numerous to list who so loyally stayed with the author through thick and thin, dark and light, low and high; and here to Fr. Slavko who in a superlative and truly extraordinary way was the definition par excellence of a guide, a father, a brother, a true friend and the most trusting and thus most freeing of all passengers to have had along on this ride.

And finally to J.& S.B., I & M.B., P.& D.G., Z.& L.J. and D.& C.N. who harbored the author during his nomadic years and in doing so supplied him with the most basic needs for this book to become reality.

And finally, completely and eternally to: God the Father,
God the Son, Jesus Christ,
God the Holy Spirit
& Their
Chosen Servant in Total Humility and Obedience,
Our Most Beloved Mother
MARY

(Addendum)
THE
DIVINE SUBSTANCE

Nicky Eltz

CAUTION !!

This Product Contains Information Repulsive To The New
World Order, and Therefore Simply Too Dangerous
For Mass Diffusion.
READ IT ONLY AT YOUR OWN RISK OF BEING
WELL-INFORMED.

A SHORT DISCUSSION ON

THE
DIVINE SUBSTANCE

HOLY COMMUNION
ON THE TONGUE
WHILE KNEELING

AS COMPARED TO

COMMUNION IN THE HAND
WHILE STANDING

Nicky Eltz

*"But I say that I cannot be for it (Hand Communion),
and also cannot recommend it."*

*The Priest has, "as servant of the Holy Eucharist
and all Holy forms, a primary responsibility
— primary, because it is complete."*

*"To touch the Holy Creations is a privilege of the ordained."
Laymen can only get such permission "for a true emergency."*

Pope John Paul II

Dear Catholic!

This Addendum represents only a modest attempt to bring a flicker of light onto an extremely delicate, hazy, confusing, volatile and, to many also, painful subject. Good, simple and true information is dearly lacking or, to be more precise, is well hidden from the majority of good Catholics by this subject's so well broadcast and therefore highly influential opponents.

In this excessively technology-ridden world, so infested with misand disinformation, it is often very difficult to get to the core of any truly worthwhile subjects. This is just one such case, yet still Holy Communion is the only subject without which the world, in the holy opinion of St. Padre Pio, would cease to exist.

What follows is only a fraction of the vast amount of information available in Catholic history and mysticism, and it is this with which, it seems, surprisingly few Catholics of today, religious as well as lay, are familiar. This Addendum merely outlines what, in the opinion of millions, our Holy Mother Church, under the guidance of her Mother, Mary, wishes of its Bishops, Priests and laity when it comes to distributing and receiving of Holy Communion. May Mary intercede and, through these pages, speak to many hearts so that this small effort will bear good fruits.

ABOVE ALL ELSE, this Addendum is a call to prayer, persistent and deep prayer, regarding this most Holy subject.

In all fairness to potential readers of THE DIVINE SUBSTANCE, let it be known already now that it mirrors unwavering support for Holy Communion on the tongue while kneeling and near to none for any other form of receiving Jesus in the Holy Eucharist. Moreover, it shows five cases where Satan, through different individuals, spoke up for Holy Communion in the hand.

If you, dear Catholic, consider yourself a well-informed protagonist of Communion in the hand and can therefore find as much credible and, yes, holy information as is presented here which speaks in its favor, then do not read this Addendum. Were you now to try to find it, you will, considering that it does not exist, simply NOT be able to do so.

May God bless you and Mary protect, lead and intercede for you when it comes to receiving Jesus in Holy Communion,

The Author

"He is unworthy who celebrates the mystery otherwise than as Christ delivered it."

St. Ambrose

THE BIBLE

"Abraham fell down on his face." (Gen 17:1-3)

All Israelites "threw themselves onto the ground before their tents." (Ex 33:10f)

"At the name of Jesus all knees should bend, in Heaven, on earth and under the earth." (Phil 2:10)

"They fell down and adored it." (the Divine Child, Mt: 2,11)

"Accept it and eat it." (Mt 26:26) "Accepting" or receiving (Greek = lambanein) is passive, passively accept; not "actively take". "Every knee shall bend before Me." (Is 45:23)

"The twenty-four oldest fell down and adored Him." (Rev 5:13f) According to Luke (22:19), out of principle only consecrated hands may "take" and "give to" the people. The laity remains passive.

Christ gave the dipped piece to Judas (Jn 13:26f) and the eucharistic meal to the Apostles. (Lk 22:19) Implication, they did not "take it".

...and many others.

In the Semitic culture during the time of Christ there was no such thing as getting the meal placed into the hand. If the host wished to honor a guest in a special way, he placed a piece of the meal onto the guest's tongue.

Regard for such Jewish customs allows for Communion on the tongue to follow. This historical evidence confirms the biblical conclusion that Christ took a "basic norm" and adjusted it to become a "Divine principle".

THE EARLY CHURCH

Saint Pope Sixtus I, *(117-126)*

Reminded the Christians of the Apostolic rules and installed that only servants of the cult, Priests, could touch the Holy Mysteries.

Origenes, Doctor of the Church, † 250

"...be aware with all care and reverence that not the smallest particle of it fall to the ground, that nothing be dropped of the Consecrated Gift. You believe, and correctly so, that you have sinned when some is dropped out of carelessness."

Saint Pope Eutychian, *(275-283)*

"No woman may come close to the altar nor touch the Chalice of the Lord."
Some of the reasons for the temporary appearance of Communion in the
hand in the Early Church were, among others, these:

1) *Heresies:*

In the 2nd and 3rd Centuries there occurred influential philosophical/theo-
logical streams of thought to deny the Divinity of Christ and to make the
Christian Community unsure of itself. The writers of the Church, with the
true faith, were in that time still having theological troubles explaining the
mystery of the Holy Trinity, and besides this there were dangerous omissions
(Subordinationism).

2) *Practical Conditions:*

The shapelessness thereof, and therefore the danger of particles crumbling
from the broken and leavened eucharistic bread, made, among other things,
placing it into mouths difficult.

3) *Bloody Persecutions:*

With this often being the case, a legitimate handling of Holy Communion
(for instance House Communion) occurred alongside provable mis-uses and
forbidden diffusion of it (for instance, Communion brought to the sick by the
laity).

4) *Religious Laxity:*

After 313 AD the Church experienced an outward peace. It came to a rapid
growth of Church members, yet, despite their being baptized, many remained
with their old (immoral) customs.

5) *Loss of Faith:*

Despite the banishment of Arianism (denial of the Divinity of Christ) at
the Council of Nicea (325 AD) the arianistic beliefs soon touched the entire
Church. Emperor Constantine II (337-361 AD) persecuted correctly believing
Bishops and caused that most Bishoprics were still occupied by Arians. The
Catholic Church was, for the first time, in danger of going under due to an
internal decrease in the true faith. Only very few Bishops, including the often
banished Saint Athanasius, offered any resistance.

There is no evidence to be found that any early Pope at any time ever permitted or distributed Holy Communion into the hands of the laity.

When Arianism was finally defeated, when the present shape of Communion wafers was installed, and when many horrible mis-uses of Hosts due to Communion in the hand had been reported, it led back to Communion on the tongue. Communion in the hand was rejected by the Church in 5th and 6th Centuries. In the furthest parts of Gaul (later to become France) it took a bit longer until the Councils of Rouen (650 & 878 AD). Also in Spain, where Communion on the tongue experienced strong opposition from the heretical Sect of the Casians, it was finally installed again at the Synod of Cordova (839 AD).

Council of Trent *(1545-63)*

"...that the power was handed to the Apostles and their successors in the Priesthood to consecrate His Body and Blood and to distribute it." The laity, again, remains passive.

SAINTS

Saint Augustine, † 430

"...but no-one eats this flesh, before he has not adored it. ..., we sin if we do not adore it."

Saint Francis, † 1226

"And when He is offered by the Priest at the altar and is carried somewhere, then all the people should bend their knees and show the Lord, the living and true God, praise, glory and devotion."

Saint Thomas Aquinas, † 1274

He emphasized that the Most Holy could only be touched by Consecrated hands, except for "emergencies".

(Jesus to...)
Saint Bridget of Sweden, † 1373

"Look, my daughter, I left behind five gifts to my Priests, ... and fifth, the privilege to touch My Most Holy Flesh with their hands."

Saint Catherine of Sienna, † 1380

She received Holy Communion from Jesus Himself into the mouth.

Martyr & Saint Cardinal John Fisher, † 1535

"Times of flowering or collapse within the history of the Church were always associated with the handling of the Holy Eucharist."

Saint Jean-Marie Vianney, Curé of Ars, † 1859

A Consecrated Host left his fingers and flew by itself into the mouth of a First Communicant. A doubter who witnessed this converted and thereupon became a Priest.

EUCHARISTIC MIRACLES

Lanciano, Italy, (750)

Scientists have proven that the material conserved in the church of Lanciano is true human flesh and blood. Both are of the same blood type, the flesh is that of heart muscle, and it is alive.

Sr. Crescentia Höss, † 1744
(stigmata)

The consecrated Host flew out of the Tabernacle, through the length of the Church, and landed in her mouth.

Sr. Maria Columba Schonath, † 1787
(stigmata)

The consecrated Host flew out of the Tabernacle, through the length of the Church, and landed in her mouth.

Therese Neumann, † 1962
(stigmata)

The consecrated Host flew out of the Tabernacle, through the length of the Church, and landed in her mouth. Also, while blinded by blood emanating from her eyes while suffering Christ's Passion, she could tell that a layman had sneaked into her room dressed as a Priest, and she thereupon spoke up and sent him out of the room (which was off limits to all but Priests at that moment).

Marthe Robin, † 1981
(stigmata)

"When I began to bring the Host toward Marthe's mouth, I could not. The Host itself flew toward her mouth and placed itself onto her tongue." Fr. Joseph Marie Jacq, 1974. Also, Our Lady told Marthe that she would conquer Freemasonry in France. Remember this as you read on.

Julia Kim of Naju, South Korea

When receiving Communion on the tongue, the Host has turned into flesh and blood. This miracle started in June 1988, on the Feast of Corpus Christi, yet it has continued into the '90s and been witnessed by the Holy Father in Rome.

There are even Eucharistic Miracles recorded where simple animals knelt down before consecrated Hosts. What does that say about the callousness that many church-going human-beings of today show toward the Eucharistic Jesus?

Moreover, nowhere can one find a Eucharistic Miracle where a consecrated Host landed in someone's hands. Might there be a reason for this?

POPES

Pope Leo XIII, † 1903

"As soon as the order of reason contradicts Eternal Life and the Authority of God, it becomes permitted to disobey, people that is, in order to obey God."

Saint Pope Pius X, † 1914

"In the moment of receiving Holy Communion one must kneel."

Pope Paul VI, † 1978

Hand Communion started in Holland in 1965/66, as a result of some LAITY QUESTIONING WHETHER JESUS WAS TRULY PRESENT in the Consecrated Host. This sounds similar to: "denial of the Divinity of Christ." Pope Paul VI in the Encyclical MYSTERIUM FIDEI already rejected so-called "Hand Communion" as an "already spread false opinion". He thereupon asked the Dutch Bishops to write to all their Priests and "to give them directives to once again return to the traditional manner of receiving Holy Communion". He also wrote against the increasing mis-use of sex in marriages (pill, etc...) three years later in his Encyclical HUMANAE VITAE. NEITHER of these instructions was passed on by the Dutch Bishops and their Priests remained uncensored and unpunished. (Note: While acknowledging that nothing except Hell is ever beyond reparation, today, only 30 years later, Holland has, under the banner of liberal individualism, become a spiritual and moral tumor of a terminal nature. E.g., 9% of all deaths there are today the result of active euthanasia. Even a young girl with multiple sclerosis was killed in this way.)

In 1969 the ever-increasing number of Bishops who pushed for Communion in the hand (including by then in Germany, France and Belgium) requested of Pope Paul VI to give special permission for it in order to "sanction the disobedience". Surprisingly, and after much hard-fought resistance, he seemed to give in, and later in 1969 gave certain Bishops' Conferences, where the opposing manner of receiving Holy Communion had (in disobedience) taken hold, "special permission" to allow it. Then this "special permission" was ONLY granted to "certain communities and certain towns", and most certainly NOT in all Dioceses and also NOT "as a custom", and therefore its illegal inception as well as its spreading throughout so many countries is misleading, invalid, erroneous and, finally, wrong. The limited permission that Pope Paul VI gave was dragged out of him under force and deceitful conditions. Is there any wonder why he said that the "smoke of Satan" had entered the Church?

In order to stem this ever-increasing "custom in disobedience" the Pope then (also in 1969) turned to the whole Church, wherein he warned seriously (vehementer hortatur) of the dangers of Communion in the hand and advised "for the good of the Church itself" that all Bishops, Priests and Laity once again conform with the again confirmed manner of Holy Communion on the tongue. This warning and the resulting advice have full validity until today!

In 1975 Pope Paul's cherished liturgical expert and advisor on this very issue, Archbishop Annibale Bugnini, the very author of LITURGICAL RE-FORM (NOVUS ORDO MISSAE), was dismissed by the Pope when Bugnini's Masonic affiliation was exposed. Bugnini had, back when the issue was being handled, far over-stated the opinions of the minority and, at the same time, far understated that of the over-whelming majority. He had advised the Pope with outright lies and wild distortions, but the damage had already been done and all Catholicism was well on its way to being undermined by this betrayal.

So, rather than reading LITURGICAL REFORM, co-advised as it was by a team of Protestants, read instead, when submersed in prayer, the Bible, read the writings of this Holy Father, and then read and live Our Lady's messages from locations around the world where at least veneration has been approved.

It was reported that a few hours before his death, Pope Paul VI, when Holy Communion was brought to his room, got out of his sick bed and dropped onto his knees to receive Jesus.

Pope John Paul I, † 1978

The night he was murdered by another Freemason in the cloth, Pope John Paul I had in the drawer of his desk a list of some 30 Cardinals and Bishops who were Freemasons and whom he was going to dismiss the following day.

Pope John Paul II

After 11 years of Hand Communion, he said: "In several countries Communion in the hand has become the norm. At the same time voices expressing the lack of reverence of eucharistic forms are becoming louder — a lack that not only must be shouldered by those demonstrating it, but also by the Shepherds of the Church."

Do we now understand why, as Our Lady has said, our Holy Father suffers?!

In Germany, in 1980, he said: "But I say that I cannot be for it (Hand Communion), and also cannot recommend it." Also that the Priest has, "as servant of the Holy Eucharist and all Holy forms, a primary responsibility — primary, because it is complete."

"To touch the Holy Creations is a privilege of the ordained." Laymen can only get such permission "for a true emergency".

"But, I myself have seen the Pope distribute Holy Communion in the hand," you might be saying to yourself right now. This is true. However, when he does so, it is ONLY because he at that moment finds himself in a country where the Conference of Bishops has decided to disobey his and his predecessor's relevant instructions and he therefore does not wish to antagonize the Conference of Bishops, thereby giving rise to possible schisms on this issue. When Bishops disobey the Pope, there is, OF COURSE, no culpability on the behalf of the laity, that is, IF all the information that they have received is ONLY from their bishop.

The Holy Father, when visiting France in the 1980s, refused to give Holy Communion into the hand of then President of France, Giscard d'Estaing, and his wife who, prior to the meeting, had so boldly announced that she would stand up to the Pope in this regard! The Pope did not give in, and all this was shown on French television.

While in Zagreb, Croatia, in September 1994, the Holy Father had assisting Priests (in lieu of altar boys) using enormous patens to catch any possible particles that might have fallen while he distributed Holy Communion. The author, and therefore also millions of others, saw that when communicants still attempted to raise their hands, they simply had to stop and receive Communion on the tongue from the Pope or otherwise bump into those large patens. In so doing, HE GAVE THEM NO CHOICE. Not one person received Communion in the hand that day, at least not from Our Lady's Holy Father.

While in Krakow, Poland, in June of 1997, again, no Hand Communion was distributed by the Priests concelebrating at the Papal Mass.

CARDINALS

Cardinal Julius Döpfner, † 1976

Shortly before his death he said: "Had I known that through Communion in the hand so much lack of reverence was to be practiced, I would have never spoken for it. ... Today one goes to Holy Communion like one took holy water in the past. For two years I fought for Communion in the hand. Now that I have seen the results, I would never again do it. But now, I know of no way to rescind what has occurred. Get rid of Communion in the hand!"

Cardinal Franjo Šeper, † 1981
(former Prefect, Congregation for the Propagation of the Faith)

"The question of Hand Communion is for me not a question of the form, but ... a question of faith and therefore truly a decision of conscience for the Priest."

"No-one, having asked his conscience, can thereupon feel the need to request Communion in the hand."

Please ask yourself, dear Catholic, when and why you ever started with Holy Communion in the hand. Do so honestly, and then take the answer into prayer. Was it a good reason or was it simply, as so much else in our generation, because "everyone else was doing it"? Had you been informed correctly and thoroughly at the time? Please listen to this important Cardinal, and you too ask Jesus whether he might have been right? Or were you perhaps, like so many others, merely swept along "by the times" and were thereby never given a true chance to really ask or listen to Jesus about this. If so, PLEASE do so now.

Cardinal Joseph Ratzinger
(Prefect, Congregation for the Propagation of the Faith)

"We must reconquer the dimension of Holiness in the Liturgy." (1988) The obvious implication is that "the dimension of Holiness" has been lost.

19ᵀᴴ AND 20ᵀᴴ CENTURY MYSTICS

Katharina Emmerich, † 1824
(stigmata)

Considered the most famous of all German mystics, Katharina saw Jesus distribute the bread into the mouths of the Apostles.

Therese Neumann, † 1962
(stigmata)

She lived only on the Consecrated Host for some 35 years and also saw Jesus distribute the bread into the mouths of the Apostles.

When 'Resl' was being asked by Fr. Joseph Naber to describe what she saw while having visions of the Christ being removed from the Cross, the following exchange occurred:

Naber: And they were the ones who held Him up there?

Resl: Yes. The old man was up there and the other one, a pious one also, he was one of those who are not always with the Savior (disciple). They had a good grip on the Savior, from behind, the ladders stood firmly, and they could fold over the long linen cloth, he (Joseph of Arimethea) gave all the orders. They, by the way, were not allowed to touch the Savior with their bare hands, they had a real, what's it called?

Naber: Reverence?

Resl: Yes, I surely liked that, surely liked it. It was good for the Mother (Mary) also. ...

St. Padre Pio, † 1968
(stigmata)

"How often is ... this kiss of peace given to us in the Holiest Sacrament! Yes, we must burn in yearning for this kiss of the Divine mouth, moreover let us be even more grateful!"

Maria Simma of Sonntag, Austria
(Suffering Soul for and Visionary of the Poor Souls in Purgatory)

In carrying their suffering either mystically or with prayer, she has, since the 1960s, delivered 40 to 50 Priests (incl. Bishops), most of whom were in Purgatory due to spreading the practice of Communion in the hand or similar irreverent practices. Maria calls Hand Communion, "the work of the devil." She also repeats often what the Poor Souls tell her, and an often expressed worry of theirs is that "the Church of today is in the worst shape that it has been since its very beginning."

Reminder: As St. Louis de Montfort advised us, a true Marian devotion includes a love and better understanding for the Poor Souls in Purgatory. [51]

Sr. Agnes Sasagawa of Akita, Japan *
(stigmata)

While her Sisters were all receiving Holy Communion in their hands, the stigmata of her left hand forced it shut with horrible pain, and she was therefore forced to receive Jesus on the tongue. At the same instant the wound in the right hand of the wooden statue of Our Lady bled from the identical spot. Could these sufferings respectively have been reparation for the abuses in the left hands of the laity and the right hands of Priests? Of course. Since then Sr. Agnes and all her Sisters receive Holy Communion only on the tongue.

 * Recognized by the Church.

Sr. Anna Ali of Kenya
(stigmata)

Sr. Anna converses with Jesus and her revelations focus on Eucharistic devotion. Jesus has told her that Freemasonry has agreed to abolish Him from the Holy Mass.

CHURCH DOCUMENTS

THE DOCUMENTS OF VATICAN II

These contain nothing at all about this so crucial subject, and yet millions of people wrongfully associate Hand Communion with Vatican II.

THE CREED OF GOD'S PEOPLE
by Pope Paul VI

I, II, III, IV. REVERENT RECEPTION
1) ... 2) The required eucharistic fasting for at least one hour prior to Holy Communion (medicine and water exempted); becoming, respectful attire. One should only come to the table of the Lord with great reverence, the hands folded, the eyes sunken.

THE CATECHISM OF THE CATHOLIC CHURCH, 1993

The Catechism also has nothing at all concerning this matter, and this lack of any pertinent information in 1993 is in itself of great interest. Why is there no mention of it? Certainly not because its main authors, Cardinal Joseph Ratzinger and Cardinal Christoph Schönborn, are protagonists of Hand Communion, but then again they are both very close to the present Holy Father.

RECENT PAPAL INSTRUCTIONS

MEMORIALE DOMINI *by Pope Paul* VI
The Pope's Letter (DOMINICAE CENAE)
to All Bishops & Priests
October 18-22, 1968 & May 29, 1969

This includes:

"In view of the state of the Church as a whole today, this manner of distributing Holy Communion (on the tongue) therefore should be observed, not only because it rests upon the tradition of many centuries, but especially because it is a sign of reverence by the faithful toward the Eucharist. The practice of placing Holy Communion on the tongue of the communicants in no way detracts from their personal dignity. This traditional manner of administering Holy Communion gives more effective assurance that the Holy Communion will be given to the faithful with due reverence, decorum and dignity."

And this then is followed by the votes of all the world's Bishops that were overwhelmingly against Communion in the hand. Then follows an excerpt in which the strict conditionality of this tolerance is very clear:

"Yet, if the opposing practice, meaning the placement the Holy Communion in the hand, is already spread widely, then the Apostolic Seat, in order to alleviate the assignment of the pastoral office, that in today's situation is becoming ever more difficult, conveys the instruction and the burden of responsibility of considering the special conditions in each case, yet only under the condition that every danger of a deterioration of reverence and the increase of false opinions about the Holy Communion are kept away and that deficiencies are avoided."

"Opposing practice" and "only under the condition"? Do these expressions and all the rest sound to you as though the Princes of the Church (including the Pope, whose decree this afterall was) and particularly the men at the Congregation for the Holy Liturgy, were so enthusiastic about Hand Communion? It certainly does not. This paragraph, as does the rest of the document, burns with an all-inclusive anxiety that Holy Communion does not lose its holiness in the way it is handled by both the Priests as well as the faithful.

This is the ONLY document where a tolerance of Hand Communion can be found, yet does this in any way change how it came about that the Church was forced into letting it occur? It does not. There was blatant dishonesty, manipulation and sedition on the behalf of Bugnini, and he certainly was not operating alone. This was subversion in the Church. Can that lead to good fruits? No, it cannot, and it has not. Were something comparable to occur in a government or industrial environment, the resulting aftermath would naturally have been corrected a long time ago. And, it is here that our own consciences MUST start functioning and we must thereupon quickly start to also act accordingly.

also

THE MYSTERY & THE CULT OF THE HOLY EUCHARIST
by Pope John Paul II
The Pope's Letter (DOMINICAE CENAE) to
All Bishops & Priests
February 24, 1980

This includes:
"How eloquently the rite of the anointing of Priests' hands in our Latin ordination tells that a special grace and power of the Holy Spirit is necessary precisely for Priests' hands! To touch the Holy Eucharist and to distribute them with their own hands is a privilege of the ordained."

also

INESTIMABLE GIFT (INAESTIMABILE DONUM)
On Some Norms Concerning the Cult of the Eucharistic Mystery
by Pope John Paul II
The Holy Congregation for the Sacraments and Divine Worship

(Holy Thursday) April 3, 1980

This includes:

"The Holy Eucharist is the gift of the Lord, which should be distributed to laymen THROUGH THE INTER-MEDIATION OF CATHOLIC PRIESTS who are ordained especially for this work. Laymen are neither permitted to take the Sacred Host by themselves nor the Consecrated Chalice."

What has become clear by now is that the present Holy Father did attempt, in a very gentle way, to rescind the earlier-mentioned tolerance into which his predecessor had been coerced by constant pressure and misand disinformation. What do we do? Do we try to unravel the political infighting inside the Vatican some 25 to 30 years ago, or do we simply do what the present Holy Father wishes of us? Ask Our Lady what we today should be doing, if you on your own are still confused. She will ever so gently, yet also firmly and permanently instill in you the form that is in God's wishes. Let her lead you also in this regard.

OTHER TESTIMONIES

Martin Luther, † 1546

He rejected receiving the Lutheran Lord's Supper with the hand as being "an expression of lack of faith". Considering the real presence in the moment of the Lord's Supper (Lutheran formulation), Luther also accepted God's principle of Communion on the tongue.

Anneliese Michel, † 1976
(incorrupt)

As this girl from a pious German family was, at 16, suddenly afflicted with demonic Possession, the demon was (during an Exorcism ordered by the local Bishop) forced to give the following account: "The thing (Holy Host) may not be placed into the hands. The Priests must be courageous. The laity may not distribute it. During the distribution of that stuff (Holy Communion) one must kneel. On the order of that one there (pointing at a statue of Mary nearby),

Hand Communion must be gotten rid of, for it is my work. The Bishop must forbid Hand Communion, if he can achieve it."

Mother Teresa of Calcutta, † 1998

The Sisters of Charity allow only Communion on the tongue, and, when asked about this, one of her senior Sisters responded: "Mother Teresa has asked for this because she wishes her Sisters to be obedient to the Pope." (1996)

It is also reported that when a group of Bishops, while visiting Mother Teresa in Calcutta, asked her what, in her opinion, the worst evil in the crisis of the Church was, she answered, surprising them all, that it was the "modern form of receiving Communion."

Mother Angelica, EWTN TV

"Very few children I have met have ever been taught that He is really, truly, present in the Holy Eucharist. ... We find Hosts in missalets, we find Hosts under pews under chewing gum... I have seen a 9 year-old girl go to Communion and pop one like an M&M. (An American candy.) I have seen people put it into their sleeves, put it in their pockets, and leave it on the pew."

Try putting chewing gum under the pew with your mouth.

Professor Klaus Gamber, † 1978
(Liturgical Expert)

"Hand Communion stands in crass opposition to the long ago determined reverent and fearfully careful handling of the Most Holy."

Helmut Thielicke
(Evangelical Prof. of Theology)

"If the Transubstantiation, or the changing form of the bread and wine, were to be correct, then one ought never again get up from kneeling!"

Granted, this is unnecessary outside of Holy Mass and Adoration, yet, then again, this is also a most holy expression for someone who, in fact, is still searching. Certainly God will bless this man profusely. This remark is dramatic confirmation, dear Catholic, for the fact that often recent converts make better Catholics than born Catholics.

Chaplain Schallinger & 242 other Priests
(In a letter to Pope John Paul II in 1979)

"We can, due to questions of conscience, not distribute Hand Communion."

Fraternity of Priests of St. Peter
(formed by Pope John Paul II in 1988)

Their Priests distribute "no Hand Communion."

PSYCHOLOGY

Are we not also responsible to pass true reverence for the Most Holy of Holies on to our children and grand-children? It makes an enormous difference to children whether they, for instance, see their most respected and often idolized grand-parents kneeling humbly in front of the Eucharistic Jesus or whether they see them standing and again just receiving "something in the hand". We are responsible for our children!

"BRING MY CHILDREN TO ME, BLOCK THEM NOT."

Are we not also responsible for evangelizing and spreading God's love as well as word to those many who have yet to experience them? And what more reliable way is there to do this than by our respectful, loving and, yes, reverent example when we find ourselves directly before God — God in the Most Holy Eucharist? None.

Human psychology is such that anything that many touch becomes profane. Already in the Old Testament God requires, when it concerns the laity, the prohibition of touching all that is holy. Only those called to attending to the holy are exempted. Examples: Mt. Sinai; Case of the Covenant; Consecration at the Temple; and others.

If museums never let the people touch their most cherished exhibits (just try touching the Mona Lisa, the Hope Diamond or the Declaration of Independence without prior permission!), and if armies of security never let the people touch their Presidents (just try touching Clinton, Schroeder, Jelzin or Chirac without prior permission!), WHY DO SOME PEOPLE STILL THINK THEY MAY TOUCH THE EUCHARISTIC JESUS, OUR GOD AND OUR SAVIOR, without such a permission and privilege having been bestowed upon them by the Church, and thereby through the Holy Spirit? Those exhibited treasures mentioned above are most likely fakes themselves, while Jesus never is! Concerning those Chiefs of State, comments are unnecessary.

When the Consecrated Host is touched by the general public then subconsciously it becomes denigrated to the level of another general blessed thing or object. And, the thereby resulting unconsciously denigrated and, therefore, incorrect association toward the Holy Eucharist is a hidden danger for the faithful, whose WILLING ACCEPTANCE OUR TRUE FAITH ITSELF FORBIDS. On the other hand, the human psyche values an act of touching it with the lips as a clean and thus sacred act of love (a kiss).

When your grand-mother, or any other more honored guest, asked for something on the other side of your dinner table and, because of impractical circumstances of the moment, you took it with your hand rather than taking hold of the dish itself, remember, you said: "Pardon my hands." Are you an honored guest at Jesus' table?

Moslems keep their left hand off the table during all meals. This is because other natural functions are attended to with the left hand. When a thief is punished in any of the more radical fundamentalist Moslems countries, the right hand, the one with which he eats, is then chopped off.

MEDICAL ASPECTS

It is medically proven that saliva has anti-bacterial properties, and 1 to 2 liters of saliva wash and cleanse the mouth in a single day. The hand, however, as an outer member, is always a carrier of dirt and illness due to contact with doorknobs, money, greetings, *ETC*...

When some people, as a somewhat feeble retort, ask whether you sin more with your hands or your mouth, you can, with the same frailty of human logic, respond to them with the question whether they clean ... ?

For that matter, sin only emanates from our hearts, minds and wills and that is afterall the reason for our coming to Jesus' Sacred Heart in passively attending and receiving from His Sacred Table at Holy Communion in the first place. In short, to heal our hearts, minds and wills, not our hands.

Some people have expressed worries that in these times of A.I.D.S. and similar illnesses, Holy Communion on the tongue might increase the chances of such conditions spreading. Any doctor will tell us, for A.I.D.S. to become dangerous in this respect, open wounds (broken skin) would have to be present around the mouth. In 99% of Communions distributed onto the tongue, no contact of any sort occurs. Were this fear warranted, then by now all physical contact of any kind ought to be forbidden. Moreover, searching for a Priest who has contacted such an illness through distributing Holy Communion on the tongue will remain fruitless.

As we saw earlier, the Divine Substance in Lanciano is that of live human heart tissue. The next time you are at a large hospital with the capabilities for cardiac operations, go in and ask its senior staff whether you may handle some live human heart tissue. You will be escorted to the next exit, if not to the closest Psychiatric Ward. Are they perhaps being "unbrotherly" in forbidding it, or are they insuring that it stays clean or, as some might prefer to say, sacred?

HISTORY OF ART

While not having access to the necessary sources, Old Master Paintings often show Jesus putting the bread, having dipped it first into the wine, into the Apostles' mouths, as was the Jewish custom. Most contrary to the so-called art of today, the Old Masters, their schools and their students were all meticulous in representing every subject that they tackled with uncompromising exactitude. The precision of these paintings can also be confirmed in the present Catechism, under The Seven Sacraments. Museums around the world, that own 'Old Masters', exhibit this scene repeatedly, and this subject alone would warrant a separate discussion if not a research paper or even a full-fledged book with many sacred illustrations. (See Tiepolo, Tintoretto, etc...)

THE ANTI-CHRISTIAN OPPOSITION

Already in the 19th Century, we may quote Stanislas de Guaita. He was a fallen away Priest, a kabbalist, a satanist and a model for all Freemasons.

"When we have succeeded in having Catholics receive Communion in the hand, then we will have met our goal."

The following can be quoted from a Masonic Plan in the year 1925:

"How can one rob the faithful of their belief in the true presence? ... First one must bring people everywhere to receive communion while standing, then one must place the Host in their hands. Prepared in this fashion, they will come to see the Eucharist as a mere symbol of a general brotherly meal and will thereby fall away."

And the following can be quoted from a list of Masonic directives in the year 1962, as given by an American Grand Master. Of 34 separate anti-Catholic suggestions made in it, here is...

#6 "Stop Communicants from kneeling to receive the Host. Tell Nuns to stop the children from folding their hands to and from Communion."

Today, when Ireland, Croatia and Poland are being especially targeted by the Freemasons, just one anti-Christ(ian) outgrowth of this will be that Hand Communion, now more than ever before, will encroach even deeper yet into their churches, today three of the sturdiest left in Europe. Other eastern European countries, beware!

Please understand very clearly, and for the sake of your very soul, that the ultimate goal of Freemasonry is the total destruction of the Church and the Eucharistic Jesus is the very core of the Church, IS HE NOT? How immense will Mr. Bugnini's reparation be?

SO PLEASE, STOP IMMEDIATELY FROM HELPING THEM WITH THEIR DOOMED ATTEMPT TO DO SO!

The case of Anneliese Michel was discussed throughout the world press in the late 1970s. The most detailed study of her case was made by the American Anthropologist, Dr. Felicitas Goodman, who was not Catholic. The demons were under orders of the attending Priests as well as Our Lady herself. Again, they said:

"THE THING MAY NOT BE PLACED INTO THE HANDS. ... THE LAITY MAY NOT DISTRIBUTE IT. DURING THE DISTRIBUTION OF THAT STUFF, ONE MUST KNEEL. ON THE ORDER OF THAT ONE THERE (MARY), HAND COMMUNION MUST BE GOTTEN RID OF, FOR IT IS MY WORK."

"...IT IS MY WORK," says the demon. Please pray about this and ask either Jesus or Mary to confirm or correct this. Trust in Them and They will, in Their time, do one or the other; but, first you must open yourself to Them in this regard. When, as a result of legal proceedings brought on by the Government against both Anneliese's family and the attending Priests and Bishop, her earthly remains were later disinterred and found to be incorrupt.

Every western press today reports an epidemic of satanic practices, and even the New York Police Department has in recent years come to the Catholic Church for advice in dealing with it. The lowest of all such practices is the socalled 'black mass' where each time consecrated Hosts are offered to Satan for desecration. Does it then not follow that getting those needed Hosts has become so much easier due to someone's sloppiness? Somebody in our ranks will be held responsible for every one of those!

MY IMMACULATE HEART WILL TRIUMPH

FATIMA
Sr. Lucia, Jacinta *(†),* & Francesco *(†)*

In 1916 these three visionaries received Holy Communion from the hand of an angel: "...he held a chalice in his hand, over it a Host from which drops of blood dripped into it." He then placed the Host in Lucia's mouth and gave the contents of the chalice to Jacinta and Francesco. Sr. Lucia: "Moved by the power of the supernatural that surrounded us, we all imitated what the angel did, this means we all knelt down like him."

"...LIKE HIM"! We humans are not allowed to do something that the angels do not do when in the presence of Jesus, that is, IF we wish to speak here about the SAME angels — God's!

AMSTERDAM
Ida Peerdeman, † 1995

In the picture of "The Lady Of All Nations" *, Mary's feet stand on Holland and Germany. Our Lady warned of a great peril that, because of false doctrine and heresy, would befall the Church. Through Ida Our Lady asked that Rome be made aware that this error would have its origin in Holland.

* Approved for veneration by the Bishop of Haarlem, May 1996.

GARABANDAL
Concita Gonzáles

She received Holy Communion from Archangel Michael on July 18, 1962. As above, she also "suddenly fell to her knees." Those around her could watch as "a small Host started becoming visible on her tongue, and then grew larger until the size of a Host that a Priest has at Holy Communion, although thicker." This was filmed, a copy of which is in the Vatican.

And even if this was in 1962, Concita has NOT changed her ways regarding this matter, and she never will.

AKITA
Sr. Agnes Sasagawa *
(stigmata)

REPEAT: While her Sisters were all receiving Holy Communion with their hands, the stigmata of her left hand forced it shut with horrible pain, and she was therefore forced to receive Jesus on the tongue. At the very same instant the wound in the right hand of the wooden statue of Our Lady bled from the very same spot. Could these sufferings respectively have been reparation for the abuses in the left hands of the laity and the right hands of Priests? Yes, they could have, moreover since then Sr. Agnes and all her Sisters receive Holy Communion only on the tongue. * Recognized by the Church.

MEĐUGORJE
Marija, Vicka, Mirjana, Ivanka, Ivan and Jakov,
Jelena and Marijana *

There Our Lady said during one of her first apparitions that the reason she went to Međugorje was that "here the true faith is being practiced." Does not "true faith" perhaps also include that when Our Lady started appearing there ONLY Communion on the tongue was the local practice? It was the western pilgrims who brought Hand Communion to Međugorje. "True faith" concerns, ABOVE ALL ELSE, the appropriate reverence toward the presence of Jesus, our Savior and God, in the Consecrated Host. For if it does not, then for true Catholics it means nothing at all, and we can all go bowling instead of receiving the Lord. * Approved for veneration.

In the first weeks of Međugorje, and while the children were forced to have the apparition in many different places around the village, it happened that Our Lady appeared to them out in the fields. On one such very well documented occasion, someone in the crowd asked of Marija Pavlović whether they too could touch Our Lady. Marija then took people's hands and placed them where Our Lady was. After having done this for a while the visionary started crying and when asked why, she responded that each touch left a dirty spot on Our Lady. At that point THEY STOPPED doing this. If they stopped doing so because the Blessed Mother was becoming dirty, does this not tell us that we should not touch Jesus in the Eucharist either? Yes, it does.

Also, in the message in which Our Lady advised the faithful there to pray the "seven Our Fathers" after the evening Mass, she included the word "kneeling". Today the great majority of faithful there do kneel during "the sevens", as they so naturally also do up on the two mountains or when in one of the visionaries' houses for an apparition, and this must tell us that those same ones, the greatest majority that is, would in fact much prefer to also do so during Holy Communion. Might these facts not also be gently nudging, gently advising something about how Holy Communion itself, which happens either

60 to 80 minutes later or about 5 to 15 minutes before or 2-3 hours before, ought to be received? Of course it does, and the need for kneeling there is even so very much greater than at either "the sevens" or during any of the many apparitions, because Jesus is our God, not Mary — the same Mary, that is, who advised the children many years ago that were they to have the choice between an apparition and Holy Mass that they were to opt for Holy Mass. Remember, Our Lady leads, leads us to Jesus, yet still never antagonizes, demands, or judges.

Voices of local administrative authority have, while in visible distress, stated that this so very crucial issue "...has nothing at all to do with Međugorje!" This author begs to differ and does so most vehemently, for the above situations alone are ample proof for his heartfelt concern.

Here already we have three separate mystical events in Međugorje (or, if we dare, "messages by implication") that occurred in its earliest days, and these, when summarized, are "true faith", "not to be touched" and "kneeling". And naturally this combination ought to point us unhesitantly toward the traditional form of receiving Holy Communion.

The former Bishop of Mostar, the diocese in which Međugorje is to be found, permitted Hand Communion to be practiced, so this is by no means a suggestion or, even much less, a call that the Franciscans there should change anything at St. James' Church. But Our Lady's messages there, both the direct ones as well as those given by her images or example, are afterall far more important to us Marian laymen than the innumerable confusions and conflicts within the Church Hierarchy. Mary is calling us to change our hearts and to do so toward Jesus, and only from there, from within our hearts, will all outer behaviors then also naturally change. Mary is coming to us to protect and to lead her Church, and we, her children, are her Church! Do not pester the already over-worked Međugorje Priests or visionaries about this, but, go ahead, pester Jesus or Mary to speak directly to your open heart.

When the visionaries there say, as happens quite often, that Our Lady wishes for us to receive Holy Communion with the heart, this means with love. With love, when it afterall concerns God Himself, means with a loving and thus true reverence. Yes, the inner content is initially more important than the outer form, yet the outer form IS A RESULT of a more reverent inner content. Moreover, when it concerns the others, for whom we ARE, remember, also responsible, our outer form, based on our own reverent inner content, leads the others to better inner content as well.

Without even trying to ask Međugorje pilgrims outside his regular circle of friends and acquaintances about this issue, this author can testify that he alone knows at least a dozen westerners who, due to their prayer-lives having deepened exponentially in Međugorje, changed over from Hand Communion to the traditional form of receiving on their very own, yet he knows of not a single one who ever changed in the other direction. There must be a good reason for this and considering that Our Lady's presence in Međugorje is the one and only new message to be found there, this just has to do something with her rather than with anything else.

Yet at the same time, in never mentioning this crucial issue in a public message in Međugorje directly, is Our Lady just possibly doing exactly the same as the Holy Father, whom she herself said she "chose for our time", when having to deal with the above mentioned (disobedient) Conferences of Bishops? This author believes so.

Is the message in which Our Lady mentioned having chosen THIS HOLY FATHER not alone a sufficient reason that all Catholics ought to follow his God-given loving guardianship for Jesus, for his Mother (Totus Tuus), for their Church, for their Priests, for all their "dear little children," and for the world; and to follow it always? YES, IT IS. If he is the successor to The Rock on which the Church would rest, then please let us stand with it rather than standing up to it!

Before the unforgettable weekend of November 24-26, 2000, Fr. Slavko had undoubtedly been the most reverent priest in Međugorje. Already back in1985, just four years after Mary had begun appearing in Međugorje, he announced the following before a Mass, "Because this is a very holy place, please let us receive Holy Communion on the tongue." This so persevering child and thus imitator of Mary's said to the author a few years later, "Never in my life would I receive in my hand," and, at another time, "yes, I do have a problem with it." (Hand Communion) He too, as a persistent student of Our Lady's, tried his utmost also never to antagonize, demand or judge, but his behavior around the Most Holy of Holies made him the giant Priest among Priests that he was. Now that Mary has told us that Father Slavko was "born into Heaven" immediately, let us take his example.

Before and during the latest Balkan war a fellow, 55 or so, was often seen walking around Međugorje. He never talked with , anyone, always wore a construction-type 'hard-hat', and carried a brown leather bag with a strap. One evening a local resident saw him, after receiving the Host in the hand, placing it into his jacket pocket rather than consuming it. After a silent confrontation, whereupon the fellow was forced physically to finally consume it, he was followed out into the dark by another Croatian pilgrim. His bag proved to be empty that evening. In late 1992 he, after having stolen a machine-gun out of a Military Police car, was shot and killed by soldiers at the intersection in Tromeđa, right next to the local gas station. He was known in Siroki Brieg, Ljubuπki, Grude and as far away as Livno for the same thing. He always seemed to have plenty of money and was known for staying in the best hotels around. Often hundreds of dollars are paid in the West by the organizers of satanic 'black masses' for Consecrated Hosts. This, as the reader might already know, is also approximately the price of a machine-gun. Let us try to pray for that poor soul.

When someone refers to the so crucial issue that this short discussion attempts to address as, perhaps, questionable spirituality, the author again suggests to the reader that, instead of getting all entangled in someone else's own entanglement in Church legalities rather than blazing in love for Christ, and thereby getting you quite exhausted and confused, listen instead to the words of the powerful Pope Leo XIII. As Pope Leo XIII advises, listen to God when he speaks to your conscience. It is purely YOUR conscience, not someone else's. Or, at the very least, listen to and act upon Our Lady's message concerning the present Pope.

FRUITS OF HAND COMMUNION

First, how then did Hand Communion arrive, for instance, in Italy? If you can believe it, it was due to the tourists, or so said the Priests who then pressured the Conference of Bishops with this so vacuous and self-serving argument. They said that tourists were coming from Germany, France, Belgium and Holland who wanted to receive Communion in the hand and so, not to disturb their (well endowed) holidays, the Priests agreed with them, and then finally so did some Bishops. So, in short, the tourists' spending money triumphed over the true reverence for the Eucharistic Jesus!

Other than what has already been mentioned, Hand Communion has only further spread severe reservations among the faithful, and here especially among the young, concerning the true presence of Jesus in Holy Communion.

It has, in many parts of the West, caused and then strengthened the idea that the so-called "peace-greeting" is the most important part of the Mass. The peace-greeting too was another idea out of the time of Bugnini et al, and it too has badly weakened the true reverence when the laity is directly in front of the Eucharistic Jesus.

Oh, pardon, did someone mention the peace-greeting? Yes, you're right, they did have a peace greeting in the Early Church; but back then it was BEFORE the Consecration, and NOT right after it, when Jesus is already with us, and when He and His mother both want Him and ONLY HIM to enter our hearts! You and your good neighbor, when it comes to Jesus' and Marys' wishes, can both wait until you're out on the sidewalk or, better yet, in the café. Remember, we are meant to bring Jesus into the cafés with us, and NOT bring the cafés in to Jesus! When one has a toothache, one seeks the dentist, yet when one has a broken car one seeks the mechanic; and therefore, woe to those who take their toothaches to a mechanic! Our Lady, moreover, most definitely concurs; and here is why.

Once Mary appeared to Marija of Međugorje, and it happened to be only a few minutes after a Consecration. She came at the usual preset time, yet, on this occasion, Mary neither prayed with nor spoke to the visionary, and left after a mere few seconds, having ONLY blessed the small group that was at this Holy Mass. When the attending Priest later asked Marija why it had happened so very quickly, her answer, emphasized by a graceful move of her outstretched hand directed toward the front of the altar, was: "She didn't talk to me because Jesus was standing, ...here." Further explanation ought not to be necessary. A digression...

Hand Communion has also spawned a school of thought in the U.S. Church, spurred on, as is almost everything else in the West, by liberal individualism, that one ought to stand even during the Consecration! The same spirit has recently led the American Bishops to pronounce that the American way of receiving Holy Communion is while standing. And why not cheer, whistle, stomp our feet and bring along garish cheer-leaders with pom-poms flying?! And why not, as this author has himself already witnessed in western Catholic Churches, have coffee, watch television and bring one's dogs into church?!

It has also indirectly helped remove the Tabernacles from the center of churches, first to a side area, then to a side room, and finally into another building where few, if any at all, can find Jesus, even if they wanted to adore Him. It has also led to the removal of all kneelers from many western church-es. Satan is a very sly predator, and as any truly praying individual already knows, he is persistent at attempting to break us and to pull us down, step by step by step by step.

In Europe laymen have occasionally organized themselves into groups whose sole responsibility it is to carefully gather up the many crumbs that are left strewn about after Hand Communion. Never before was this a true need, and what used to be taken care of perfectly well by the traditional form of Holy Communion, including the use of patens, is now being done by very loving and reverent souls who do, thank God, still exist.

But is it really a wonder by now why so many western churches stand cold, prayerless and empty when Jesus has first been stood up to, then ignored, then replaced, then moved, then removed, and finally discarded altogether?!

Has not the 1925 Masonic Plan done its job very well?! All too well, dear Catholic, and now is the time when we must return to true reverence and, if we wish for our Church to experience the Renewal of which the Holy Father speaks, then do so in crowds. Many have tried a Renewal without Our Lady, and today that one is fragmented beyond repair. Others have experienced a Renewal with Our Lady but have tended more to her than to true reverence toward her Son, Jesus. ONLY if all of us come back to true reverence toward her Son will we really be with her, and then a true Renewal will become unstoppable.

One of these above-mentioned faithful who collects crumbs after Holy Mass is a Deacon who is not only an extraordinary exorcist, but also an inner-locutionary of Our Lady's (these with the supportive guidance and authority of an Archbishop). About half-way through this little document, the author asked this valiant Child of Mary's whether or not Mary wanted the author to continue putting THE DIVINE SUBSTANCE together with the eventual intention of having it published. Our Lady's response was: "Yes, he may go ahead." And well before that, the author once asked this saintly man why he thought he was given the graces that he had. His humble answer was that he really did not know for sure, but that he suspected a combination of the mystical influence of his spiritual director, St. Padre Pio, and that he himself had been gathering up the Eucharistic Jesus in this manner for some thirty years.

And when Communicants today, adherent to one or the other of today's two forms of receiving Holy Communion, are either bypassed entirely or even verbally abused by Priests (e.g., being scoffed at for "obsessive behavior"), to which group will they belong? ALWAYS to the group trying their best to adhere to Holy Communion on the tongue while kneeling, and never to the other group. This fact also should tell us something. Whose doing, dear Catholic, is this — Jesus' or Satan's?

FURTHER DISCUSSION

When the all-too-generic argument, "But that (and, we must presume, most of the above) is old-fashioned," is heard, then remind them gently that such a belief is often the seed of many sins of apostasy. The "New Agers" say that "Jesus is old-fashioned," and considering that we are speaking of Him here IN the Divine Substance, that argument, the author sincerely hopes, instantly voids itself.

313

When the argument, "But the Church has allowed it," is heard, remember please, you are the Church, and not the entangled intricacies of disobedient, dishonest and betraying bureaucrats in some far-off and unattainable places. The Church has not "allowed it", it has ONLY under back-handed duress tolerated it, and you are NOT "a true emergency." Or do you perhaps, at some later date, want to become one?

When the all-too-democratic argument, "Don't make waves, don't be different, don't be singular. Those may lead you to pride", is heard, remember, to Jesus YOU ARE different, to Jesus YOU ARE singular, and ONLY WITH JESUS do you become free. So, again, OUT OF THE WAY, Satan!

To quote a simple and thus lucid thinker who quite obviously, like this author, is not all too impressed with the world-wide Masonic call for counterfeit "equality, brotherhood and liberty" among all the world's people:

"The religion of our society is democracy, brother-hood, socialization, conformity, agreement (and) popularity. Today Christian ethics are not as distinctive as Christian faith. Everyone admits the claims of love (in principle, if not in practice), but not everyone admits the claims of faith. Everyone agrees (again, in principle) with Jesus' ethical teachings, but not everyone agrees with His claim to divinity. If only we can classify Christ with other ethical teachers and Christianity with other religions, we will have removed the odium of distinctiveness, the scandal of elitism, and the terror of being right where others are wrong."

Like it or not, and even more so than other Christians, we Catholics ARE distinct, we Catholics ARE an elite, we Catholics ARE right; and herein lies THE ENTIRE ISSUE!

While it is true that Christ is present in His word, and in the people of God gathered together, and while certainly every living person is truly a Temple of the Trinity, what gives an extraordinary distinction to the Presence of Christ in the Holy Eucharist is that there, as His words state so very exactly, His Presence is The Pledge Of The New Covenant between God and His people. In any culture and at any time, the Pledge of the Covenant MUST be enshrouded in a very distinct reverence!

This very distinct reverence toward God is, in any religion and at any time, primarily shown by the act of kneeling toward God while praying to Him. Even the most moderate of all practicing Moslems kneel and pray toward their God five times a day while we Catholics, who today kneel so rarely, are at the same time so prone to worry about our young who today are joining other religions or, just as often, sects whose members even kneel before their socalled Gurus! God hears the others' prayers as He does ours, but if we do not show our love for Him, how true, how heartfelt can our prayers really be? Might we Catholics who over these decades have been pulled away from kneeling before God not ourselves unknowingly be assisting our youth in their search for this true reverence, for this penitent position of love for God, for which all souls while still here on earth, both young and old, so naturally yearn? We Catholics, the Catholics who have Jesus Himself in every Holy Communion, therefore have no reason at all to even go to Church if we ourselves are not lovingly prepared to kneel before Him.

As the Poor Souls in Purgatory themselves once told Maria Simma: "Many wish to be good Catholics; but to strain for holiness, that seems too much for them! And still God's Holy Church needs truly holy and not somewhat holy men! The tide of ruin is stronger than the mediocre, so how should it be conquered by mediocrity?!"

Only our own holy reverence can conquer the "tide of ruin", so please let us all stop being mediocre!

Renewed Hope

The Bishops' Conference of the Philippines has returned to Holy Communion on the tongue due to the increase of sacrilege that had occurred with Communion in the hand.

Yet Another Prayerful Opinion

Hand Communion is an inequity against God that has already badly damaged the unity in, as well as the respect for, our Sacred Catholic Faith.

The so urgent need for this Addendum is in itself more than sufficient proof for the validity of this statement.

Now, rather than talking about it, PRAY ABOUT IT and listen well to your conscience. God put a conscience into every one of us, not a library full of weighty books or the infinite justifications of some influential highbrows. When, as a fruit of much prayer, this God-given conscience becomes more and more well-honed, the first of all most obvious fruits is TRUE REVER-ENCE. Jesus came, not to make us all equally clever or more alike, but to have us love Him and through Him each other. ONLY with true reverence and love for Him, ONLY when we have understood and begun practicing the First Commandment, will we ever even begin to be able to love one another! That is why it is the First Commandment, and all opposing teachings are simply fraudulent and thus a huge waste of our time.

Especially when discussing this topic with western Priests or Bishops, arguing produces only distressed fruits. This discussion is not meant to antagonize western Priests or Bishops, their good parishioners, or anyone else, but here again...

Please read, listen, watch, reflect and pray about what Our Lady's Pope is doing! Or did she perhaps not know what she was doing when she chose him?!

The Holy Father, when appointing some 30 new Cardinals in 1995, chose almost exclusively men from former 'Iron Curtain' countries and from Africa. Did he perhaps have holy reasons for doing so? He most certainly did!

And now, pray about it even more.

CONCLUSION

When we look at the above names and situations as compared to the vast number of Communicants who today are receiving Holy Communion in the hand, it becomes abundantly clear that this holy issue is far from settled. Now it is left, once again, for Mary's children to give the best example to the whole world, and to follow her where their prayer-lives lead them — closer to Jesus in an ever more reverent manner.

The evidence, the undeniably holy evidence, is not only strong, it is truly overwhelming, and that is overwhelmingly in favor of the traditional form — Holy Communion on the tongue while kneeling. And who is it who constitutes that other much, much smaller group of, yes, dissidents? While this situation is not one where the majority automatically prevails, we will, of course, in the end have to leave that to Jesus. But one thing is still certain, Jesus gives us the Saints and holy mystics as role models, and not so that we then consider them "old-fashioned", "out in vogue" or even "misguided".

Their graces were given to them because they had been so virtuous and not, as so many people today seem to think, democratically or, God forbid, even randomly or equally.

The author does not in any way or form suggest that all the faithful who receive Communion in the hand are, on the other hand, themselves necessarily misguided, for he knows quite well that there are holy individuals among them, as there are anywhere else. But he does, however, suggest that they haven't been guided at all, and that is why he has taken the time to write THE DIVINE SUBSTANCE.

When we merge what Our Lady told Marthe Robin about the demise of Freemasonry with the fact that it certainly seems as though it was, in fact, the Freemasons who brought about the "false opinion" in spreading Hand Communion, we may also conclude, already now, that when Our Lady does finally conquer Freemasonry that Hand Communion will also have fallen away for the second time. Let's take her numerous hints and nudges already today, rather than waiting until something cataclysmic occurs.

Moreover, when names such as Augustine, Francis, Thomas Aquinas, Catherine of Sienna, Bridget of Sweden; Leo XIII, Pius X, Jean-Marie Vianney, Therese Neumann, Marthe Robin, Katharina Emmerich, Bl. Padre Pio, Lanciano, Mother Teresa, Maria Simma, Fatima, Garabandal, Akita and Međugorje roll by our ears, it can only make sense that we should listen well, learn from them all, follow and imitate them all now. In not doing so we are, by this point, blatantly admitting our callousness toward the Eucharistic Jesus.

Wouldn't Our Lady greatly prefer that ALL her contemporary children also listen, trust, imitate and thus privately as well as officially act upon the wishes of her Holy Father in Rome, and therein possibly join the ranks of these above names?

As the Međugorje visionaries testified about Purgatory in January of 1983: "The majority of people go to Purgatory, many go to Hell and a small number go directly to Heaven."

LET US ALL GO DIRECTLY TO HEAVEN!

Nicky Eltz

317

POSTSCRIPT

1)   While still putting the final touches on THE DIVINE SUBSTANCE, the author received a letter from a gifted Australian Franciscan Priest who is also very active among Charismatics. Two thirds of the way through the letter he suddenly wrote: "I do not know why I am hearing this, but, 'Show many Priests how to be Priests.' Are you by chance considering the Priesthood?" "No," responded the author in due haste, "but I am writing a piece on the confusion that circles around the proper form of receiving Holy Communion." Those of us who say we listen to charismatic Priests ought to take this remark very seriously.

2)   The author published THE DIVINE SUBSTANCE without the sanctioning of any Parish Office or any Bishop and so it, of course, remains unofficial wherever it is read. It only represents the well-founded and prayer-assisted opinion of its author and his friends. If this little document brings extra dimensions onto the author's cross, he accepts it, and hopefully without whimpering, for his love for Christ, for His Mother and all their Parish Offices; and therefore, so be it.

INSTRUCTIONS

Now that you have so courageously risked being better informed than you were prior to having read THE DIVINE SUBSTANCE, the Author believes Our Lady herself would advise the following:

Always move gently, yet, at the same time, persistently and always ONLY one step at a time.

1) Take this issue first into your own prayers.

2) Only then take it gently into your families.

3) Only then take it gently into your prayer-groups.

4) Only then take it gently, and ONLY AS A PRAYER-GROUP, to your Priests. Search out older and thus more experienced Priests with a rich prayer-life already behind them. Forget, for now, all female 'eucharistic ministers' and any Priests under 50. Only go up the spiritual ladder, not the bureaucratic ladder.

5) Ask them to confirm what is written here. They can, that is, IF they want to. Come armed with other books that you have collected from among your private Marian libraries.

6) Only once you have found equally courageous and active friends among your good Priests, then ask them to take this issue to your Bishops. Suggestion: Perhaps have representatives of your prayer-groups accompany your Priests to your Bishop. Watch out for satanic interference, and to deflect that call upon ST. MICHAEL ALONG WITH OUR LADY. ALWAYS help your Priests in doing things, like this, that can become somewhat difficult. Expect vigorous resistance at any least-expected moment. Go only armed with prayer! Again, always go gently.

7) Along with your Priests, ask your Bishops now to confirm the contents of this booklet. Yes, THEY CAN, that is, IF they want to.

8) Once you have found amenable spiritual direction in this regard, write about it yourselves and then spread it in your bulletins and Marian journals.

9) Keep praying, and...

**MARY WILL HELP YOU,
FOR IN TAKING THE ABOVE PATH
OU ARE HELPING HER SON!**

"To touch the Holy Creations is a privilege of the ordained."
Laymen can only get such permission "for a true emergency."

Pope John Paul II

IN HONOR
OF
FR. SLAVKO BARBARIĆ, OFM
1946 -- 2000

"Pregare, pregare, non fotographare!"

THE TRUE AND PEACEFUL ORDER

What could after all be so remarkable about a disorderly collection of, say, 1,000 brick and stucco houses and their 7,000 full-time residents in one of the most volatile and enigmatic areas of the globe? As recently as in early summer of 1981 it was only a lazy sun-baked basin of vineyards and patches of tobacco surrounded by five small rudimentary stone hamlets, supplied by one dark little grocery store. The two common denominators of its population were that they found themselves in a Parish called "place between the hills" and that the majority of them were boldly aware of their Croatian and thus ancient Catholic blood. Today it hums, murmurs and rumbles in activity, including buses full of foreigners, a daily plight of construction workers, 100 gaudy souvenir shops, a gaggle of guides, UN, NATO and OSCE vehicles, humanitarian aid convoys, a few too many shiny new German sedans, an army of taxis, a dozen or more grocery stores, a spanking new Post Office, a drug-store, too many cafés to count, a handful quasi-hotels, two bus companies, four or five rather risky banks, a dozen or even more jewelry stores, several clothing stores and boutiques, book-stores, a furniture store, a lamp store, even an art and antiques gallery, and the ever-meandering groups of pedestrians from every corner of the world following their appointed umbrellas.

However, despite of all that, the shepherdess can still today lead all her loyal sheep across its dangerous roads.

What has caused this sensational change and, when we have found it, what exactly is it, from where exactly is it and is it real or a contrivance on the part of one or several potential orchestrators?

For 12 years now this inquisitor has been dealt the fortune or misfortune, privilege or restraint, grace or disgrace to have been intimately observant of and peripherally participatory in its daily workings. The stage is only that, a "place between the hills", and its players, described as follows, are easy to identify and easier yet to observe:

-- A slowly revolving staff of five to ten rather independent, tough, fun, earthy, intelligent and, thank goodness, somewhat rebellious Franciscan Priests attended to by a tenacious flock of Sisters.

-- Three to six (depending on familial, social, seasonal or invitational circumstances) young adults who are, at least initially, the center of attention for all the towns' newer visitors. All but one of this loosely knit group are married today and they vary widely in degrees of education, worldliness and spirituality. At closer observation they could, in their being clearly defined individuals, come today from any part of the world and, as some experts have claimed, would never work well as a group.

-- An ever circulating element of foreigners from a few dozen on windy and paralyzingly cold winter days to a veritable sea of heads on its anniversaries and other big days.

-- An also revolving force of "keepers of the order" who, depending on the year and the political surroundings it brings with it, wear anything from badly cut mustard polyester suits of the UDBA (former communist secret police) to camouflaged fatigues of the Croatian Army (aka HVO or Croatian Defense Council) to overly decorated uniforms showing various national colors but always topped off by either the baby blue beret of the UN or the divers plumage of NATO. Although for a variety of different reasons, each of these showed or still shows a nearly amusing ineptitude in bringing about order to anything in those parts.

When one locates a peaceful order -- as welcome there as anywhere else in the world -- it is gentle yet strong and, surprisingly, concentrates upon three very unpretentious things.

The first is the visitors' being permitted or invited to meet around any one or more of these unconventional young adults at 5 or 6:00 p.m. depending on whether it is winter or summer time. There one murmurs quietly or recites poetry-like verse for a while and then the perceived highlight of that entire "place between the hills" occurs. It remains unseen by the conventional among us (so let us call the unusual group "seers") and happens daily somewhere in the village when these again entirely unpretentious stars of the silent show stare at a wall, over a table or through a book-case. There they look slightly upward, move their lips without an audible result and show a broad variety of emotions. When it is over they "return" to being among us and again show clearly that something enormous has just happened to them. According to the written notes that one of these seers brings to the world on the 25th of every month, the second source of order is far more crucial than the first.

This occurs at the heart of a long solemnly held ritual in the huge local church that is accompanied by talks, singing and more murmurs. All of this, however, finally concentrates upon a small, round and white flour-based wafer that is later on held high over the heads of the gathered crowd and finally brought down among the attendees for consumption to all who freely wish it.

The third, if we today still take the opportunity to seek it out, is to be found in any one of the many residential houses where the large and truly extended local families still live. The family is still well defined there as the nucleus of everything that happens in the "place between the hills" and it also is often referred to in the notes that are broadcast to the world at the end of every month. These families are to be found around their large tables and huddled in their over-sized sofas, or out in their vineyards preparing them for the upcoming season, or all working together at building a new house, or at their raucous and spicy weddings, or at the ,bocanje' pits on the weekends, or in the names of each of this Parish's hamlets, or in the local paper and, at death, in the long processions that slowly wind their way through the streets following a squeaking cart that carries the coffin. The family is of such primary importance there that the following remarks were once made by a loyal and thus much respected resident: "See that fellow over there? He is again expanding his store, but he's not all that sound. D'you see, he is 40 and has yet to get married."

That "the place between the hills" has, as do all other popular places, its excessively passionate friends as well as fanatical enemies but is, despite either of these equally unreliable and erratic groups, very real for simply remaining in the world's spot-light now for some 21 years. There Princes and Presidents, Archbishops and Ministers, philosophers and sports heroes, artists and theistic meta-psychiatrists, body-builders and car-dealers, neo-writers and actors, lawyers and criminals, Green-Peacers and ex-patriot intellectuals, beggars and inventors, AIDS victims and billionaires, healers and Satan worshippers have all come and gone and this picturesque parade continues with no end in sight.

What makes it do so?

Money? No, for it continued very well, thank you, as a bestial war -- with its Russian-built MiGs bombing towns on all four sides of it, with mortar shells whistling through the air over it and Mujahedins' heads being shattered by their own men near it -- came to within four miles of its doors.

Power? No, for it demands nothing more from anybody's mind, body or pocket than any other unpolished town on earth.

Easy living? No, for it has no street signs, no hospital, no train station, no laundromat, no theater, no library, no bowling alley, no credible clean-up crew, its lodging, food and amenities are still well below the western average, and it is often affected by interruptions in power and water.

Entertainment? Not for anyone who has ever owned merely a black and white television set without even a Remote Control.

Easy fame and fortune? Uneasy and sometimes painful fame for a handful and short-lived fortunes for a few, but what about the other 99.99% of the 23 million people who have gone there over these last 21 years? No, not fame or fortune either.

Why does it not fail? It will not permit itself to be dispersed and those who have either tried with all their cunning or investigated their mostly paranoid need for possibly doing so -- a Communist Regime, the U.S. State Department, the fourth largest army in Europe, a succession of psychiatrists and counselors, all conceivable modern media, well-paid professional investigators, and the Church Hierarchy -- are all historically proven experts at exposing suspicious situations that could, with or more often without good reason, threaten their own stability. The Pope and several of his most trusted have often spoken and/ or acted for it, yet still its clerical enemies use all methods imaginable to squash it. At the same time it can only be adjusted to, but not stopped, slowed down or sped up, by anybody who has internally anything in the slightest to say about it.

Why does it not by itself, as such, succeed? The success of something brings with it its beginning, its acceptance, its zenith and its end as well as other clear definitions. These then write themselves into history and by nature always blend into a fog when its ingenuity has worn off. Worn off? The "place between the hills" simply does not wear off despite its being in the midst of a veritable flood of contrasts. For the most part the Priests and Sisters have come and gone. So have the municipal, state and federal governments, their chosen courts, their police and even their currencies. The lives of the seers have made their normal but definite changes and the faces of the towns' visitors never remain the same. Still it simply prevails and gently slides along as the "place between the hills".

One can love the place, one can hate it, one can write about it, one can sell it, one can shoot at it, one can photograph it, one can cry for it, one can pervert it, one can invent upon it, one can make films of it, one can live it but one cannot kill it, and there it stays -- quietly in its somewhat dusty yet friendly and calming basin.

Those who love the place are mostly wise enough to carry it quietly within themselves and then act upon it by changing their lives from top to bottom, from inside to out.

Those who hate it very soon locate the painful holes that they themselves have, by analyzing or attacking personalities, shot into their own feet and thus into their own credibility.

Those who write about it either help others to understand it or, if they do so negatively, waste much precious time, and therefore also much grace.

Those who sell it paralyze their own growth and are as shallow as their pockets will soon again be.

Those who shoot at it have been unable to see their targets and even less so their own consciences.

Those who photograph it take home good memories, fun light games or vivid imaginations.

Those who cry for it show far too little hope in it.

Those who pervert it are merely further damaging their own already psychopathically fragile health.

Those who invent upon it are either blinded or must be extremely bored or insecure.

And those who make films of it need to cover their vast costs and thus feel a distrustful need to attempt to democratize it.

Democratize it?! Never!

While those who live it thereby prove its simple reality and reflect from within themselves what is hidden in those three mostly invisible and entirely unpretentious events, and it is these that nobody can kill.

Some of those who live it in its most loyal and thorough form are also those accused most often of contriving it. So, have they contrived their own lives, contrived their own slander, contrived their own commotion, contrived their own pain, contrived their own unpaid 15 to 18 hour work-days, contrived their own war, contrived their own merciless wear and tear and contrived their own ridicule?

As any healthy, testing and thus still exploring child knows, liars are soon entangled in their own stories. This story, however, entangles no-one while touching millions and the more one searches for lies down there in the "place between the hills", the more one loses sight of them for they simply are NOT there.

In observing and then following the footsteps of this invisible stream that creates the only true and peaceful order in that place, one will soon come upon the direction that everything that happens there takes. First this stream is gleaned from the lessons that have been collected from these seers and then read by millions around the world. In that local microcosm, as in millions and millions of cases today around the entire globe, it then, one could say, is fertilized at the ritual in the church and finally permitted to take hold in their families.

So, what is this invisible stream?

Is it bad, is it impartial or is it good? Nothing bad has yet been found in its message, while it clearly has not stayed impartial, and thus it must be good.

Is it self-serving, is it vacuous or is it giving? Self-serving only in the void left by Communism and in the so useless frills the West has brought to it lately, while vacuity has by its nature no growth, and thus it must be giving.

Is it destructive, is it innocuous or is it creative? Never has it destroyed anything, unless destruction itself has there faced its own demise, while innocuous it is only to the self-important, and thus it must be creative.

Is it dangerous, is it lethargic or is it healing? Only communists, atheists, materialists and all their bankers find it dangerous, while nothing that is threatening to them has ever been lethargic, and thus it must be healing.

Is it droll, is it dull or is it important? It is droll only to those who hold the family as such and they themselves will, by their own unnaturalness, soon be gone, while dull only to those who wish to remain isolated and sad, and thus it must be important.

Is it temporary, is it sporadic or is it persevering? Nothing that has so deeply impressed every continent but the Antarctic can be called temporary, while the indescribable pressures that it has overcome also invalidate its being sporadic, and thus it must be persevering.

Is it man-made, is it natural or is it supernatural? Were it man-made then the also man-made flaws within its message would have by now been unearthed by many, while were it merely natural then nature today would not be as marred as it is, and thus it must be supernatural.

And finally, is it then demonic, neutral or Divine? Were it demonic, then its world-wide reputation would not be one for being a place that heals hearts, while neutral spirits do not exist, and thus it must be Divine.

So, what is there to this gentle yet strong order that certainly must have been urgently needed, hoped for, looked for, and finally found if 23 million have so far traveled through thick and thin to reach it?

It is good, giving, creative, healing, important, persevering, supernatural and Divine!

Moreover, can and do its visitors attest to this and if so, then how do they follow through with it? Yes, they can and they do, and this is how.

Already many years ago now an Italian Institute along with one of the chief local investigators, and for a very long time now one of its most convincing and balanced protagonists, of that place asked 250 first-time pilgrims this question, "Why have you come?" To this they received a wildly varying collection of answers that included, "I came because my aunt told me about it", "I came so that Mary would heal my dying son", "I came because there suddenly was an opening in the group", "I came to visit Mostar", "I came to see the sun spin", "I came to take a break from my hectic city life", "I came hoping to see the Blessed Mother myself", "I came to pray for my father", "I came to see Fr. Jozo" and "I came to find out my mission in life." The answer, which ever it was, that held the highest percentage accounted for less than only 5% of the total. Then they asked the same question of 250 second-time pilgrims. Between the first and second visits the answers had dramatically changed for this time over 80% of the responses to this simple question were all only slight variations on the SAME theme of, "I came back to learn how to pray."

Pray?! Only Aunt ... what's her name ... does that. Daddy, who is she anyway? Tell me.

Well, she believes. She puts her faith into practice. She simply is a part of all of us and always says, "God, You who are pure love, I want and need You and Your Mother all year long!" and it is THIS that makes her who she is! Oh, she's wonderful, so safe and so strong. Our whole family and, for that matter, the whole town considers her theirs.

Where does she get all that love and ... where is she now and ... ?

She replenishes it over and over again whenever and wherever she finds Mary alongside Jesus at Holy Mass and right now she's gone to Međugorje ... again.

Nicky Eltz
Međugorje

"...its most convincing, balanced and persevering protagonist..."

REFLECTIONS ON THE MESSAGE OF
NOVEMBER 25, 2000

"Dear children,
Today when Heaven is near to you in a special way, I call you to prayer so
that through prayer you place God in the first place. Little children, today I am
near you and I bless each of you with my maternal blessing, so that you have
the strength and love for all people you meet in your earthly life; and that you
can give God's love. I rejoice with you and I wish to tell you that your brother
Slavko has been born into Heaven and intercedes for you. Thank you for hav-
ing responded to my call."

Fr. Slavko greets us all, loves us all, blesses us all, and is now interceding for
each one of us with his prayers before the Father in Heaven, and that is why
each of us will also continue to follow Our Lady's messages in the best way
that we can. We, as his millions of spiritual children throughout the entire
world, will, of course, also continue with the innumerable projects that were
either inspired or in any way assisted by our dearest Fr. Slavko. Now that
he is in Heaven next to God, our Father, he will be able to do so very much
more than he already did while he was still among us, and it most certainly
needs not be said that already here on earth he was a true and indisputable
giant among men and an untiring Summa cum Laude Post-Graduate Student
in Mary's School as well as the greatest teacher possible on Our Lady's messages here in Međugorje. As usual, let us first reflect -- as Father would also
want us to -- on what Mary told us last month. There she expressed her wish to
open her motherly heart to us and only once again called us all to pray for her
intentions. She wished to again renew prayer with us and also to call us to fast
and that she would offer these to her Son, Jesus, for the coming of a new time
-- a time of spring. Then she told us that many hearts have been opened to her
during this Jubilee Year and that in this way the Church was being renewed.
She then expressed her joy for this and thanked God for this gift and then only
once again gave us the three-fold call to prayer, which, if we listen to her, will
mean until we find true joy in prayer. Nothing can possibly be more powerful
and effective than to pray in any way that we can for Mary's intentions. This
is because her intentions are, like any mother's intentions when she speaks to
her little children, that we listen to her, that we decide to do what she wishes

of us, and that we can, by way of deciding to listen to her, then also discover and experience how great God's love for each of us is. Being always purely "full of grace" and being the most powerful intercessor in Heaven, Mary's intentions are far more important and wideand far-reaching than ours could ever be. When enough of us around the entire world have experienced God's love for each of us, then this new time, this time of spring, will have arrived. To see what is happening in this Jubilee Year, all one needs to do is watch the immense program that our Holy Father in Rome has organized and led during each and every day throughout this year. Almost no day goes by without St. Peter's Square being filled to capacity and it is no one other than Mary who has given him the unwavering strength to continue, and exactly this, and nothing less, was also the case with Fr. Slavko. One needs only to see the huge Youth Festivals and Priest Retreats, or any of the other so very many Holy Masses and accompanying talks given by the Holy Father or given by Fr. Slavko, because we will then have also witnessed for ourselves what has been happening during this Jubilee Year. Mary who has been leading and who all along has been teaching, leading and protecting our Holy Father in Rome sees all of this all at once; and it is this that makes her joyful. Even when we are broken, even when we suffer, even when we mourn most deeply, even when we might feel that we have been thrown into a confusing vacuum without yet being able to understand how we are supposed to continue, we can still have joy in our hearts because we know that Fr. Slavko is now with us in a still much stronger way than ever before. Many of us, no matter of what age, no matter of what race, nationality or social strata, now feel like orphans, many of us seem somewhat lost and disoriented, but if we do what Mary, what the Holy Father in Rome and what Fr. Slavko all want us to do, then we will soon discover and experience in fullness that we are not at all alone, but simply strengthened by their love and prayers for us.

Fr. Slavko, having finished leading the Way of the Cross up Križevac, did not go up alone to the base of the huge cross as he normally did, but rather moved back to the left to the large bronze relief of the Resurrection. There he briefly prayed for the Souls in Purgatory and then again moved downward when his knees slowly buckled beneath him. Rita was at his side quickly, then he collapsed in her arms, and died at around 3:30 p.m. of a massive heart attack on Friday, November 24. He had sat up one more time taking a giant gasp for air, but he was by then already in Our Lady's arms on his way to Heaven. Friday evening during the apparition Marija Pavlović-Lunetti, while crying, asked Mary, "what are we NOW supposed to do?!" …and Mary's loving answer was, "Simply continue." Five of the six visionaries -- Vicka, Marija, Mirjana, Ivanka and Jakov -- were here in Međugorje for Fr. Slavko's funeral on Sunday, the Feast of Christ the King, at 2:00 p.m.; and the newspapers reported that some 10,000 people attended it in prayer, while CNN reported that it was 20,000. It was probably closer to 5 or 6,000, but what does that matter? Because of the Thanksgiving travel crush in the USA, Ivan tried the best he could, but was still unable to find a flight that was fast enough to get him here in time. The Holy Mass for Father was held on the outside altar with a crowd as large as any summertime Mass, which, in this case, means that there was a veritable sea of black clothing reaching almost all the way around St. James' Church. Some 200 Franciscans and many Priests from other countries concelebrated the Holy Mass, with the Bishop of Mostar being its main celebrant, and while the local choir sang songs of praise. Although unnoticed by some, Jesus in the Most Blessed Sacrament remained exposed along with a Chalice right behind Fr. Slavko. Huge bouquets and wreaths were lining the entire eastern wall of the church, and many deeply loving and extremely moving talks were given. All businesses in town remained closed on both Saturday and Sunday, and Croatian flags decorated light-poles along the main avenue. After the beautifully organized and deeply prayerful Holy Mass the huge procession that followed his coffin then moved slowly out through the front plaza of the church while praying out loud, and then -- as Fr. Slavko would also have wanted it -- turned southward along the street to Krizevac, to his Cross Mountain. He was then laid to rest in the small cemetery right behind the church that faces his Krizevac.

Being November and the cold and wet winter having now finally arrived here in Međugorje, the stream of pilgrims had receded somewhat, but still we have had groups here from Austria, France, Italy, Korea, Japan, and some smaller groups from Germany, the USA and Poland. The huge crowd coming in honor of Fr. Slavko certainly made up for the receding number of the regular pilgrims coming to Međugorje. Private jets arrived at local airports, cars were rented all over Europe and many of his loyal non-Croatian students of prayer seemed to come out of nowhere, all stunned by the immense loss of a very, very great friend and of an equally great Priest. Croatian Television and Newspapers were here and a true storm of e-mails and faxes arrived in the Međugorje Parish Office from all over the world. Now Međugorje will only become more alive than ever before and people from all over the world will continue to pray and decide to be renewed in their efforts for true peace in the world. Our Holy Father in Rome had already been notified by Friday evening and it is known in the Vatican that the world-wide emotional response has been huge beyond anyone's imagination. This vast explosion of love for him is the best witness possible for what Fr. Slavko had done for the whole world during his 18 years of service for Our Lady here in Medugorje, and that, as we all know so well, also included repeated and especially venomous persecutions from various quarters that always seemed at least to finally land on his small bent shoulders. Still he never broke his stride, he never tried to give his huge cross to anyone else, he never ceased learning, his huge hands never ceased blessing, his heart never ceased absolving, and he never once was found off duty, no matter what the circumstances, no matter what the weather, no matter what was happening during the entire war, and no matter whether already very near death. As we saw earlier, he was always available for an unending parade of Princes, Presidents, Archbishops, Ministers, Philosophers, sports heroes, artists, Theistic Meta-Psychiatrists, Generals, neo-writers, actors, beggars, inventors, AIDS victims, billionaires, lawyers, criminals, healers, Satan worshippers, intellectuals and the dying; and he never stopped to take even the shortest break. "Pregare, pregare, non fotographare!" Once during an Adoration he prayed that we should learn to wear ourselves out for Jesus, and it was this that he finally did -- all the way directly into Heaven. In the words of a world-renowned Prayer, Healer, Surgeon and Psychiatrist, Fr. Slavko was, "O so free, O so very free!" In the words of a world-class Brain Specialist, Psychiatrist and Para-Psychologist, he was the Chief of Medugorje "simply because of the way he celebrates Holy Mass and because he has no edges". In the words of a well-known Catholic Scholar and Priest, he was "pure fidelity and absolute dedication". In the words of a famous American Catholic Philosopher and author: "The sage has unusual insight into the human heart, into character, into human nature as well as into the peculiar and particular needs and aspirations of the individual. He is a pioneer and his radical new insights become the platitudes of future generations. He tells us things that we need, but do not wish to hear. He makes enemies through his wisdom, and is often ‚assassinated'. He feels at home with you. He is thinking about you all the time, and not of himself. He has space within himself for you because he has roomy selves and hospitable houses in his spirit. He is adaptable to changing human needs and situations. One never knows what answer will be given because he sees the questioner's needs, and because he sees that the real question is always the questioner, not the question. Much, other than matters of the soul, therefore bore him. He has love, compassion, selflessness, humility, perseverance, earthiness and is neither left nor right. He is challenging, often surprising, often unpredictable, often upsetting, entirely unprogrammable, unpin-downable, unemployable, unrecruitable, and yet always creative for the other. He is unclassifiable...", and such a sage was our dear friend, Fr. Slavko Barbarić, OFM. O Father, please keep praying for us!

TODAY WHEN HEAVEN IS NEAR TO YOU IN A SPECIAL WAY

This expression alone should, unless we are made of stone, tell us very simply and clearly how well Mary knows each and every one of us. For those many of us who knew Fr. Slavko well, for those many of us who at some time worked alongside him, for those many of us who knew him only briefly, and for those many of us who knew him only by sight, we had, all together, grown equally so very accustomed to his presence here, that Međugorje only a few days ago now had been quite unthinkable, completely unthinkable without him. Mary knows this, Mary sees all this, and as any good mother knows, Mary knows whom her children love and that their many different needs for him have now quite naturally also traveled with him to Heaven. While we now still yearn for him, we are now at the same time yearning for Heaven, and that is why Heaven is now especially near to us today.

I CALL YOU TO PRAYER SO THAT THROUGH PRAYER YOU PLACE GOD IN THE FIRST PLACE

Only through prayer can we come to learn to place God in the first place and this means to place love, mercy, trust, forgiveness, and our faith in the first place so that all else will become easier for us to carry during this lifetime. By placing God in the first place we will quickly realize that everything that we have, every talent we may have, that everything that we experience, and everyone we will ever meet is only a gift from God, and with this realization we will always become ready to begin anew to build new loving relationships, and at the same time experience God's enormous love for us all. Here too our dear Fr. Slavko was our best possible teacher, simply because he lived what he preached, he loved and lived Mary's messages beyond the point of ridicule;

and, as any good teacher knows, setting a true example is what his or her students will cherish most thoroughly and therefore also remember the best.

TODAY I AM NEAR YOU AND I BLESS EACH OF YOU WITH MY MATERNAL BLESSING

While it is true that Mary is always near us when we try to pray and try to be close to God, she wishes to repeat it here because she is, like any good mother, consoling all her children when they are sad or suffering, as so many of her children are after this weekend of breath-robbing grief. A maternal blessing is a consoling, warm, safe, strong and protective presence which all children can remember from when they were still small and very dependent, just as we today are so dependent on the faith and knowledge that we have Jesus' mother to run to, to lean onto, to hide behind, and to speak with. A maternal blessing is a mother who speaks and acts lovingly for us and toward us, and who in Heaven is always ready to be near us. A maternal blessing can never be more special or less special because our mother did afterall give us life, and our faith tells us that Mary gave life to Jesus and is therefore live-giver for every one of us, and here is meant that she is the mediatrix of all graces.

O THAT YOU HAVE THE STRENGTH AND LOVE FOR ALL PEOPLE YOU MEET IN YOUR EARTHLY LIFE

When we have decided for prayer and have therefore experienced God's infinite love for each one of us, and most especially for us who have been called to believe and to trust in Mary's presence here in Međugorje now for some 19 years, 5 months and 3 days, this will always give us the strength to love and to be alive for the others around us during this earthly life, and here too Fr. Slavko has been an incomparable example to follow and to remember for the rest of our lives. For so many of us around the whole world Father was a model of service for everyone who ever was given the grace and the privilege to even just watch what immense output he contained within himself for those around him. He was the living witness to the truth that "lost time is lost grace", and as simple as this thought in fact is, it was he, before all others, who made this expression come alive with love and with light. He was the living witness to the truth, as Bl. Padre Pio already told the world, that each one of our souls was worth more to God than the entire universe.

AND THAT YOU CAN GIVE GOD'S LOVE

Although no one would ever express this idea in words, by saying, "I give you God's love", anyone who has faith knows intuitively that all true love comes to us from God, and that their well-being is therefore not dependent on them, but rather on God's grace. Fr. Slavko was known to pray to God for the grace of being able to recognize when his person would be needed and truly necessary for someone, and then to be available for them at that very moment. This should show us how we may become freer of ourselves through our always deeper contact with God through our prayers. The more we turn to God, and the more we call on Him, the more we will be led by Him in a clear way to give our brothers and sisters that which they really need to continue on their path. Consolation, encouragement, simplification of something, a blessing, a nudge this way or that, or simply a hug, all these things are a part of all this. Someone once was able, in one brief instant, to see that Fr. Slavko, while walking from his confessional around the front of the church, communicated with no less than four people at the very same instant. Without even slowing down his gliding stride, he said good-bye to someone with his left hand stretching back, he greeted someone else with his out-stretched right hand toward the front, he spoke a few short words to someone in back to his right, and he glanced lovingly at a fourth person in front to his left. This explosive flash of a picture told its observer everything that ever needed to be known about Fr. Slavko.

I REJOICE WITH YOU

Mary rejoices with us even when we are crying, but our human sorrow will now, with Mary's motherly help, turn into eternal joy which no one will ever be able to take from us. Those of us who tried to meet with Fr. Slavko know very well how short this time always was, even when it was in fact many hours in a car, in an airplane or at a conference. It was, no matter how much time we in fact had with him, always all too short a time! His quiet presence alone alleviated things for others so dramatically that when he was no longer there life quickly became heavier again. But now our time, if we seek it, can be unlimited with him and that is because prayer is the strongest way to communicate with someone, and afterall we are all united in prayer; and most especially with those whom we love most deeply. Fr. Slavko was tangible proof for the truth that love is far stronger than even death, and this too must make us rejoice.

AND I WISH TO TELL YOU THAT YOUR BROTHER SLAVKO HAS BEEN BORN INTO HEAVEN

Once again Mary shows so clearly here that she knows everything about us, that she sees everything that we are living, that she, as our mother, knows how we feel about someone as close to us as Fr. Slavko was, and still is. She does not say, as she did about the Holy Father in the message of August 1994, "my most beloved son", but rather, she says "your brother". Because he was in fact here among us ONLY for his brothers and sisters, precisely this is what made it possible for him to go to Heaven directly. There was no 'I' left in his person, when he used the word 'I' in his texts, he did so only very hesitantly, and the only time when he used 'I' verbally he was always already in the process of giving it to someone else. Many of us who tried to make him a gift were soon somewhat frustrated because we knew intuitively that he would give the same gift to someone else the very next day, where he must have known that it would be much more valuable to someone else, rather than collecting dust in his tiny messy corners. "Your brother", yes, "our brother", yes, "my brother" was the exact thought that so very many of us carried away with us after we had been given the privilege of being with him for only a few short moments. Yes, when our brother celebrated Holy Mass -- Holy Mass with which he had blended himself so completely, so naturally, so spontaneously, and so very lovingly -- we were immediately pulled along with him into a deeper level of prayer, a deeper level of mystery, a deeper level of grace and a deeper level of love for Jesus. This and only this is what makes for a great Priest -- a Priest according to Mary's great heart.

AND INTERCEDES FOR YOU

When someone was asked to translate for Fr. Slavko for a while, Father whispered to him that he always tries to address that somewhat deaf and almost asleep person in the last pew behind that last column there in the very back of the church. The idea being that if he reaches that deaf and asleep person, he will have reached everyone else present. He always chose the most simple ways to present something to us, because he knew that all of us would be able to understand it this way, for we are afterall all living the same life with all its many burdens, its many crosses, its joys and its sorrows. He intercedes for us, and that every time that we, in any small way, reach for him in our prayers; and even when we are a little deaf and somewhat asleep! Each one of us may keep saying this to ourselves, each one of us may keep hearing and seeing him before us with that very boyish, almost naughty little smile, and those huge deep and loving eyes that exuded such gentle but strong authority -- an authority that he had earned so very well, because it was purely meant to help us on our way along the path with Mary. Now let our hearts keep yearning for him in the same way that he always yearned to help even more people than he already was helping. And now with Fr. Slavko before our eyes, in the way that we may remember him the clearest, and while seeing those enormous hands blessing all of us, let us pray the way he always prayed at the closing of his reflections...

God, our Father, thank You for sending us Your Son, Jesus, to open our way to salvation. Thank you for sending us Your most humble and obedient servant and His mother, Mary, so that she could, over these many years, teach us, lead us and love us through her messages that have become a School of Prayer and a University of Love. Thank You, O Father, for the grace that we may, in these days of deep grief and loss, learn even more deeply than before what it means to place You in the first place in our lives. Thank You, O Father, for the grace that we may be told by Mary that Heaven is especially near to us during this vast explosion of love for Fr. Slavko that has shown itself everywhere in the world. We ask You, O Jesus, along with Mary, for the grace that we may all quickly have the strength and love to continue all that Fr. Slavko showed us during his exceptional life here on earth. Forgive those of us, O Lord, who tried what we could to understand him only with our minds and therefore failed, and please give all those the grace now to understand him with our hearts -- the only way that one could possibly understand him completely. Give us the grace, O Lord, to be able to love all those around us in the same way that You taught Fr. Slavko to love them. Give us the grace to be available for all our brothers and sisters, no matter who they may be, as Fr. Slavko was always available, day and night, for those who needed him. Show us, O Mary, how we can become able to wear ourselves out for Jesus, and, Jesus, please give each of us the grace to understand deeply that this is truly a time to rejoice because now Fr. Slavko can do infinitely more for this distressed world than he could while he was still among us here. May each of us receive the grace, O Holy Spirit, to be able to place Fr. Slavko with our hearts before our very eyes, and that, in so doing, he may continue to nudge each one of us along on the right path to You, O Jesus. Let us see his huge hands blessing us and everyone else around us, let us feel his loving slap on our backs just when we feel miserable or weak, let us see his deep, gentle and all-seeing eyes before us, let us always see his ever-moving glide to his next appointment, let us hear his beautiful, dry, deep and soothing voice in prayer and in song, let us see him moving up his two mountains with his flock so very close around him, let us see him directing our large Masses, and, above all else, O Lord, let us never forget that what he did the best of all was: pregare, pregare, pregare. Through the intercession of Mary and in the name of the Father, the Son and the Holy Spirit, let us all love and pray the way Fr. Slavko has taught us so well to do! Andate in pace. Andate con joia. Amen.

Nicky Eltz
Medugorje; November 28, 2000